GCSE

HUMAN BIOLOGY

Morton Jenkins
Curriculum Manager in Science
Coleg Glan Hafren, Cardiff

D1465316

Letts

Letts Educational
Aldine House
Aldine Place
London W12 8AW
Tel: 0181 740 2266
Fax: 0181 743 8451
E-mail: mail @ lettsed.co.uk

First published 1983
Revised 1987, 1992, 1994, 1997
Reprinted 1995

Text: © Morton Jenkins 1997
Design and illustrations: © BPP (Letts Educational) Ltd 1997

British Library Cataloguing in Publication Data
A CIP record for this book is available from the British Library

ISBN 1 85758 5844

Printed in Great Britain by Ashford Colour Press
Letts Educational is the trading name of BPP (Letts Educational) Ltd

Acknowledgements

I am grateful to the London Express News and Feature services for permission to use their reference for the illustration on page 86, and to the following Examination Boards: Northern Examinations and Assessment Board, Southern Examining Group and Northern Ireland Council for the Curriculum Examinations and Assessment, who gave their permission to reproduce questions from their examination papers.

Please note that the Examination Boards accept no responsibility for the accuracy or method of working in the answers given to sample questions.

Morton Jenkins 1997

Contents

Variation and the mechanisms of inheritance and evolution

Populations and energy flow within ecosystems

Hygiene and healthy living

Test yourself

Introduction

How to use this book

help in reaching a standard of work appropriate to a GCSE examination in Human Biology. It has been written for the requirements of all the British examination boards which will be offering the subject for assessment at Key Stage 4 of the National Curriculum. Information is given concerning:

- learning and remembering
- devising a revision programme
- syllabus requirements
- the GCSE system
- topics to be learned and understood
- advice on answering examination questions
- types of examination questions to be expected
- acceptable answers to examination questions
- advice on experimental skills and coursework assessment
- last minute help.

First, find out which syllabus you ar   school or college. Your teacher will be the first person to ask if you cannc   cond, obtain an up-to-date copy of the syllabus from the examinati   ncn is offering it. There will be a charge for this but it will be a good investment. The addresses of the examination boards are given on pages 6–8. Third, look up the syllabus analysis on pages 6–8. Here you will find the following information:

1. details about the tiers of entry which are available for the syllabus;
2. the lengths of papers for each tier;
3. the available grades for each tier;
4. the percentage of the assessment given to coursework.

If you are a private candidate not attending a school or college, you may wish to contact the exam board for which you intend to enter, for advice on completion of coursework and to find a centre where you can take the examination.

The General Certificate of Secondary Education (GCSE) National Curriculum, Key Stage 4

The GCSE has been modified to support the National Curriculum and to benefit from its operational experience, gained over at least eight years. In 1990, the Secretary of State for Education and Science instructed the former Schools Examinations and Assessment Council (SEAC) to develop GCSE as a means of assessing Key Stage 4 of the National Curriculum.

In 1994, the National Curriculum core subjects (English, Mathematics and Science) were first examined via the GCSE. Since 1995, the separate sciences, including Biology (Human) have been assessed to meet the requirements of the new National Curriculum.

Each new syllabus describes what is to be assessed and what methods of assessments will be used to judge achievement in the final years of compulsory education. However, the examinations are available to all who can meet the requirements, regardless of age or whether the candidate is studying in a school, in a college, or under other circumstances. The GCSE will continue to be available to mature and private candidates and will achieve a balance between investigation and the acquisition of knowledge and understanding via theory.

The aims and objectives of the syllabuses in Biology (Human) and Human Physiology and Health remain fundamentally the same for all examination boards.

Aims

In Biology, Human Biology and Human Physiology and Health the aims describe the educational purposes of following a course for the GCSE examination. They are:
1   To develop an interest in, and enjoyment of, the study of living organisms.
2   To encourage an attitude of curiosity and scientific enquiry.
3   To promote an appreciation of the importance of experimental and investigatory work in the study of Biology (and Human Biology).
4   To promote respect for all forms of life.
5   To develop knowledge and understanding of fundamental biological concepts and principles.
6   To develop an awareness of:
    (a) relationships between living organisms,
    (b) relationships between living organisms and their environment,
    (c) the effect of human activities on these relationships.
7   To develop a range of manipulative and communicative skills appropriate to the subject.
8   To develop an ability to use these skills to identify and solve problems.
9   To promote an awareness and appreciation of the development and significance of biology in a personal, social, economic and technological context.
10 To provide:
    (a) a worthwhile educational experience for all, whether or not they are intending to study biology beyond GCSE level;
    (b) a suitable preparation for careers which require a knowledge of biology;
    (c) a suitable foundation for further studies in biology and related disciplines.

Objectives

These reflect the aims that are measurable.
1   Knowledge and understanding. Candidates should be able to:
    (a) demonstrate knowledge and understanding of biological facts and principles, practical techniques and safety precautions;
    (b) demonstrate knowledge and understanding of the personal, social, economic and technological applications of biology in modern society;
    (c) use appropriate terminology in demonstrating this knowledge.
2   Skills and processes. Candidates should be able to:
    (a) make and record accurate observations;
    (b) plan and conduct simple experiments to test given hypotheses;
    (c) formulate hypotheses and design and conduct simple experiments to test them;
    (d) make constructive criticims of the design of experiments;
    (e) analyse, interpret and draw inferences from a variety of forms of information including the results of experiments;
    (f) apply biological knowledge and understanding to the solution of problems, including those of a personal, social, economic and technological nature;
    (g) select and organise information relevant to particular ideas and communicate this information cogently in a variety of ways;
    (h) present biological information coherently.

Learning and remembering

The best way to learn about any science is through an investigatory approach, and most teachers agree that students remember most facts if they have learned and understood them through experiments which they have carried out themselves. Unfortunately, there are some topics in Human Biology which cannot be learned in this way and you need to use second-hand data and certain well-known aids to memory. Repeated reading of notes and texts is one way of remembering certain facts. The construction of simple flow diagrams using key words is another commonly used method. Topics are summarised by using key words, linked logically with arrows. But whichever method you use, none is a substitute to *understanding*. This book is structured in such a way that it can be used to learn, understand and revise Human Biology in a simple and straightforward manner.

Devising a revision programme

The importance of beginning your revision well in advance of your examination cannot be overemphasised. You can obtain a fair idea of your memory capacity by reading a part of a text which is new to you and, after 40 minutes, writing a list of the facts you can remember. The average person will initially recall about 50%, then after an interval of 10 minutes, 25% of the original material will be remembered. After two days you will probably recall no more than 15%. These are average figures, of course, so do not be depressed if your scores are lower, or complacent if they are higher. Your capacity for retention will be influenced by the amount of sleep that you have had, what other matters are on your mind, and your interest in the topic. Even 15% of the original information may seem to be a very small amount but the percentage can be dramatically increased by revising the original text after one week, and then again after two weeks. By this time, the facts will now be retained by your so-called long-term memory store and up to 80% of the original material may be recalled in this way. Bearing in mind that the time each student can maintain concentration will vary considerably, there are certain revision principles which can be followed:

- Make a realistic estimate of how much you can revise each week over a period beginning perhaps three months before your examination.
- Divide your revision time into 30-minute periods separated by intervals of about 10 minutes.
- Use the revision notes and summary tables in this text to help you.

Check list of revision tips

"You can recall something without understanding it, but you cannot really understand something without recalling it."

Learning facts This is most time-consuming task of all.

1. Look up to the appropriate topic in this book and read it to familiarise yourself with the principles discussed there.
2. Make simple flow diagrams, using key words and arrows.
3. Summarise topics, using key words as headings and sub-headings.
4. Copy your summaries and diagrams from memory.
5. Then repeat the four suggestions given above.

Understanding This is essential for mastering skills other than recall, for example, data handling, deduction and application.

1. If you are in a school or college, ask your teachers for explanation of topics you do not understand.

2 Use the past examination questions in this study guide to judge the depth of knowledge you will need for each topic.

3 After revising a topic, try to answer the questions set on the topic **before** looking at the answers.

4 If you still do not understand a topic, do not try to remember it like a parrot. Go back to the beginning of the topic and build up your understanding step-by-step.

Last minute help

Examiners assess candidates by awarding a percentage mark based

the ability to record information in a concise form with a balanced and logical arrangement.
- The ability to handle information in a variety of forms and make deductions from it.
- The ability to solve problems based on biological data.
- The ability to use investigatory and experimental skills in a laboratory-based situation.

Improve your technique

All those who have had experience of marking examination scripts know that the majority of candidates could have improved their performance had they followed these simple rules of technique:

(a) Check that the correct exam paper has been received. This may sound obvious, but in an examination room, where several examinations are going on at the same time, mistakes could be made. Also GCSE examinations often involve a choice of differentiated papers. The choice will have been made before you enter the examination room and so it is essential that you know which paper you have chosen and that you receive the correct paper.

(b) Read the instructions at the top of the paper carefully. Look at the number of questions that are to be attempted and whether any of them are compulsory.

(c) If there is a choice, read all of the questions before deciding which to answer.

(d) Having read all the questions and selected the ones you wish to answer (if there is a choice), consider which ones can be answered by direct recall with the least amount of reasoning. These are the questions which usually can be answered in the shortest time (provided you know the facts).

Allocate your time carefully

Choosing questions which require the shortest time to answer is a sound idea. Time gained at the beginning of the examination will be of great value later when it can be used for those questions which need skills of reasoning and understanding.

It is common practice to include an indication of the number of marks carried by each part of the questions set in GCSE examinations. The breakdown of marks is usually given in the right-hand margin after each question. Candidates are advised to take special notice of this mark allocation because it shows the maximum mark available for a specific part of a question. There should be a direct relationship between this mark and the time taken to answer the question. For example, if a question is divided into three parts, carrying 5, 5, and 10 marks, respectively, it would be pointless to spend more time on either part 1 or 2 than on part 3. A moment spent on planning just how long to take on each part of a question in relation to the allocation of marks is a sensible use of time.

Make sure you answer the question set

Carefully judge the relevance of your answers. No marks are awarded for irrelevant material, even though it might be accurate. Each question will have an objective mark scheme which is used by all the examiners marking that particular paper. Include only that information which is vital to answer the question. Also it is essential to make your meaning clear. Examiners are not mind readers and will give no credit to the candidate whose statements are not intelligible. Do not pad or fill out answers with flowery language. Write to the point and as concisely as possible. If diagrams are specifically requested in a question, they too will have objective mark schemes. Marks will be awarded for accuracy of proportions, clear lines and clear arrangements of labelling arrows. An untidy sketch will not gain marks and is a waste of your valuable time. In order not to smudge and make unclear an otherwise good diagram, use pencil rather than ink. Diagrams should be large enough to show all the necessary details and should be fully labelled. Unless a question specifically asks for a diagram, consider the relevance of labelled drawings or graphs during the initial planning of the answer. Where diagrams would be useful, again at the planning stage, decide which to use and where in your answer to use them.

Understanding the question

Sometimes candidates have difficulty in understanding the meaning of instructions given in questions. The following table contains a list of common terms which often introduce questions on examination papers, together with an explanation of what they mean.

Instructions in questions	Meaning
Describe/give a description of …	Explain, by the use of prose and diagrams, the nature, form or function of a particular object or concept
Give an account of …	Write an explanatory description
Discuss …	Give an account of the various views on a topic
Compare …	Put side by side, one or more similarities
Contrast …	Put side by side, one or more differences
Distinguish between …	State the essential features of objects which make each different from others. A combination of 'compare' and 'contrast'
Explain/Account for …	Make known in detail, make understood
Indicate/Show …	Point out, make known, make understood
State …	Present in a form of a concise statement
Define …	State precisely and concisely what is meant by
List …	Write, one after another, in the form of a catalogue
Summarise …	Give a brief account of
Survey/Outline	Give a general (as opposed to detailed) account of
Write an essay on …	Write a full account, subdivided into paragraphs, of the subject
Comment on …	Make explanatory remarks or criticisms upon
Illustrate by reference to …	Use named examples to demonstrate the idea or principle

After completing an answer, read through it immediately. Check carefully that, as a result of writing at high speed, no words have been omitted, particularly any which might alter the sense of a sentence or passage.

Syllabus analysis

Southern Examining Group (SEG)

Address: Stag Hill House, Guildford, Surrey, GU2 5XJ
Telephone: 01483 506506

Science: Biology (Human) 2650

Core paper

Syllabus topic	Covered in Unit
Life processes and cell activity	
Life processes	1.2, 1.3, 1.4, 1,5, 1.6
Cells	1.1
Humans as organisms	
~~Breathing~~	3.1, 3.3, 3.4, 3.5, 3.6
Respiration	3.2
Nervous system	8.1, 8.2, 8.3, 8.4, 8.5, 8.6, 8.7, 8.8, 8.9, 8.10
Health	3.6, 9.6, 12.10, 13.5, 13.6
Hormones	8.11, 9.3
Homeostasis	7.1, 7.2, 7.3, 7.4, 7.5, 7.6, 7.7
Green plants as organisms	
Photosynthesis	11.3
Water and minerals	4.1, 4.2
Variation, inheritance and selection	
Growth	9.9, 10.5, 10.7
Reproduction	9.1, 10.4, 10.7
Inheritance	10.1, 10.2, 10.3, 10.6, 12.17
Evolution	1.7, 1.8
Living things and their environment	
Adaptation and specialisation	11.5
Energy flow and cycles in ecosystems	11.1, 11.2, 11.3
Humans and the environment	11.4, 14.4, 14.5

Additional paper

Syllabus topic	Covered in Unit
Maintenance of circulation in humans	
The heart	6.2, 6.3, 6.4, 13.3
Blood groups	6.7, 6.8
Support and movement in humans	
The human skeleton	2.1, 2.2, 2.3, 2.4, 3.6, 2.7, 2.8
Muscles and joints	2.5, 2.9, 2.10, 2.11, 13.3
Human reproductive system	9.2, 9.3
Human growth and development	9.4, 9.5, 9.7, 9.8, 9.9
Causes and control of human diseases	
Causes of disease	12.1, 12.2, 12.3, 12.4, 12.6, 12.9, 12.13, 12.14, 12.15, 12.16, 12.17, 12.18, 12.19
Control of disease	12.5, 12.6, 12.12, 14.1, 14.2, 14.3

Exam breakdown

All candidates complete coursework: 25%
There are two written papers worth: 75%
These are:
1. Core paper worth 50% (1.5 hours): Life processes and living things
2. Additional paper worth 25% (1 hour): Additional human biology
There are separate papers for Foundation tier (Grades C–G) and Higher tier (Grades A★–D).

Science: Human Physiology and Health (non–National Curriculum) 2690

Core paper

Syllabus topic	Covered in Unit
Relations between man, other organisms and the environment	
Dependence of man on other organisms	11.1, 11.2
The importance of hygiene and healthy living	12.1, 12.2, 12.3, 12.4, 12.5, 12.6, 12.10, 12.11, 12.12, 13.1, 13.2, 13.3, 13.4. 13.5, 13.6, 14.1, 14.2
Influence of man on the environment	11.4, 11.5, 14.4, 14.5
Organisation and maintenance of the individual	
Structure and functioning of cells	1.1, 1.2, 2.11, 3.2, 7.5
Life processes	
Nutrition	4.1, 4.2, 4.3, 4.4, 4.5, 4.6, 5.1, 5.2, 5.3, 5.4, 5.5, 5.6, 5.7
The blood circulatory system	6.1, 6.2, 6.3, 6.4, 6.5, 6.6, 6.7, 12.12
Breathing and gaseous exchange	3.1, 3.2, 3.3, 3.4, 3.5, 3.6, 12.18, 12.19, 12.21
Excretion	7.1, 7.2, 7.3, 7.4
Sensitivity and coordination	8.1, 8.2, 8.3, 8.4, 8.5, 8.6, 8.7, 8.8, 8.9, 8.10, 8.11
Principles of homeostasis	5.4, 7.2, 7.6, 7.7
The skeletal system, muscles and movement	2.1, 2.2, 2.3, 2.4, 2.5, 2.6, 2.7, 2.8, 2.9, 2.10, 2.11, 13.2
Reproduction, growth and development	
Sexual reproduction	9.1, 9.2, 9.3
Healthy development, pre- and post-natal	9.4, 9.5, 9.6, 9.7, 9.8, 9.9, 12.21
Chromosomes, cell division and genetics	10.1, 10.2, 10.3, 10.5, 10.7, 12.17
Variation, its causes and significance	10.4

Exam breakdown

All candidates complete coursework: 25%
There is one written paper worth: 75%
There are separate papers for Foundation tier (Grades C–G) and Higher tier (Grades A★–D).
Each paper is 2 hours long.

Northern Examination and Assessment Board (NEAB)

Address: 12 Harter Street, Manchester M1 6HL
Telephone: 0161 953 1170

Syllabus topic	Covered in Unit
Human life processes	
Cells, tissues and organisms	1.1, 1.2, 1.4, 1.5, 1.6
Nutrition	4.1, 4.2, 4.3, 4.4, 4.5, 4.6, 5.1, 5.2, 5.3, 5.4, 5.5, 5.6, 5.7
Circulation	6.1, 6.2, 6.3, 6.4, 6.5, 6.6
Respiration	3.1, 3.2, 3.3, 3.4, 3.5
Movement	2.1, 2.2, 2.3, 2.4, 2.5, 2.6, 2.7, 2.8, 2.9, 2.10, 2.11
Sensitivity	8.1, 8.2, 8.3, 8.4, 8.5, 8.6, 8.7, 8.8, 8.9, 8.10, 8.11
Excretion	7.1, 7.2, 7.3, 7.4
Homeostasis	7.5, 7.6, 7.7
Human continuity and development	
Reproduction	9.1, 9.2, 9.3, 9.4, 9.5, 9.6, 9.7, 9.8, 9.9
Controlling fertility	9.3, 11.6
Inheritance	10.1, 10.2, 10.3, 10.4, 10.5, 10.6, 10.7, 12.17
Health, lifestyle, hygiene and disease	
Food hygiene	12.5, 12.6
Personal hygiene	13.1
Disease	12.1, 12.2, 12.3, 12.4, 12.6, 12.9, 12.15, 12.21
Protection against disease	6.7, 9.6, 12.10, 12.11, 12.12, 13.5, 13.6
Biotechnology	
Growing microbes	12.2
Using microbes to make useful substances	12.7
Using microbes in sewage treatment	14.2
Biotechnology and disease	12.7, 12.10

Human influences on the environment	
Fuels and the environment	14.4
Transfer of energy and materials through ecosystems	11.1, 11.2, 11.3
Human population	11.4, 11.5

Exam breakdown
All candidates complete coursework: 25%
There is one written paper worth: 75%
Foundation tier (Grades C–G) 2 hours
Higher tier (Grades A★–D) 2 hours 15 minutes

Northern Ireland Council for the Curriculum, Examinations and Assessment (NICCEA)

Address: Beech House, 42 Beechill Road, Belfast, BT8 4RS
Telephone: 01232 704666

Syllabus topic	Covered in Unit
Diversity of organisms	1.3, 1.5, 1.6, 12.1
Relationships between man and the environment	
Energy flow	11.1, 11.3, 11.4
Decomposition cycles	11.2
Water and sewage treatment	14.1, 14.2
Diseases	12.1, 12.2, 12.3, 12.4, 12.5, 12.6, 12.10, 12.11, 12.12, 12.13, 12.14, 12.15, 12.16, 12.19, 12.20, 14.6
Beneficial microorganisms	12.7
Humans and the environment	14.3, 14.4, 14.5
Organisms and maintenance of the individual	
Structure of plant and animal cells	1.1, 1.2, 1.3, 1.4
Photosynthesis	11.3
Nutrition	4.1, 4.2, 4.3, 4.4, 4.5, 4.6
Digestion	5.1, 5.2, 5.3, 5.4, 5.5, 5.6, 6.7
Transport	6.1, 6.2, 6.3, 6.4, 6.5, 6.6, 6.7, 6.8, 6.9
Gas exchange	3.1, 3.2, 3.3, 3.4, 3.5
Excretion	7.1, 7.2, 7.3, 7.4, 7.5
Sensitivity/coordination	8.1, 8.2, 8.3, 8.4, 8.5, 8.6, 8.7, 8.8, 8.9, 8.10, 8.11
Homeostasis	7.8, 7.9
Support and movement	2.1, 2.2, 2.3, 3.4, 3.5, 3.6, 2.7, 2.8, 2.9, 2.10, 2,11
Development of organisms and continuity of life	
Chromosomes	10.5
Cell division	10.7
Cancer	12.21
Reproduction	9.1, 9.2, 9.3, 9.4, 9.5, 9.6, 9.7, 9.8, 9.9, 12.4, 12.6
Inheritance and variation	10.4
Mendelian inheritance	10.1, 10.2, 10.3, 12.17
Selection	1.8

Exam breakdown
All candidates complete coursework worth: 25%
Exam papers are worth: 75%

Tier A (Papers 1 + 2) C–G
Tier B (Papers 2 + 3) A★–D
Paper 1 (1 hour). Compulsory short answer questions
Paper 2 (1 hour 30 minutes). Compulsory structured questions with some free response.
Paper 3 (1 hour 30 minutes). Compulsory structured questions with a larger element of free response.

Chapter 1

Man's position in the living world

1.1 The cell as a unit of life

A cell is the simplest organised unit of living matter and can maintain itself at a higher energy level than its surroundings, grow and reproduce. For this reason, cells are recognised as the basic units of life. All cells are enclosed in a thin membrane that surrounds a fluid with a consistency of the white of an egg, known as the **cytoplasm**. With the notable exception of the red blood cells of mammals, cells have a nucleus which acts as a control centre. The cytoplasm, together with the nucleus, is called **protoplasm**. Electron microscopes provide the most detailed pictures of cell structure and reveal the contents of cells as a collection of **organelles**. Each organelle has a particular function to perform and uses special chemicals, called **enzymes**, to help it carry out the chemical reactions which go on inside it.

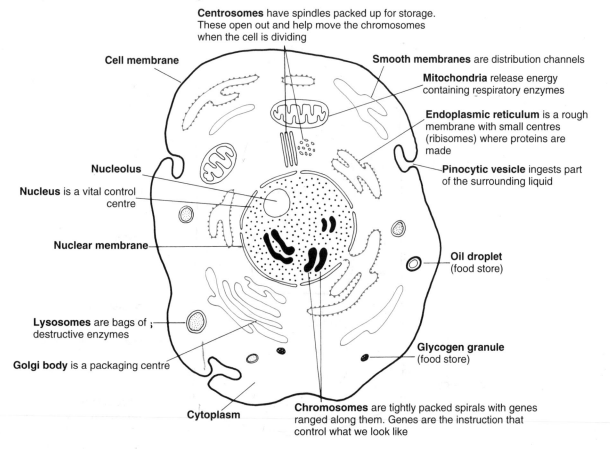

Centrosomes have spindles packed up for storage. These open out and help move the chromosomes when the cell is dividing

Cell membrane

Smooth membranes are distribution channels

Mitochondria release energy containing respiratory enzymes

Endoplasmic reticulum is a rough membrane with small centres (ribisomes) where proteins are made

Pinocytic vesicle ingests part of the surrounding liquid

Nucleolus

Nucleus is a vital control centre

Nuclear membrane

Oil droplet (food store)

Lysosomes are bags of destructive enzymes

Golgi body is a packaging centre

Glycogen granule (food store)

Cytoplasm

Chromosomes are tightly packed spirals with genes ranged along them. Genes are the instruction that control what we look like

Fig. 1.1 Section of a generalised animal cell as seen with an electron microscope

Table 1.1 Summary of cell structure and function

Organelle	Structure and function
Cell membrane	Thin **'skin'** of a cell. This gives the cell its characteristic shape. It **controls the entry and exit** of all materials.
Mitochondria (–singular, mitochondrion)	Sausage-shaped bodies, with a highly folded interior. These are the **power houses** of the cell. Within mitochondria most **energy is released** during the process of respiration.
Ribosomes	The small centres where **proteins** are made by the cell. The proteins may be used inside the cell for growth or they may be transported out of the cell, e.g. digestive enzymes.
Lysosomes	Spherical bodies which **store** certain enzymes for use within the cell
Endoplasmic reticulum	A series of membranes continuous with the cell membrane. It **increases the surface area** for the attachment of ribosomes and may help in the exchange of materials between the inside and outside of the cell
Golgi body	A collection of flattened sacs. The **packaging department** of the cellular factory. It is here that enzymes and other materials are packaged in 'envelopes' of endoplasmic reticulum for transport to the exterior
	present
Centrosomes	These are paired rod-shaped structures at right angles to one another near the nucleus. They help in **spindle formation** during cell division and are found in animal cells only
Nucleus	This is the **control centre** of the cell. It is surrounded by a porous double membrane which allows exchange of materials and is made largely of nucleo-protein
Cytoplasm	A complex mixture of chemicals of which 80% is water. The main constituents are proteins, fats, carbohydrates and mineral salts. It is the **basic living material** of all cells
Pinocytic vesicle	An infolding of the cell membrane concerned with **ingestion** of part of the surrounding liquid

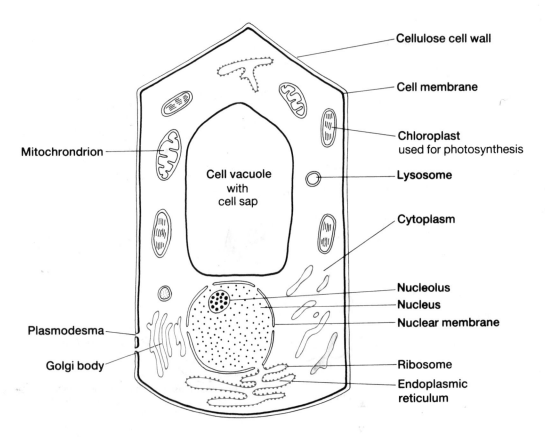

Fig 1.2 Section of a generalised plant cell as seen with an electron microscope

Labels: Cellulose cell wall, Cell membrane, Chloroplast used for photosynthesis, Lysosome, Cytoplasm, Nucleolus, Nucleus, Nuclear membrane, Ribosome, Endoplasmic reticulum, Mitochondrion, Cell vacuole with cell sap, Plasmodesma, Golgi body

1.2 The importance of enzymes

Enzymes are chemicals produced by living cells which have the power of altering the rate of chemical reactions occurring in the body.

Properties of enzymes

1. They are all **proteins**.
2. They all require **water** before they are able to function.
3. They are only produced by **living cell**s.
4. They are **specific** in their action, one enzyme speeding up one reaction only.
5. The enzyme molecule is only **temporarily changed** during its action and can be used repeatedly. Large quantities of enzyme are not necessary.
6. They work within only a **narrow range of acidity or alkalinity**.
7. They work within only a **narrow range of temperature**.
8. As they are proteins, **high temperatures** will coagulate or denature them.

Investigating the action of the enzyme, catalase

Every living cell contains **catalase** which acts on certain chemicals to release oxygen. This process is often necessary to change harmful waste products into harmless substances.

Procedure

1. Place 10 cm³ of hydrogen peroxide in a test tube.
2. Add a small piece of fresh liver to the hydrogen peroxide and note the result.
3. Expected observation: vigorous bubbling in the liquid.
4. Test the gas being evolved by using a glowing splint. It should re-light when inserted in the test tube near the bubbles.
5. Repeat stage **1** but add a small piece of liver which has been *boiled* and then cooled.
6. Expected observation: no bubbling of the liquid.

Deduction

(a) The enzyme in fresh liver (catalase) can break down hydrogen peroxide into water and oxygen:

$$2H_2O_2 \xrightarrow{\text{Catalase}} 2H_2O + O_2$$

(b) Boiling denatures catalase.

Summary of enzymes used in detergents

The following enzymes are all produced by bacteria:

Table 1.2

Name	Acts on	pH	Use
Alcalase	Protein	7–10	Soaking preparations and general purpose detergents
Esperase	Protein	7–12	General purpose and heavy duty detergents in liquid form
Savinase	Protein	7–12	Liquid detergents
Termamyl	Starch-containing foods	7–9.5	At high temperature (up to 90°C). Dishwashing machine detergents for removing starchy food remains.

1.3 Comparison of green plants and animals

Cells

A typical plant cell	*A typical animal cell*
Cellulose cell wall	No cellulose cell wall
Chloroplasts	No choroplasts
Large vacuole	No single large vacuole
No centrosomes	Centrosomes present

Organisms

Plant	*Animal*
Photosynthesis takes place	No photosynthesis
Body is often branched	Body is compact rather than branched
Chlorophyll is present	N~ ~hl~ ~h~ ll

Stores protein	Protein is not stored

1.4 Distinction between cells, tissues and organs

- **A cell** is the basic unit of all living organisms consisting of cytoplasm bounded by a membrane and usually with a nucleus.
- **A tissue** is a collection of similar cells subject to the same laws of growth and development, e.g. muscle tissue, bone tissue.
- **An organ** is part of a living organism which acts as a functional unit and is composed of a collection of tissues, e.g. kidney, liver, heart.
- **An organ system** is a group of organs which combine to perform certain functions, e.g. the digestive system, endocrine system and nervous system.

1.5 Characteristics of living organisms

1. **Movement** *The ability to move* as a result of expenditure of energy released by cells is present in all living things. All animals move in search of food at some stage of their lives. All plants move towards or away from certain stimuli such as light or gravity.

2. **Nutrition** *The ability to obtain food* is present in both plants and animals but the methods by which they do this form a basic difference between them.

3. **Growth** This is *the irreversible increase* in size which occurs by incorporation of new cytoplasm. It happens when the rate of manufacture of living material is greater than the rate of breakdown.

4. **Respiration** This is *the release of energy from glucose sugar* present in all living cells of the body. *It does not mean breathing.* Breathing is just the exchange of gases at the respiratory surface, e.g. the air sacs of the lungs.

5. **Excretion** This is *the elimination of waste material* which has come from chemical reactions taking place in the cells of the body. *The elimination of faeces via the anus is NOT excretion – it is egestion.*

6. **Reproduction** This is *the ability to produce new individuals* resembling the original parents. It ensures the continuity of the species.

⑦ **Sensitivity** This is *the ability to react to changes* in the surroundings – stimuli – and to changes within the organism.

If you read the above definitions carefully, you will see that none of them can be applied to non-living things, e.g. movement of inanimate objects will only take place if energy is applied to them in some form. It is never released within themselves. In chemistry, growth of crystals does not involve the manufacture of new protoplasm and it is reversible.

1.6 Conditions necessary for all forms of life

1 **A suitable temperature.**

2 **A source of energy** In other words, a means of obtaining food.

3 **Water** This is necessary **in order for enzymes to work** and **as a solvent** for all the chemical reactions taking place in the body.

1.7 Man as a mammal

Characteristics of mammals in general and man in particular

Mammals are **warm-blooded vertebrates** that possess **hair**, **sweat glands**, **a four-chambered heart**, a **diaphragm** and **external ears**. A **hard palate** separates the nasal from the food passage, allowing simultaneous breathing and chewing, and the **teeth are differentiated** into four distinct types (see Section 5.2). Most mammals **do not lay eggs**. Instead, the young develop inside the mother's body in the *uterus* until they are ready to be born. The exceptions are members of a group of mammals, the *monotremes*, which includes the *duck-billed platypus* and the *spiny anteater*.

All mammals **suckle their young on milk** and show some degree of **parental care** after the young have been born. This reaches its most developed form in humans. Finally, mammals have a **more developed brain** than other animals, and in man the brain reaches a level of development not found in any other creature.

1.8 Man as a product of an evolutionary process

Man belongs to a group of mammals, the primates, that also includes monkeys and apes.

Characteristics of primates

① Hands and feet are well adapted for **life in trees**.
② An **opposable thumb and index finger**.
③ **Well-developed eyes and ears** with a corresponding development of the areas of the brain concerned with vision and hearing.
④ **An enlargement of the frontal region of the skull** to accommodate a large brain.

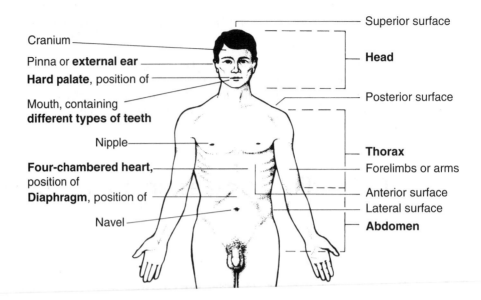
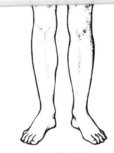

Cranium

Pinna or **external ear**

Hard palate, position of

Mouth, containing **different types of teeth**

Nipple

Four-chambered heart, position of

Diaphragm, position of

Navel

Superior surface

Head

Posterior surface

Thorax

Forelimbs or arms

Anterior surface

Lateral surface

Abdomen

Fig. 1.3 Mammalian features of man

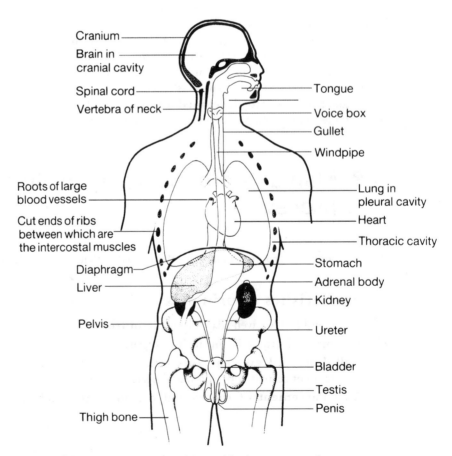

Cranium

Brain in cranial cavity

Spinal cord

Vertebra of neck

Roots of large blood vessels

Cut ends of ribs between which are the intercostal muscles

Diaphragm

Liver

Pelvis

Thigh bone

Tongue

Voice box

Gullet

Windpipe

Lung in pleural cavity

Heart

Thoracic cavity

Stomach

Adrenal body

Kidney

Ureter

Bladder

Testis

Penis

Fig. 1.4 Some of the more important cavities and body structures of man

Both man and present-day apes – the gorilla, orang-utan, gibbon and chimpanzee – had a common ancestor many millions of years ago. Although man is closely related to present-day apes and to fossil forms of apes and ape-men, he has some features which distinguish him from them all. The chief ones are:

(a) **Brain size** in relation to the size of the rest of the body. This is expressed as cranial capacity, i.e. the size of the part of the skull that houses the brain. Modern man has a cranial capacity of 1600 cm³ whereas that of apes is 600 cm³.

(b) Man is **bipedal** (i.e. he walks on two legs).

(c) Man has always **manufactured tools**.

(d) Man is the only animal to use **spoken language** and to communicate via the **written word**.

(e) Man devotes time to **cultural activities**.

Summary

Man's position in the living world

1. The cell is the basic unit of structure and function of living issue.
2. Enzymes are biological catalysts. Some are used in industry in detergents.
3. Living things are organised according to different levels of structure. Some are made of single cells, others are made up of many cells as tissues, organs and organ systems.
4. Living things have seven basic characteristics. These are: movement, nutrition, growth, respiration, excretion, reproduction and sensitivity.
5. All life requires a suitable temperature, water and a source of energy.
6. Humans are products of evolution and show characteristics of mammals, in particular primates.

Quick test

(a) Which of the following is not part of an animal cell?

A a nucleus   **B** a cell membrane   **C** cytoplasm   **D** a cellulose wall

(b) Enzymes:

A are biological catalysts   **B** work independently of pH   **C** are not involved in respiration   **D** do not alter the rate of a chemical reaction

(c) One difference between green plants and animals is that green plants have chlorophyll. For which of the following processes is it essential to plants?

A digesting food   **B** making mineral salts available   **C** making carbohydrates   **D** speeding up respiration

(d) Which of the following is a tissue?

A muscle   **B** a leucocyte   **C** the stomach   **D** the skeleton

(e) Which of the following is not a characteristic of all living things?

A respiration   **B** excretion   **C** nutrition   **D** hearing

(f) Which of the following is needed for all forms of life?

A oxygen   **B** water   **C** chlorophyll   **D** starch

(g) Man is a mammal because:

A he moves in search of his food   **B** he is a vertebrate   **C** he has hair   **D** he is warm-blooded

(h) Some living cells were broken into fragments and arranged into two groups:

Group I – all fragments lacked a nucleus

Group II – all fragments possessed a nucleus

Each group was maintained under uniform conditions and examined at regular intervals.

	Group I	Group II
Fragments examined	200	200
Surviving 24 hours	160	158
Surviving 48 hours	120	148
Surviving 72 hours	60	144
Surviving 96 hours	6	144

The best conclusion that can be made from this investigation is that

A the nucleus is normally necessary for the continued life of the cell

B nucleated and non-nucleated cell fragments have an equal chance of survival

C cell fragments cannot live long

D the removal of the nucleus injures the cytoplasm of the cell fragments

Chapter 2
The skeleton and movement

2.1 Functions of the skeleton

1. To act as a **framework** and to support the soft tissues of the body.
2. To enable **free movement** by the action of **muscles**.
3. To **protect** the delicate internal organs.
4. To **produce blood cells**. This is the function of *bone marrow*. In infants the red marrow of *all* bones is involved but in adults blood cells are produced in the red bone marrow of only the sternum, ribs, vertebrae, cranium and the 'heads' of the femur and humerus.
5. To **store calcium**. The calcium in *blood* is in equilibrium with that of bone.

2.2 The skeletal system

- **Axial skeleton.** This forms the axis of the body and has two parts: the *skull* and *backbone* (vertebral column).
- **Appendicular skeleton.** This is made up of the *limb girdles* (shoulder and hips) and the *limbs* (arms and legs). The limbs are attached to the limb girdles with ball-and-socket joints.
- **Thoracic skeleton.** The two parts of this are the *breast bone* (sternum) and the *ribs*. (see Fig 3.2(a) p. 21.)

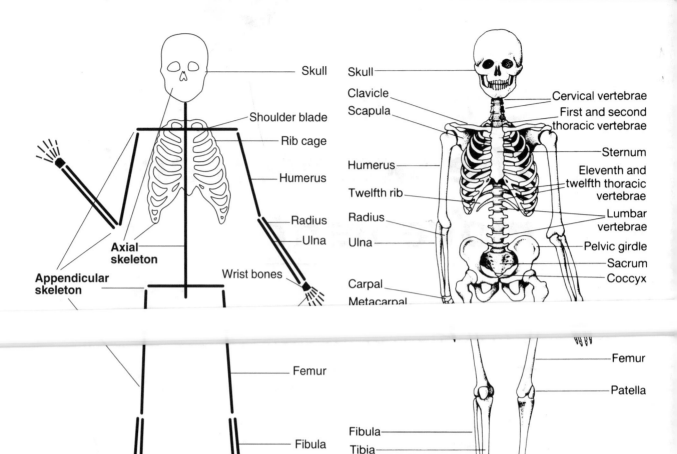

Fig. 2.1 The basic structure of the skeleton **Fig. 2.2** The human skeleton

2.3 Axial skeleton

The skull

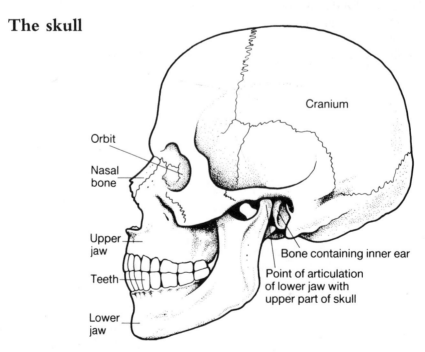

Fig. 2.3 Lateral view of the skull

The **cranium** houses the *brain*. Underneath, towards its posterior (back) end, is a large opening, the **foramen magnum**, through which the *spinal cord* passes from the brain.

There are paired *sense capsules*. The **auditory capsules** are bony cases which protect the middle and inner ears and are fused to the cranium near its posterior end. The **nasal capsules** are fused to the anterior (front) of the cranium and make up most of the **facial region**. They protect the delicate lining of the *nasal passages*. The *eyes* are without bony capsules but are protected by the **orbits**.

There is an upper and a lower **jaw**. The **upper jaw** is fused to the anterior half of the floor of the skull. The **lower jaw** articulates with the cranium on each side near the auditory region. Its function is to house the teeth used for chewing.

Vertebrae

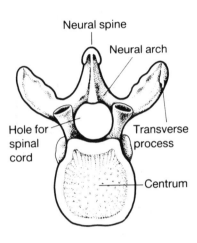

Fig. 2.4 The basic plan of a vertebra

Table 2.1 Structure and function of vertebrae

Part of vertebra	Function
Neural spine	Attachment of back muscles
Neural arch	Protection of spinal cord
Centrum	Support
Transverse process	Attachment of muscles

Table 2.2 Different types of vertebrae

Name of vertebra	Number	Function
Cervical/Neck	7	The first, the **atlas**, articulates with the skull and enables the head to move up and down. The second, the **axis**, articulates with the atlas and enables side to side movements of the head. The remaining five are for the *attachment of neck muscles* for movement of the head
Thoracic/Chest	12	To support the *ribs*
Lumbar/Abdominal	5	To support the whole weight of the body
Sacral	5 (fused)	To support the *pelvic girdle*
Coccygeal/Tail	4 (fused)	No function. A vestigal structure, the **coccyx**

Ribs

There are *12 pairs* (see Fig. 2.2). The last two pairs are *floating ribs* because their anterior ends are not attached to the sternum. The flexibility of the cartilages of the *sternum* and of the ribs, together with the joints with the vertebrae, enables the ribs to move when the *intercostal muscles* contract, thus allowing the volume of the thorax to be increased during inspiration.

2.4 Appendicular skeleton

Limb girdles

These consist of the bones with which the limbs articulate (Fig. 2.2). They are:

① The **pectoral/shoulder girdle**, which consists of the two *clavicles* (collar bones) and two *scapulae* (shoulder blades).

② The **pelvic/hip girdle**, which consists of two halves, the *innominate bones*, fused together. Each innominate bone is composed of three fused bones. These are the *ilium*, *ischium* and *pubis*.

Limbs

The limbs of all mammals are made from a basic plan, the **pentadactyl limb**.

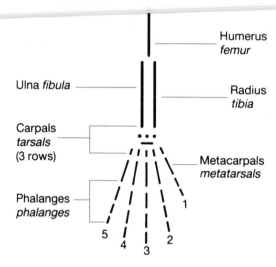

Fig. 2.5 The pentadactyl limb (bones of the fore limb (arms or front legs) are in normal type; those of the hind limb are in italics)

2.5 Joints

There are three main types of joints:
- **Fixed** or **immovable** (fibrous) joints, e.g. sutures between skull bones.
- **Slightly movable** (cartilaginous) joints, e.g. the *pubis, sternum/ribs* and between the *vertebrae.*
- **Freely movable** (synovial) joints.

Table 2.3 Types of synovial joints

Joint	Position in body
(a) **Gliding**	Articular processes of vertebrae
(b) **Hinge**	Elbow, knee (see Figs 2.6, 2.16)
(c) **Ball-and-socket**	Hip, shoulder
(d) **Condyloid**	Radius / carpal in wrist
(e) **Pivot**	Atlas / axis in neck
(f) **Saddle**	Metacarpal of the thumb and the carpal of the hand

The structure of the synovial joint

● Joints are needed where two bones meet and will move against each other.

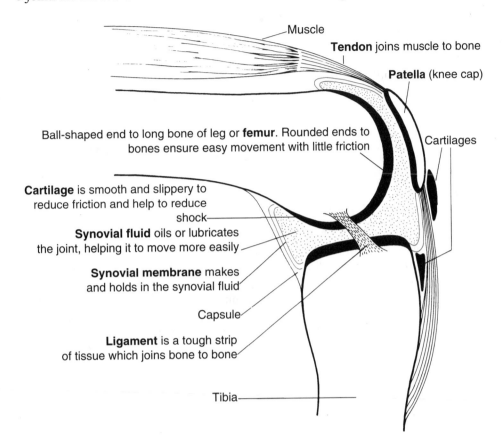

Muscle

Tendon joins muscle to bone

Patella (knee cap)

Ball-shaped end to long bone of leg or **femur**. Rounded ends to bones ensure easy movement with little friction

Cartilages

Cartilage is smooth and slippery to reduce friction and help to reduce shock

Synovial fluid oils or lubricates the joint, helping it to move more easily

Synovial membrane makes and holds in the synovial fluid

Capsule

Ligament is a tough strip of tissue which joins bone to bone

Tibia

Fig. 2.6 Diagram to show the structure of the knee joint. This is shown as if it had been cut in half

Table 2.4 Structure and function of parts of a synovial joint

Part of joint	Function
Cartilage	Helps to absorb shock
Synovial fluid	Helps to reduce friction
Synovial membrane	Secretes synovial fluid
Synovial capsule	Keeps synovial fluid in place
Ligament	Joins the bones together
Tendon	Joins muscle to bone allowing movement

2.6 Principles of levers applied to the skeleton

Forces acting on a lever produce movements centred at a point, the **fulcrum**. Two forces are generally involved: the **load** and the **effort**. The effort is the force applied to hold the load in **equilibrium**. For example, it is the muscular effort needed to lift a weight or to hold the head still in an inclined position.

The **effect of a force** in a lever system is called its **moment** and equals the *product* of the *force* and the *distance* between the force and the fulcrum. At equilibrium

effort × distance of effort from fulcrum = load × distance of load from fulcrum.

Some levers are more efficient than others. Levers can be grouped into first, second and third order levers.

First order levers

The *effort* and the *load* are on *opposite* sides of the *fulcrum* and a movement of the effort results in movement of the load in the *opposite* direction. When the fulcrum is central, at equilibrium the effort must *equal* the load. This type of lever produces movements of the trunk and head with very little contraction of the muscles involved.

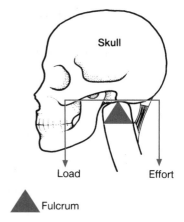

Skull

Load   Effort

Fulcrum

Fig. 2.7 First order lever

Second order levers

load in the *same* direction. The *effort* is *less* than the *load*, and to maintain equilibrium, any distance the effort moves from the fulcrum must be *greater* than the corresponding distance moved by the load. This type of lever action is seen when the body is raised on tiptoe.

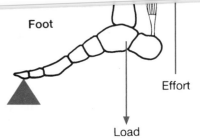

Foot

Effort

Load

Fig. 2.8 Second order lever

Third order levers

The *effort* is exerted between the *fulcrum* and the *load* and movement of the effort results in movement of the load in the *same* direction. The *effort* is *greater* than the *load*, and to maintain equilibrium any distance the effort moves from the fulcrum must be *less* than the corresponding distance moved by the load. This is seen in the arm and is the commonest type of lever in the body. A variety of large movements can be made with very little shortening of the muscles involved.

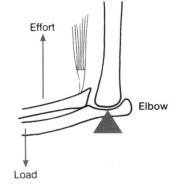

Effort

Elbow

Load

Fig. 2.9 Third order lever

2.7 Bone

Functions

1. To act as a strong framework to **support** the weight of the body.
2. To provide a secure **attachment** for the internal organs.
3. To provide a **store** of calcium, phosphorus and other essential minerals.
4. To **produce blood cells** (bone marrow).

Composition

50% water, 50% solid matter.
The solid matter consists of 67% calcium carbonate and calcium phosphate, 33% organic matter (gelatine and collagen).

General structure

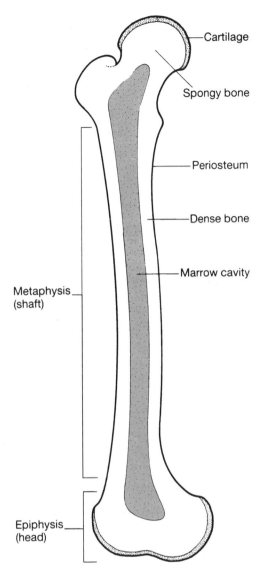

- Cartilage
- Spongy bone
- Periosteum
- Dense bone
- Marrow cavity

Metaphysis (shaft)

Epiphysis (head)

Fig. 2.10 The general structure of a long bone

Microscopic structure

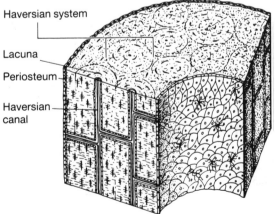

- Haversian system
- Lacuna
- Periosteum
- Haversian canal

Fig. 2.11 A microscopic view of bone

The **Haversian system** contains the *Haversian canals* which run in a longitudinal direction parallel with the surface of the bone. The bone substance surrounding the Haversian canals contains concentrically arranged spaces, the **lacunae**, which contain the bone cells. Minute canals (canaliculi) join up the lacunae, and also communicate with the Haversian canals. *Blood vessels* and *lymphatics* run throughout the Haversian canals and nourish the bone cells.

Development of bone

① **In the developing fetus** special connective tissue gives rise to a skeleton made entirely of cartilage. As the fetus grows, the cartilage is gradually replaced by bone and becomes harder as *calcium salts* are deposited within its substance. Later, special bone cells, **osteoblasts**, enter the calcified cartilage together with other cells which remove the cartilage. The osteoblasts proceed to lay down bone in place of the cartilage which is then absorbed.

② **Membranous bones**, principally the flat bones of the skull, develop from special groups of connective tissue.

2.8 Cartilage

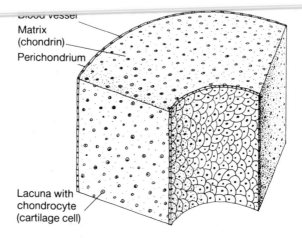

Blood vessel
Matrix (chondrin)
Perichondrium
Lacuna with chondrocyte (cartilage cell)

Fig. 2.12 A microscopic view of cartilage

Cartilage is firm bluish-white tissue, sometimes called **gristle**, that is made up mainly of fibres of **collagen** and **elastin** with a very small amount of *mineral matter*. The surface is covered by a membrane, the **perichondrium**, which is supplied with *blood vessels*. As the membrane and the ground substance of the cartilage are permeable, no blood vessels need enter cartilage tissue: materials in blood can diffuse through to the cartilage cells, which lie in special spaces, the **lacunae. Hyaline cartilage** is found lining *joints*, **fibro-cartilage** is found between the *vertebrae*, and **elastic cartilage** is found where a certain amount of elasticity is required, for example in the *epiglottis* and *pinna* of the ear.

2.9 Muscles

Table 2.5 Different types of muscles

Type	Position in the body
Smooth/Plain/Involuntary/Unstriated	Where sustained automatic contraction is needed, e.g. in walls of the **intestine** and **bladder**. Also in blood vessels. Arranged in *sheets*.
Cardiac/Heart	**Heart**
Striated/Striped/Voluntary/Skeletal	Attached to the **skeleton** and under the control of *conscious effort*. Arranged in *bundles*.

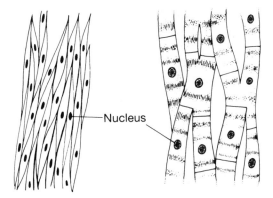

Fig. 2.13 Smooth muscle   **Fig. 2.14** Heart muscle

The structure of striated muscle

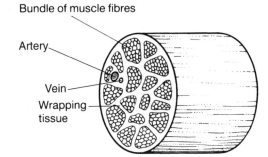

Fig. 2.15(a) Skeletal muscle

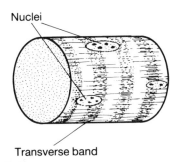

Fig. 2.15(b) Part of a muscle fibre

2.10 The antagonistic action of pairs of muscles

Table 2.6 Muscles of the arm and leg

Muscle	Origin	Insertion	Action
Biceps	Scapula	Radius	Flexes arm
Triceps	Scapula	Ulna	Extends arm
Quadriceps femoris (includes 4 muscles)	Pelvis and femur	Tibia	(a) Flexes hip joint (b) Extends leg at knee
Biceps femoris	Pelvis and femur	Fibula	Flexes leg at knee
Gluteus maximus	Pelvis	Femur	(a) Retracts leg (b) Straightens body by rotating it about the head of the femur
Gastrocnemius	Femur	Heel	Extends leg at ankle
Anterior tibial	Tibia	Metatarsal	Flexes leg at ankle

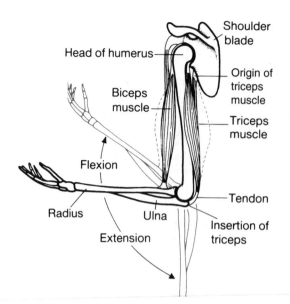

Fig. 2.16 The elbow joint is an example of a hinged joint. It is capable of flexion and extension but not rotation. The dotted lines show the change in shape of the muscles during flexion and extension

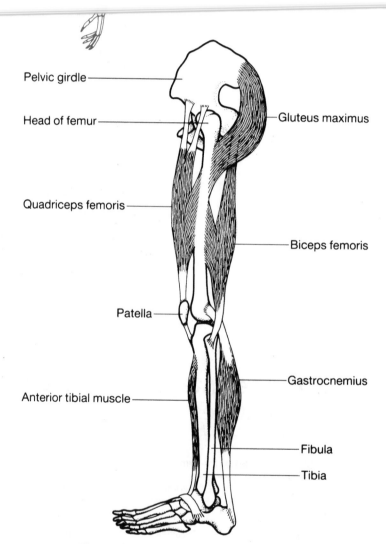

Fig. 2.17 Some human leg muscles and bones

1. The **antagonistic action** of muscles takes place when there is opposing action of two muscles such that the contraction of one is accompanied by the relaxation of the other.

2. The **point of origin** is that point of attachment of a muscle that does not move when the muscle contracts.

❸ The **point of insertion** is that point of attachment of a muscle that moves when the muscle contracts.

2.11 The physiology of muscle action

The *energy* used for the *contraction* of muscle cells comes from **adenosine triphosphate (ATP)**, which is a temporary store of chemical energy produced as a result of **respiration** (see Section 3.2).

Respiration takes place in muscle cells by **oxidation of glycogen** (a store of *glucose*). Glycogen makes up only 1% by weight of muscle and it is soon used during exercise, after which the muscle relies on fresh supplies of glucose from the *bloodstream*. To produce the maximum of ATP, **oxygen** is needed for the complete oxidation of glucose, and

lactic acid as a waste product. If exercise is vigorous or a muscle remains in a state of contraction for a long period, lactic acid accumulates. It may prevent the muscle from contracting further, causing **fatigue** and even *pain*.

When the exercise stops, the muscle *recovers* and will continue to use oxygen at a fast rate until the lactic acid is removed from the muscle via the bloodstream.

Summary

The skeleton and movement

❶ Our skeletons have several functions including support, movement, protection, blood cell production and mineral storage.
❷ Muscles produce movement of the skeleton by being attached to bones and acting across joints.
❸ Muscles which cause movement act in antagonistic pairs.
❹ Smooth muscles form layers in the walls of organs like the stomach, intestines and arteries.
❺ Special cardiac muscles is used in the heart when it pumps blood.
❻ Energy for muscle contraction is in the form of adenosine triphosphate which is a product of respiration in all cells. Anaerobic respiration in muscle cells produces lactic acid.

Quick test

(a) Cartilage in a synovial joint serves to:
  A give the body its shape   **B** protect the muscles at the joint   **C** reduce friction
  D allow for extra movement
(b) In which of the following parts of the body is a hinge joint found?
  A the shoulder   **B** the knee   **C** the hip   **D** the skull
(c) The structures which attach muscles to bones are called:
  A tendons   **B** nerves   **C** ligaments   **D** cartilages
(d) When we chew, the lower jaw is moved by the contraction of muscles. These muscles are:
  A circular   **B** smooth   **C** radial   **D** voluntary
(e) Which type of joint allows movement in more than one plane?
  A hinge   **B** gliding   **C** ball and socket   **D** saddle
(f) When the arm is flexed:
  A the biceps relaxes and the triceps expands
  B the biceps expands and the triceps relaxes
  C the biceps expands and the triceps contracts
  D the biceps contracts and the triceps relaxes.

Chapter 3
The respiratory system

3.1 The respiratory system and the exchange of gases

✓**Oxygen** must be absorbed into the bodies of animals and plants for *respiration* to occur. In microscopically small organisms, the surface area in relation to volume is sufficiently large to permit adequate gaseous exchange and no special respiratory surfaces are required. The **rate of diffusion** is *inversely proportional to the distance travelled*, and so large animals such as man require a large surface area in contact with air. The characteristics of an efficient **respiratory surface** in active animals are as follows:

- It must be **large in proportion to the animal's bulk**.
- It must be **thin enough to allow gases to pass through easily**.
- It has to be **moist so that carbon dioxide and oxygen can pass through** in solution.
- It has to be **richly supplied with blood** to transport gases to and from the surface. The more active the animal, the greater will be the oxygen requirement, so in all vertebrates, a means of **ventilating** or renewing the air at the surface is essential.

3.2 Respiration and the provision of energy

Respiration is the **release of energy from glucose** and occurs in *all* living cells.

$$C_6H_{12}O_6 + 6O_2 \xrightarrow{\text{Enzymes}} 6CO_2 + 6H_2O + \textbf{Energy}$$

Glucose   Oxygen   Carbon dioxide   Water   **ATP**

The equation is a *gross over-simplification* of the process because:

- It shows only the **reactants** and the **products** and gives no indication of the many *intermediate, enzyme-controlled reactions* which occur.
- It implies that all the **energy** is liberated in one stage whereas it is really liberated in a succession of stages, a small amount at a time.
- It implies that **oxidation** takes place *totally* by the addition of oxygen, whereas in fact most of the oxidation takes place by *removal of hydrogen* from glucose using a series of chemicals called **hydrogen carriers**. Oxygen is added during the *final* stages of oxidation only.
- It gives us no idea of the form in which the energy is made available to the cell. The energy is in **adenosine triphosphate (ATP)**, which acts as the *energy currency* of the living organism, and is released and made available to the cell when this chemical *loses* one of its *phosphate groups* to become **adenosine diphosphate (ADP)**.

3.3 The respiratory organs

Table 3.1 The respiratory organs

Structure	Function
Larynx	The **voice box** for *sound production*
Trachea	The **windpipe** to *carry air* to the lungs via the bronchi
Intercostal muscles	Used during **breathing** movements
Lungs	The organs where **exchange of gases** occurs between the blood system and the atmosphere
Diaphragm	A *sheet of muscle* separating the thorax from the abdomen and used during **breathing** movements

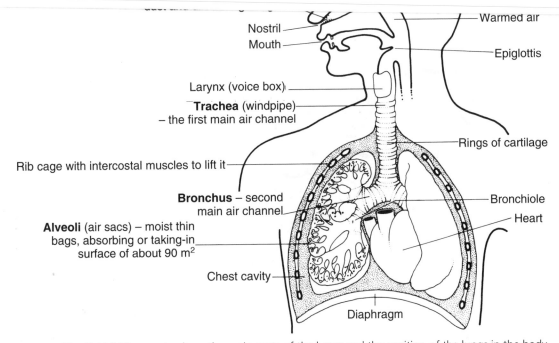

Fig. 3.1(a) Diagram to show the main parts of the lungs and the position of the lungs in the body

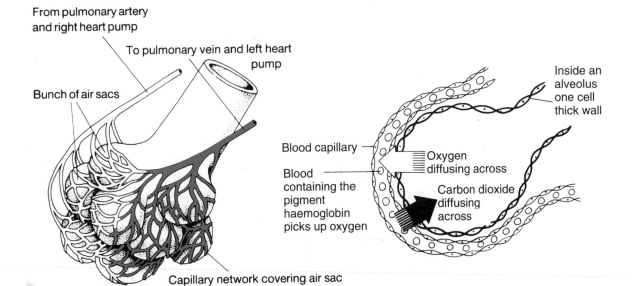

Fig. 3.1(b) The blood supply to air sacs   **Fig. 3.1(c)** Detailed section of one air sac

1. The **trachea** and **bronchi** are partially surrounded by horseshoe-shaped **bands of cartilage** which protect them from *pressure changes* during the passage of air in and out of the lungs and so keep them constantly open.

2. The **larynx** is closed by a flap of muscle, the **epiglottis**, which prevents food entering the trachea.

3. The **tubular parts** of the respiratory system are lined with cells which have minute hair-like **cilia**. The cells secrete **mucus**, which traps dust particles, and the cilia move the particles in the mucus away from the lungs to the throat. Thus the system is kept free of unwanted pollutants.

4. The **bronchi** divide to form narrower **bronchioles** which terminate in air sacs or **alveoli**. Here *gaseous exchange* takes place.

3.4 The mechanism of breathing

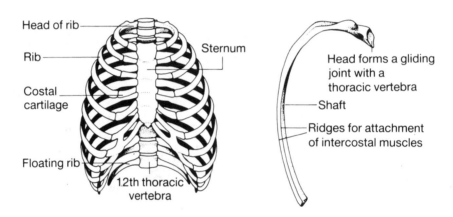

Fig. 3.2(a) The thoracic cage (left) and a left rib (right)

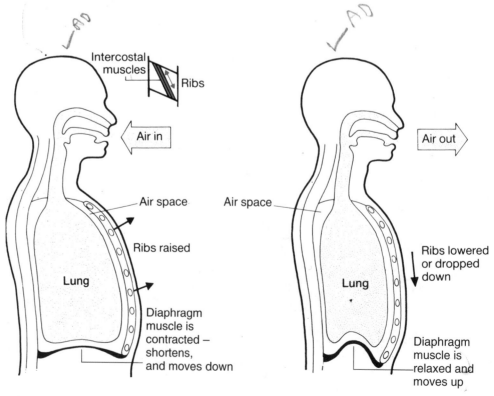

Fig. 3.2(b) Inspiration – taking air in

Fig. 3.2(c) Expiration – pushing air out

Stages of inspiration

1 **Muscles of the diaphragm** contract, causing it to *flatten*. This *increases the volume* of the thorax but *decreases the pressure* inside it.

2 **Inspiratory intercostal muscles** contract, pulling the lower ribs (which pivot at the vertebrae) *upward and outward*.

3 **A partial vacuum** is created and air is *sucked in*.

Stages of expiration

1 **Muscles of the diaphragm** relax while those of the **abdominal wall** contract. This action pushes the stomach and liver *upwards* so that the diaphragm becomes dome shaped.

2 **Inspiratory intercostal muscles** relax, allowing the ribs and sternum to fall under ~~____ This ____ the pressure~~ within the thorax but *decreases the volume*, forcing air

there is no pressure on them.

3.5 The differences between inspired and expired air

Table 3.2

Gas	Composition, as percentage of volume	
	Inspired air	Expired air
Oxygen	20.70	14.6
Carbon dioxide	0.04	3.8
Water vapour	1.26	6.2
Nitrogen	78.00	75.4

3.6 Smoking and its effects on the respiratory system

1 **The lungs are damaged** by the constant *irritation* of tobacco smoke.

2 **Smoking lessens the resistance of the lungs to diseases**, particularly to those caused by *bacteria* and *viruses*. The irritating effects of smoke gradually damage the cells which can then be attacked by *pathogens*. **Chronic bronchitis** may be linked with smoking.

3 **Heavy smoking impairs athletic performance** as it makes *gaseous exchange inefficient*.

4 **Tobacco tar produces skin cancer** when painted on the skin of experimental animals and could possibly affect human lungs in the same way.

5 **Smoking during pregnancy reduces the oxygen available to the developing fetus**, resulting in *stunted physical and mental development*.

6 **The cilia**, lining the respiratory system, are **gradually destroyed by smoke and nicotine**. Figure 3.3 shows the relationship between smoking and some lung diseases:

Smoking and health

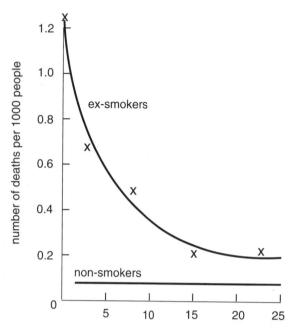

Fig. 3.3(a) Death rates from lung cancer in people who have given up smoking, and in non-smokers

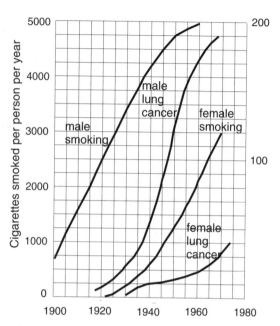

Fig. 3.3(c) Death rates from lung cancer in relation to the number of cigarettes smoked

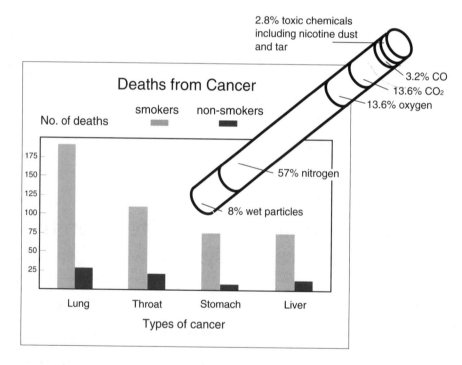

Fig. 3.3(b) Incidence of types of cancer resulting in death for smokers and non-smokers

E **xaminer's tip**

The most common
examination questions on
this topic are based on:
  The mechanism of
  breathing
  Data relating to health
  issues resulting from
  smoking.

Summary

The respiratory system

1. Breathing involves the exchange of gases between cells and the environment
2. Breathing is a mechanical process that moves air in and out of the lungs as a result of inspiration and expiration.
3. In order to be efficient, a breathing surface must be (a) large in relation to the bulk of the animal, (b) moist, (c) thin and (d) richly supplied with blood.
4. Respiration is a chemical process involving the release of energy from glucose in all living cells.
5. The carbon dioxide concentration of expired air is 100 times greater than that of inspired air.

damages your breathing system.

Quick test

(a) The approximate percentage of oxygen in expired air is
   A 0.04   **B** 4   **C** 16   **D** 21
(b) Air will enter the lungs when the:
   A diaphragm is raised
   B volume of the thorax is decreased
   C ribs and sternum are lowered
   D volume of the thorax is increased
(c) The epiglottis:
   A closes the oesophagus during breathing
   B prevents the trachea from collapsing
   C closes the trachea when swallowing
   D closes the nasal cavity when swallowing
(d) The products of tissue respiration are:
   A carbon dioxide and nitrogen   **B** carbon dioxide and water
   C carbon monoxide and water   **D** nitrogen and water
(e) The membranes surrounding the lungs comprise:
   A the pericardium   **B** the periosteum   **C** the pleura   **D** the perichondrium
(f) The processes of respiration and burning are similar but only respiration
   A releases energy   **B** produces waste gases   **C** uses up fuel   **D** occurs within cells.

Chapter 4
Food and nutrition

4.1 Classes of food

Food is required as a **source of energy** and for the **manufacture of new protoplasm** during growth. There are **six basic classes** of food required by man. These are:

- Carbohydrates
- Proteins
- Fats
- Mineral salts
- Vitamins
- Water

Carbohydrates

The chemical elements present are **carbon, hydrogen and oxygen**. They have the general formula $C_x(H_2O)_y$ and the important point to remember is that their molecules always have *twice as many hydrogen atoms* as *oxygen atoms*. They are generally divided into **sugars** (such as *glucose, fructose, lactose, maltose* and *sucrose*) and **polysaccharides** (such as *starch* and *glycogen*). Carbohydrates are used mainly as a source of *energy* (see Section 3.2).

Proteins

The chemical elements present are **carbon, hydrogen, oxygen, nitrogen** and sometimes **phosphorus** and **sulphur**. They are made of basic units, the **amino acids**, which are held together by chemical bonds called **peptide links**. Proteins are generally used for *building new cells*.

Fats

The chemical elements present are **carbon, hydrogen** and **oxygen**. Fats are made of two basic units, **glycerol** and **fatty acids**, and are generally used as a *store of energy* and for *insulation*.

Mineral salts

Besides the elements present in the above classes of foods, we need a considerable number of others. Mineral salts cannot be made by living creatures. Plants obtain them from the soil and animals acquire them, directly or indirectly, from plants. Mineral salts are required in small quantities for a variety of purposes (see Table 4.1).

Vitamins

Like mineral salts, vitamins have *no energy value* but are essential for the *chemical reactions* which take place in the body. They are needed in only very small quantities but without them we suffer from *deficiency disease* (see Table 4.2).

Water

The **protoplasm** of cells is made up of about 75% water. It plays a part in *transport* of materials around the body, *removal of waste products*, maintaining a *constant body temperature* and for *all chemical reactions* taking place in the body.

4.2 Basic food requirements

Table 4.1 Food requirements

Food substance	Chemical formula or symbol	Use	Source
Carbohydrates			
Glucose	$C_6H_{12}O_6$	Provides energy	Grapes, carrots, Honey, fruits
Sucrose	$C_{12}H_{22}O_{11}$		
Starch	$(C_6H_{10}O_5)_n$	Provides energy	Potatoes, wheat, rice
Glycogen	$(C_6H_{10}O_5)_n$	Provides energy	Liver, lean meat
Fats		Provide energy; insulation. Can be stored under the skin	Butter, lard, cheese, suet, fish oil
Proteins		Building new cells	Lean meat, fish, milk, eggs, cheese, peas, wheat
Minerals			
Calcium	Ca	Bone formation, teeth, blood clotting	Cheese, milk, bread
Phosphorus	P	Bone formation, cell division	Most foods containing protein
Potassium	K	Formation of new protoplasm	Meat and most vegetables
Sulphur	S	Protein formation	Most foods with proteins
Chlorine	Cl	Constituent of body fluids and hydrochloric acid	Common salt
Sodium	Na	Constituent of body fluids; in transport of carbon dioxide	Common salt
Magnesium	Mg	Formation of bones and teeth	Most foods
Iron	Fe	Formation of haemoglobin	Liver, kidney, eggs
Fluorine	F	Formation of tooth enamel	A trace element in some water
Iodine	I	Formation of hormone thyroxine	Sea foods
Zinc	Zn	Formation of hormone insulin	A trace element in plants
Copper	Cu	Formation of haemoglobin	A trace element in plants
Cobalt	Co	Formation of haemoglobin	A trace element in plants
Water	H_2O	Dissolving foods; a general solvent for all chemical reactions in the body	Most foods, all liquids

4.3 Vitamins

Table 4.2 Vitamins

Vitamin	Deficiency effects	Source
A (fat soluble)	Poor skin and mucous membranes. Night blindness	Green vegetables, milk, butter, fish liver oils
B₁ – thiamin (water soluble)	Beri-beri. Disorders of the nervous system, muscular atrophy	Yeast, wholemeal bread, peas and beans
B₂ – riboflavin (water soluble)	Disorders of the skin and digestive system	Yeast, meat, milk, liver, eggs
B₁₂ – cobalamin	Pernicious anaemia	Liver, fish, eggs
C – ascorbic acid (water soluble)	Scurvy – internal bleeding, swelling of gums	Citrus fruits and vegetables
D (fat soluble)	Rickets – bones soften and become pliable	Fish liver oils, eggs, butter. Formed by the action of sunlight on skin
E (fat soluble)	Embryo fails to develop. Loss of fertility (in rats)	Wheatgerm, oil, eggs, liver, green vegetables

Additional notes on the deficiency effects of vitamins

Vitamins play an essential role as **enzyme co-factors**. These are substances which help enzymes work properly, and without them the biochemical pathways that take place in the body would come to a halt. (However, not all co-factors are vitamins – *metallic ions* and other chemicals also act as co-factors for certain enzymes.) Here are some examples of the biochemical cause and the symptoms of vitamin deficiency.

- **Vitamin A** acts as a co-factor in the pathway leading to the formation of **visual purple**, a substance essential for *vision* found in the cells of the **retina**, hence the link with *night-blindness*.

- **Vitamin B₁** plays an essential role in the cellular processes involved in **respiration**, that is the utilisation of oxygen and the production of carbon dioxide during the liberation of energy from glucose. A shortage of this co-factor will interfere with one of life's most essential functions. Indeed, most of the vitamin B group are respiratory co-enzymes.

- **Vitamin C** has two specific functions:
  (a) A **respiratory** function, in which the vitamin aids in the important *energy release* mechanisms of the cell.
  (b) A **regulation function**, this concerning the formation of *intercellular material* that binds cells into tissues. Symptoms observed in vitamin C-deficient patients result from a breakdown of this material. *Capillaries rupture* because of inadequate 'cementing' between the cells.

- **Vitamin D** is essential for the metabolism of *calcium* and *phosphorus*. As these two elements are the major constituents of **bone**, vitamin D deficiency results in abnormalities of bone.

- **Vitamin E** appears to have a role in the biochemistry of the *human reproductive system*, but this is still a matter of conjecture.

4.4 The importance of a balanced diet

A balanced diet must satisfy the following requirements:

1 It must contain sufficient **energy** to be released for the *metabolism* of the individual. (On average between 10 500 and 14 000 kilojoules a day.)

2 It must contain roughly **20% protein, 20% fat** and **60% carbohydrate**.

3 It must contain some *fresh foods,* such as *green vegetables,* etc., to provide the necessary **vitamins** and **roughage** (in the form of *cellulose*) to stimulate the peristaltic action of the alimentary canal.

4 It must contain a range of **mineral elements**, especially *calcium, potassium, sodium* and *iron*.

5 It must contain an adequate amount of **water**.

6 It must be **palatable** and easily **digested**.

If a person does not receive a balanced diet, then he/she is likely to suffer from malnutrition. This may mean either *under-* or *over-nutrition*. Protein and energy (joule) deficiency is common in under-developed countries while over-nutrition, causing **obesity**, is common in developed countries.

4.5 Daily energy requirements

Table 4.3 Daily energy requirements

Person	Occupation/Activity	Requirements in kilojoules (kJ)
Newborn baby	Sleeping, moving	1900
Adult in bed	Resting	7600
Girl age 8 years	Very active in playing	8000
Boy age 8 years	Very active in playing	8400
Woman	Light work, e.g. office	8800
Man	Light work, e.g. office	10 500
Pregnant woman	Feeding the embryo	10 500
Girl age 15 years	Active in games, e.g. tennis	11 800
Woman breast feeding	Feeding a baby	12 600
Man	Moderate work, e.g. carpentry	14 300
Boy 15 years	Active in games, e.g. football	14 700

Note that the **joule (J)** is the *unit of energy* that is now used internationally. It has replaced the calorie as a unit of energy.

A **calorie** is the amount of heat energy required to raise the temperature of **1 g** of water through **1°C**.

A **kilocalorie** = 1000 calories.

A **joule** is the work done when the point of application of a force of **1 newton** is displaced through a distance of **1 metre** in the direction of the force.

A **kilojoule (kJ)** = 1000 joules. 1 kilocalorie = 4.2 kilojoules.

A simple experiment to measure the heat energy in a peanut

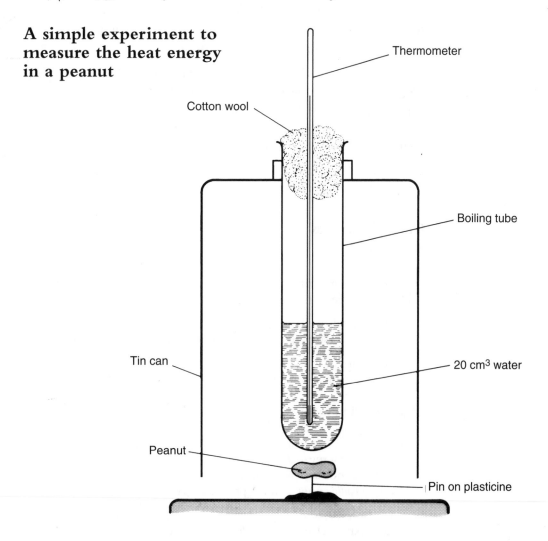

Fig. 4.1 Apparatus for determining the energy in a peanut

Procedure

1. Weigh a large peanut and mount it on a pin as shown in the diagram.
2. Place 20 cm³ water in the boiling tube.
3. Note the temperature with the thermometer.
4. Set light to the peanut with a Bunsen burner and place the boiling tube over it to catch as much of the heat as possible.
5. Read the temperature as soon as the peanut has been completely burned.
6. Record the temperature increase.
7. Work out the number of joules of heat the water has received as follows:

   4.2 J raise 1 g water 1°C
   Temperature increase = Y °C
   Mass of peanut = X g Mass of water = 20 g
   Heat gained by water = 20 g × Y × 4.2 J

   $$\text{Heat produced by 1 g of sample} = \frac{20 \times Y \text{ g} \times 4.2}{1000 \times X} \text{ kJ/g}$$

Note that possible sources of error include:
(a) heat loss around sides of boiling tube,
(b) heat loss raising the temperature of the thermometer and the glass of the boiling tube,
(c) incomplete burning of the peanut.
An improvement would be to insulate the apparatus.

4.6 Food tests

Style note: Writing Reports

When writing reports of food tests or any other investigation:

- Always keep your accounts of the **method, results** and **conclusion** separate.

- Your description of the method must be written clearly such that the reader could obtain the same results if he or she repeated your technique.

- Your results should be a clear statement of what you detected or experienced with either your eyes, nose, touch receptors or ears.

- NEVER TASTE laboratory chemicals – they may be toxic.

- DO NOT USE the terms '*positive*' or '*negative*' without qualifying the terms by saying exactly what such a result means for a particular investigation.

Carbohydrates

1. **Starch**

   Method
   Add a few drop of *iodine* dissolved in *potassium iodide* to a solution/suspension of the food believed to contain starch.

   Expected result
   The solution/suspension turns from its original colour to *blue-black*.

   Conclusion
   The food contains starch.

2. **A reducing sugar**

   Method
   Add *Benedict's solution* (or *Fehling's A & B*) to an equal volume of a solution believed to be a reducing sugar. *Boil* the mixture.
   NOTE Do not say '*heat*' or '*warm*' the mixture as these are relative terms. '*Boil*' means '*bring to boiling point*' and is a precise instruction.

   Expected result
   The mixture changes from *light blue*, through *green*, then *yellow*, to an *orange-brown precipitate*.

Conclusion
The food contains a reducing sugar. (It reduced the *copper salts* in the Benedict's solution or Fehling's to *copper oxide*.)

3 A non-reducing sugar
Method
Add *Benedict's solution* (or *Fehling's A & B*) to an equal volume of a solution believed to be a non-reducing sugar. *Boil* the mixture.

Expected result
The solution remains *blue* with no orange-brown precipitate.

Conclusion
The solution does not contain a reducing sugar.

In order to find out if it does contain a non-reducing sugar, continue as follows:

Method

solution (or *Fehling's A & B*). *Boil* the mixture.

Expected result
An *orange-brown precipitate* is formed.

Conclusion The food contains a non-reducing sugar. (The hydrochloric acid has *hydrolysed* [added water to] the original non-reducing sugar and changed it into a reducing sugar.)

$$C_{12}H_{22}O_{11} + H_2O \xrightarrow{\quad HCl \quad} C_6H_{12}O_6 + C_6H_{12}O_6$$
$$\text{Non-reducing sugar} \qquad\qquad \text{reducing sugar}$$

Proteins, fats and vitamins

Soluble proteins – the Biuret test
Method
Add 2 cm³ of *20% sodium hydroxide* to 2 cm³ of the solution containing the suspected protein. Add three drops of *1% copper sulphate* to the mixture.

Expected result
A *violet* colour is seen in the mixture.

Conclusion
The solution contains a protein.

Fat
Method
Rub a sample of the suspected fat on to a piece of paper.

Expected result
A translucent patch is seen on the paper which persists after drying.

Conclusion
The food tested contains fat.

The DCPIP test for ascorbic acid (Vitamin C)

Ascorbic acid is a powerful **reducing agent** and a dye, **DCPIP**, can be used to detect it. The vitamin causes the normally blue dye to be *decolourised*.

Method
Pour *1 cm³ DCPIP* solution into a test tube. Take a *1 cm³ syringe* full of sample material, e.g. lemon juice. Record the *volume* of sample material you need to add to the DCPIP to decolourise it.
    Repeat the test with 1 cm³ of fresh DCPIP using an ascorbic acid solution of known

concentration. Record the volume of the second, standard solution needed to decolourize the DCPIP solution.

Sample results
Volume of *lemon juice* used to decolourize 1 cm³ of DCPIP solution = 0.5cm³
Volume of *ascorbic acid* of known concentration used to decolourize 1cm³ of DCPIP solution = 0.4 cm³

Conclusion
The lemon juice was $\dfrac{0.4}{0.5}$ times as concentrated as the standard ascorbic acid solution.

If the standard ascorbic acid solution contained *1 mg ascorbic acid per cm³ water*, then the lemon juice must contain $1 \times \dfrac{0.4}{0.5}$ = *0.8 mg asorbic acid per cm³ water.*

Summary

Food and nutrition

1. Our bodies need carbohydrates, fats and protein in large quantities.
2. Our bodies need vitamins and minerals in very small quantities.
3. Vitamins are used in our bodies to help enzymes work.
4. A balanced diet should contain approximately 60% carbohydrates, 20% fat and 20% protein.
5. Daily energy requirements depend on the degree of activity of the individual.
6. Simple chemical tests can be used to determine the presence of starch, simple reducing sugars, fat, protein and a reducing agent such as vitamin C.

Quick test

(a) If you wished to show that honey contains a reducing sugar, which of the following procedures would you carry out?
   A add Sudan III   **B** boil with Benedict's or Fehling's solution
   C add iodine solution   **D** add Biuret solution
(b) Anaemia can be caused by a deficiency of:
   A carbohydrates   **B** hormones   **C** vitamin C   **D** a mineral salt
(c) Roughage in our diet is not digested, but it is useful because:
   A it helps prevent constipation   **B** it supplies vitamin B
   C it supplies calcium   **D** it provides extra carbohydrates
(d) Which of the following nutrients provides the most energy per gram?
   A carbohydrates   **B** fats   **C** proteins   **D** vitamins
(e) Carbohydrates may be stored in the muscles and liver as:
   A glucose   **B** glycerol   **C** glycogen   **D** cellulose
(f) Iodine is essential in the diet because it:
   A helps to prevent tooth decay   **B** is an antiseptic
   C is needed to produce thyroxine   **D** is needed to produce vitamin D.

Chapter 5
The digestive system

5.1 Principles of digestion

Food has to be **broken down** before it can be transported to the cells that need it. This is done both **mechanically** and **chemically**.

Firstly, in the *mouth* food is broken into small pieces that have a relatively *large surface area* for the action of **digestive enzymes** in *saliva*. These enzymes are responsible for the first stage of chemical breakdown.

After the process of **chewing**, the food is passed along the **alimentary canal** by muscular action, which also helps to mix the food with other enzymes secreted by various cells associated with the wall of the gut. There are digestive enzymes for each of three classes of food: *carbohydrates, fats* and *proteins*. These are *carbohydrases, lipases* and *proteases*, respectively. Within each category of enzymes there are several different types, each carrying out a specific function and often requiring a certain level of *acidity* or *alkalinity* that is provided by additional gut secretions.

Eventually, *carbohydrates* are converted to **glucose**, *proteins* to **amino acids**, and *fats* to **glycerol** and **fatty acids**. All of these end-products are of a molecular size sufficiently small for them to pass through the gut wall. The wall of the gut may be modified to increase the surface area for absorption of the products of digestion. Once absorbed, the materials are transported to the cells by the blood system.

5.2 Teeth

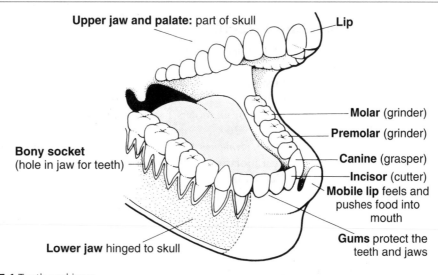

Fig. 5.1 Teeth and jaws

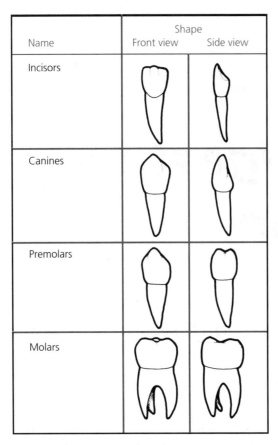

Name	Shape	
	Front view	Side view
Incisors		
Canines		
Premolars		
Molars		

Fig. 5.2 Different types of teeth

Table 5.1 Functions of the different types of teeth

Tooth	Function	Numbers (in each half of upper and lower jaw in an adult)
Incisor	Cutting	2
Canine	Grasping	1
Premolar	Grinding	2
Molar	Grinding	3

Structure

- **Dentine** is very hard and resembles *bone* in composition.
- **Enamel** is the hardest substance in the body.
- The **pulp cavity** contains *soft connective tissue, blood vessels* and *nerves* which enter the **root** through a fine canal at its base.

Milk and adult teeth

Milk/temporary teeth	*Time of appearance (months)*
Incisors	6–12
First milk molars	12–24
Canines	14–20
Second milk molars	20–24

Total number of teeth = **20**

Adult/permanent teeth	*Time of appearance (years)*
First molars	6
Central incisors	7
Lateral incisors	8
Premolars	9 and 10
Canines	11
Second molars	12
Third molars	17–25

Total number of teeth = **32**

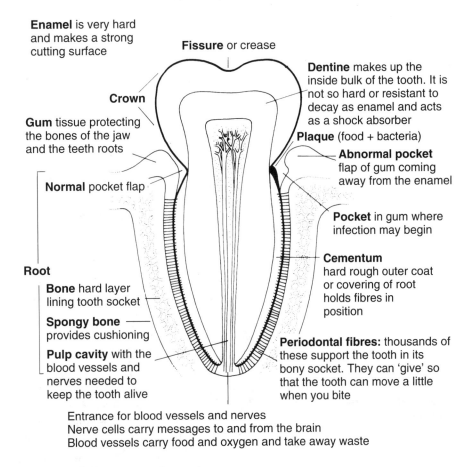

Enamel is very hard and makes a strong cutting surface

Fissure or crease

Dentine makes up the inside bulk of the tooth. It is not so hard or resistant to decay as enamel and acts as a shock absorber

Crown

Gum tissue protecting the bones of the jaw and the teeth roots

Plaque (food + bacteria)

Abnormal pocket flap of gum coming away from the enamel

Normal pocket flap

Pocket in gum where infection may begin

Root

Bone hard layer lining tooth socket

Cementum hard rough outer coat or covering of root holds fibres in position

Spongy bone provides cushioning

Pulp cavity with the blood vessels and nerves needed to keep the tooth alive

Periodontal fibres: thousands of these support the tooth in its bony socket. They can 'give' so that the tooth can move a little when you bite

Entrance for blood vessels and nerves
Nerve cells carry messages to and from the brain
Blood vessels carry food and oxygen and take away waste

Fig. 5.3 Diagram of the structure of a tooth

Care of teeth (see also Section 13.1)

A surface film, **plaque**, normally covers teeth and is difficult to remove, even by brushing with a good toothbrush. Plaque contains **bacteria** that break down *carbohydrates* into *acids* which attack the *enamel* and eventually cause **tooth decay**. Decay is undoubtedly reduced when the concentration of **fluoride** in drinking water is about *1 part per million*: fluoride helps to make the enamel more acid-resistant.

5.3 The alimentary canal

Table 5.2 The alimentary canal

Region of the alimentary canal	Function
Buccal cavity and pharynx	1 Ingestion of food 2 Mastication by teeth, food rolled into a ball and pushed into oesophagus by tongue and cheek muscles 3 Saliva added, containing: (a) water, (b) mucin (a constituent of mucus), and (c) salivary amylase (the enzyme ptyalin) 4 Food tasted by tongue
Oesophagus	Transports food to stomach by peristalsis
Stomach	1 Churns food 2 Adds water 3 Adds hydochloric acid 4 Adds various digestive enzymes 5 Secretes gastrin (hormone) 6 Absorbs alcohol and glucose 7 Stores food

Table 5.2 (continued)

Region of the alimentary canal	Function
Duodenum	1 Receives bile 2 Receives pancreatic juice 3 Secretes secretin (hormone)
Ileum	1 Secretes succus entericus (a mixture of digestive enzymes) 2 Absorbs the end-products of digestion
Colon	Absorbs water
Rectum	Stores faeces prior to removal via anus (egestion)

In the **alimentary canal** insoluble pieces of food are digested so that they become tiny soluble pieces of food that can be easily absorbed into the blood or into the lymph where they will be taken to the liver for further processing.

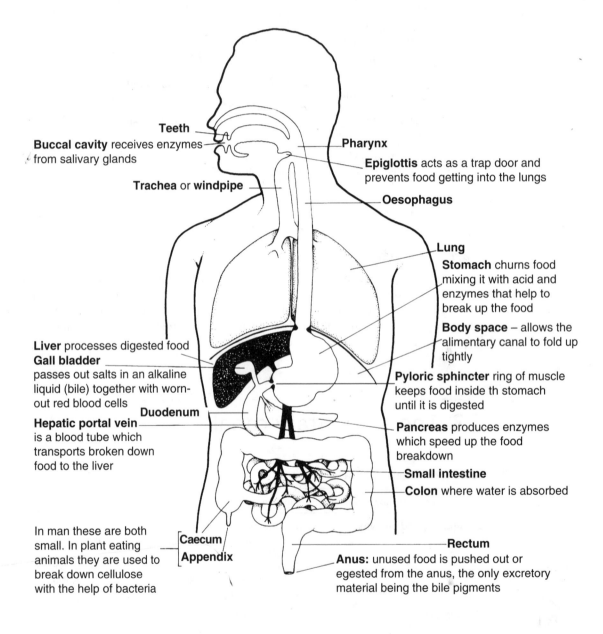

Fig. 5.4 The alimentary or food canal

Swallowing

The following diagrams illustrate the position of both the **false palate** and **epiglottis** during swallowing. Their action is *automatic* and prevents food entering the *respiratory passages* when food is passed into the **oesophagus**.

Before swallowing

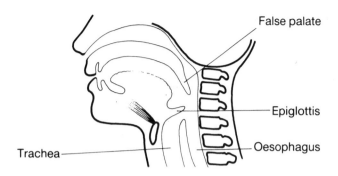

False palate

Epiglottis

Oesophagus

Trachea

Swallowing

(a) Tongue moves up and back pushing food into the throat

(b) False palate pushed back blocking the airway from the nose

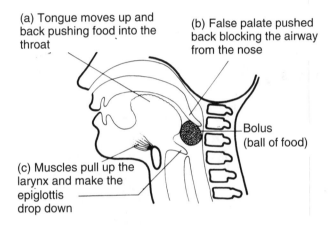

Bolus (ball of food)

(c) Muscles pull up the larynx and make the epiglottis drop down

Fig. 5.5 How we swallow

Peristalsis

This is the **automatic contraction and relaxation** of muscles along the *whole length* of the **alimentary canal** and is responsible for the movement of food. It can be simulated by pushing a marble along a rubber tube, as shown in Fig. 5.6(b).

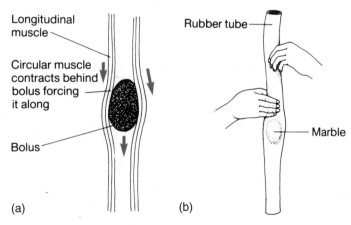

Longitudinal muscle

Circular muscle contracts behind bolus forcing it along

Bolus

Rubber tube

Marble

(a)

(b)

Fig. 5.6(a) Peristalsis is the action of circular muscles of the gut in pushing the food along

Fig. 5.6(b) Demonstration of peristaltic movement; the marble is pushed along the rubber tube by hand

5.4 The liver

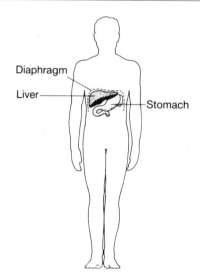

Fig. 5.7 Diagram to show the position of the liver in the body

Blood supply

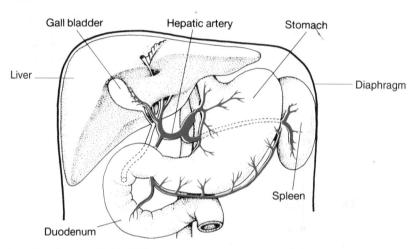

Fig. 5.8 The hepatic artery (see Table 5.3)

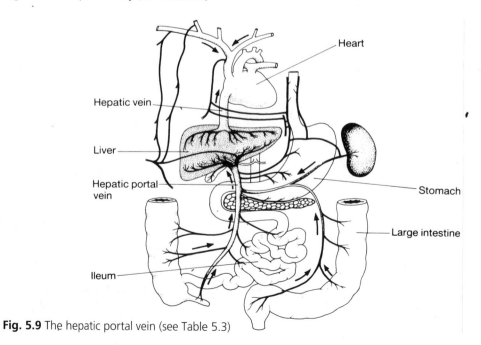

Fig. 5.9 The hepatic portal vein (see Table 5.3)

Table 5.3 Blood vessels supplying the liver

Blood vessel	Function
Hepatic artery	Carries blood containing *oxygen* to the liver
Hepatic portal vein	Carries blood containing *digested food materials* to the liver. It starts out as capillaries in the ileum and ends up as capillaries in the liver
Hepatic vein	Carries blood containing *waste products* and materials produced by the *metabolism of liver cells* away from the liver

Main functions of the liver

1. The formation of **bile**. Bile is stored in the **gall bladder** and is used to *emulsify* fats before their digestion by *lipase* in the duodenum. Bile is a mixture of *alkaline mucus, bile pigments* (breakdown products of haemoglobin), *emulsifying agents* and *cholesterol*.

2. Storage of **glycogen. Glucose** is taken to the liver in the *hepatic portal vein*. If the concentration of glucose in the blood rises above *0.1% by weight*, the excess is converted to glycogen under the control of **insulin**, a hormone produced by the *pancreas*. When the level of *blood sugar* (glucose) falls below its normal level, the glycogen is reconverted into glucose under the control of **adrenaline** (produced by the adrenal glands) and glucogen, produced by the pancreas.

3. Formation of **urea. Amino acids** are taken to the liver in the *hepatic portal vein*. Those that are in excess of the body's needs cannot be stored. The *nitrogen*-containing part of the amino acids is removed and changed to **urea**. The process is sometimes referred to as **deamination**.

4. Production of the blood proteins, **albumin** and **globulin**. These proteins are important in maintaining the correct balance of the **plasma**. They are made from *amino acids* derived from protein in the diet.

5. Desaturation of **fats**. Fats are stored in the body in a **saturated** form. This means that they cannot take any more *hydrogen* into their composition. Before saturated fats can be used by the tissues of the body, the hydrogen must be removed, and this occurs in the liver. The resultant **unsaturated fats** can be used to provide *energy* for the body.

6. Storage of **Vitamin B$_{12}$**. This is taken into the body in the diet and is used in the manufacture of *red blood cells*.

7. Storage of **iron**. In the liver, old **red blood cells** are broken down and the *iron* from the **haemoglobin** is stored for recyling in the manufacture of replacement red cells in the *bone marrow*.

8. Production of **heat**. The many *chemical reactions* taking place in the liver result in the formation of **heat**. The liver can be compared to the *boiler* in a central heating system. The heat is distributed through the *blood vessels* and helps to maintain the **body temperature** at a constant level.

9. Production of **blood clotting agents. Fibrinogen** and **prothrombin** help in the process of blood clotting and are made by the liver cells.

5.5 The chemistry of digestion

Digestion is the breakdown of large molecules of food into smaller molecules so that they can be absorbed into the blood system.

Enzymes of the alimentary canal and their functions

Table 5.4 Digestive enzymes

Region	Enzyme	Substance acted upon (substrate)	Product
Mouth (saliva)	Ptyalin	Starch	Maltose and dextrin
Stomach (gastric juice)	Pepsin	Proteins	Peptones and proteases
	Rennin	Milk protein	Coagulated milk
Duodenum (enzymes secreted by the pancreas)	Lipase	Fats	Fatty acids and glycerol
	Amylase	Starch and dextrin	Maltose (see below)
	Trypsinogen (has to be made active by another enzyme, enterokinase (see below)		
Ileum (succus entericus)	Maltase	Maltose	Glucose
	Sucrase	Sucrose	Glucose and fructose
	Lactase	Lactose	Glucose and galactose
	Erepsin (a mixture of enzymes)	Proteoses and peptones	Amino acids
	Enterokinase	Trypsinogen	Trypsin
	Trypsin	Proteins and peptones	Amino acids

5.6 Investigations with digestive enzymes

Salivary amylase (ptyalin) – investigating its action on starch

Method

Obtain a sample of **saliva** from your mouth and with distilled water make it up to 2 cm^3 in a test tube. Divide the sample into two equal parts in separate test tubes. Label the test tubes **A** and **B**. Sample A will be used for the **test** investigation. Sample B must be *boiled* to denature the digestive enzyme in it. (*Remember, all enzymes are proteins and all proteins are denatured when boiled.*) B is the **control** for the investigation.

> **NOTE**: A *control experiment* is an exact replica of the test experiment with the exception of the single material or condition under investigation. In this case, the control B has the *same materials* as the test A *except* for the active enzyme. (B is used to prove that it is the enzyme in saliva that is responsible for the breakdown of starch.)

Add 1 cm^3 of 0.5% starch suspension to test tube A. Add 1 cm^3 of 0.5% starch suspension to test tube B after cooling solution B. Place both tubes in a water bath at 37°C. Using separate pipettes, **immediately** take *one drop* from each of test tubes A and B and add the drops to separate quantities of *iodine in potassium iodide* placed on a white tile. Note the results. Repeat the tests with the iodine at one minute intervals.

Expected results

Table 5.5 Reactions with iodine

Time in minutes	Colour of sample from A with iodine	Colour of sample from B with iodine
0	Dark blue	Dark blue
1	Dark blue	Dark blue
2	Light blue	Dark blue
3	Purple	Dark blue
4	Brown	Dark blue
5	Brown	Dark blue

Conclusion

The enzyme in saliva breaks down starch completely at 37°C after four minutes. In order to find out the *product* of the breakdown of starch by the enzyme, *boil* the contents of tube A with an equal volume of *Benedict's* (or *Fehling's A & B*) *solution*. An *orange-brown* precipitate will confirm that the starch has been digested to a reducing sugar.

To investigate the action of pepsin on egg white

Method
Take the *white* (albumen) of an egg. Draw the albumen into five pieces of capillary tubing, each 2 cm long. Put these capillary tubes into a beaker of *boiling water* and leave them there for 2 minutes. The capillary tubes will then contain *hard-boiled* egg white. Measure the *lengths* of the egg white in each tube. Place the capillary tubes in test tubes as shown in Fig. 5.10.

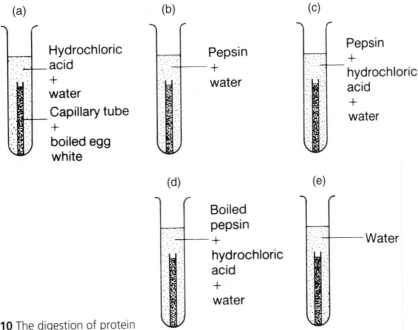

Fig. 5.10 The digestion of protein

Place these test tubes in a water bath at *37°C* for *30 minutes*. Then measure the lengths of egg white in each tube again.

Expected results
The egg white in tube (c) will have decreased in length. In each of the other tubes the egg white will have maintained its original length.

Conclusion
Unboiled pepsin, in the presence of hydochloric acid at 37°C, digests egg albumen after 30 minutes.

5.7 The fate of the products of digestion

Table 5.6 The fate of the products of digestion

End-product of digestion	Destination in the body	Fate of the end-product
Glucose	Taken to the **liver** in the hepatic portal vein	1 Sent from the liver for use by cells in **respiration** 2 Converted to **glycogen** under control of insulin and stored in the liver
Amino acids	Taken to the **liver** in the hepatic portal vein	1 Used to make **protoplasm** and other substances 2 **Repairs** worn out tissues 3 Excess cannot be stored and is **deaminated**, forming **urea** in the liver
Fats, fatty acids and **glycerol**	Absorbed by the **lacteals** and taken to the main lymph system which opens into the venous system	Fatty acids and glycerol are reformed into **fats** which are used as a store of energy and as heat insulation

Absorption

The folded internal surface of the *ileum* is covered with finger-shaped **villi**. These are lined with cells which themselves have projections, the **microvilli**. There is consequently an enormous surface area presented to the contents of the ileum for absorption of the products of digestion. The long length of the ileum and its rich *blood* and *lymph* supply are also adaptations for absorption.

Structure of the inner surface of the ileum

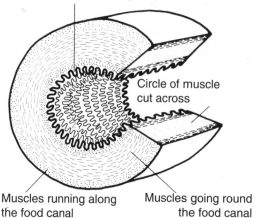

Folded wall with tiny projections called villi

Circle of muscle cut across

Muscles running along the food canal

Muscles going round the food canal

Two sets of muscles squeeze the food along using a mechanical action

Fig. 5.11 A cross-section through part of the small intestine

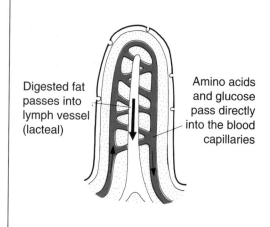

Digested fat passes into lymph vessel (lacteal)

Amino acids and glucose pass directly into the blood capillaries

Fig. 5.12 A cross-section through a single villus

E xaminer's tip

The most common examination questions on this topic are based on:
1 Causes of tooth decay
2 Digestive enzymes
3 Absorption.

Summary

The digestive system

1. The digestive system is a tube divided into various regions. Each region is specialised as an organ, adapted for performing certain stages in the digestive process.
2. Both our teeth and the muscles of the digestive system break down mechanically the food we eat.
3. Many glands secrete enzymes into the digestive system. These break down food chemically.
4. Digestion must take place before food can be absorbed and used by our cells.

Quick test

(a) Bile: **A** emulsifies fats **B** contains urea from the liver
  C contains enzymes which digest fat **D** makes conditions in the intestine acidic
(b) When digestion takes place in the stomach the conditions should be:
  A alkaline **B** neutral **C** acidic **D** basic
(c) Before it can be absorbed from the small intestine starch must be broken down to:
  A fatty acids **B** amino acids **C** glycogen **D** glucose
(d) Most human digestive enzymes work best at:
  A 37°C **B** 27°C **C** 17°C **D** 47°C
(e) The process of digestion enables us to convert food into a form which can be:
  A dehydrated **B** absorbed **C** excreted **D** egested
(f) Amino acids are produced as a result of the breakdown of:
  A fats **B** sugars **C** proteins **D** vitamins.

Chapter 6
The circulatory system

6.1 The need for a blood system

Blood is needed to *distribute* substances to the cells of the body. Very small organisms can rely on simple diffusion for this process, but in larger animals diffusion is inadequate. In man, **food, oxygen** and other essential substances are distributed to the cells, and their **waste products** collected, by the blood system. Blood can therefore be described as the **transport medium** of the human body. All mammals have a *continuous system* of vessels that conduct blood round the body. The blood is circulated by *muscular contractions* of the **heart**. It is first pumped to the *lungs* but returns to the heart to be pumped round the *circulatory system*.

6.2 Passage of blood through the heart

Blood from the veins of the head, neck and fore limbs enters the **right atrium** via the **superior vena cava**, and from the rest of the body by the **inferior vena cava** (Fig. 6.1(a)). It then passes through the **right atrio-ventricular** opening into the **right ventricle**. The opening is guarded by the **tricuspid valve**. Blood leaves the right ventricle by the **pulmonary artery**. This divides and passes to the capillaries of the *lungs*. The blood is collected by the **pulmonary veins**, which pass it to the **left atrium**. Four of these large pulmonary veins enter the left atrium. The left **atrio-ventricular opening** is guarded by the **mitral valve**. Blood leaves the left ventricle by the large, main artery, the **aorta**. Both the openings of the pulmonary artery and the aorta are guarded by **semi-lunar valves**.

6.3 The pulse

Each time the **left ventricle** contracts it forces blood into the **aorta**. The aorta, like all *arteries*, is **muscular** and **elastic** and *dilates* to accommodate the additional amount of blood. A wave of expansion is generated, and travels through the arterial system, diminishing as it reaches the *capillaries*. This wave of expansion is the **pulse**, which results from the elastic layer in the arteries *recoiling* as the heart pumps blood. The pulse can be felt and is often seen in the superficial arteries, but it is customary to measure it in the **radial artery** at the wrist.

The normal rate of the pulse, and therefore the heart-beat rate, is about *72 beats per minute* in an adult at rest, but it increases with exercise, emotional disturbance and disease.

	Normal pulse rates (beats per minute)
Adults, at rest	60–80
Infants	100–120
Children 6–10	80–100

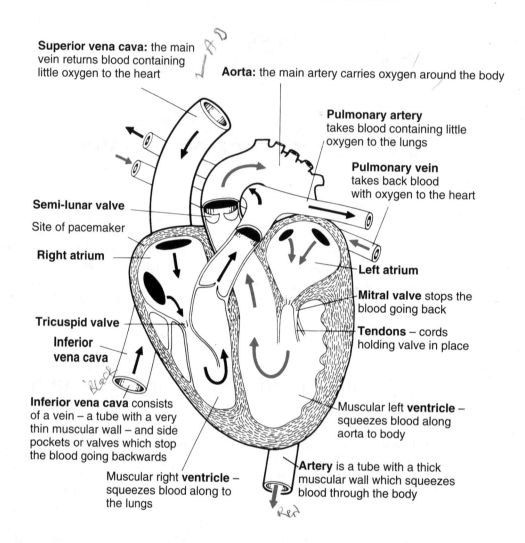

Superior vena cava: the main vein returns blood containing little oxygen to the heart

Aorta: the main artery carries oxygen around the body

Pulmonary artery takes blood containing little oxygen to the lungs

Pulmonary vein takes back blood with oxygen to the heart

Semi-lunar valve

Site of pacemaker

Right atrium

Left atrium

Mitral valve stops the blood going back

Tricuspid valve

Tendons – cords holding valve in place

Inferior vena cava

Inferior vena cava consists of a vein – a tube with a very thin muscular wall – and side pockets or valves which stop the blood going backwards

Muscular left **ventricle** – squeezes blood along aorta to body

Artery is a tube with a thick muscular wall which squeezes blood through the body

Muscular right **ventricle** – squeezes blood along to the lungs

Fig. 6.1(a) Diagram to show the structure of the heart
(The arrows show the direction of blood flow)

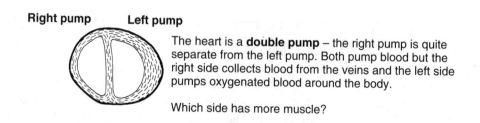

Right pump   **Left pump**

The heart is a **double pump** – the right pump is quite separate from the left pump. Both pump blood but the right side collects blood from the veins and the left side pumps oxygenated blood around the body.

Which side has more muscle?

Fig. 6.1(b) Cross-section through the heart

6.4 Structure, function and action of the heart

(a)

(b)

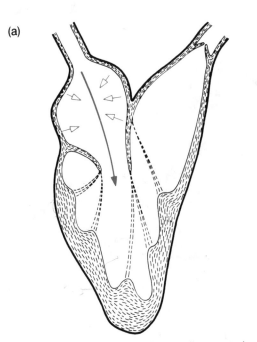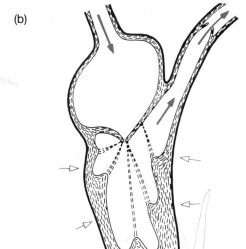

Auricular (atrial) systole: the small arrows show the contraction of the auricle which forces blood into the ventricle as shown by the large arrow.

Ventricular systole: the small arrows show the contraction of the ventricle. Large arrows show the direction of blood flow. When the semi-lunar valves open, the valves between the auricle and ventricle close.

Fig. 6.2(a) and (b) Auricular (atrial) and ventricular systole

Table 6.1 Structure, function and action of the heart

Part of heart	Function
Aorta	The largest artery in the body. Carries *oxygenated* blood to all the organs except the lungs
Pulmonary artery	Carries *deoxygenated* blood to the lungs
Pulmonary vein	Carries *oxygenated* blood from the lungs to the left atrium of the heart
Left atrium	Receives *oxygenated* blood from the lungs via the pulmonary vein
Left ventricle	The most muscular part of the heart. It *pumps blood to all parts of the body*, except the lungs, via the aorta
Bicuspid (mitral) valve	Prevents *back-flow* of blood to the left atrium when the left ventricle contracts*
Tendons of the mitral valve (chordae tendinae)	Prevents the mitral valve from turning *'inside out'* when the left ventricle contracts*
Right ventricle	Pumps *deoxygenated* blood to the lungs via the pulmonary arteries
Tricuspid valve	Prevents *back-flow* of blood to the right atrium when the right ventricle contracts*
Semi-lunar valves	Prevents *back-flow* of blood from the pulmonary arteries when the right ventricle relaxes*
Right atrium	Receives *deoxygenated* blood from the organs of the body, except the lungs, via the venae cavae
Venae cavae	The main veins of the body which return *deoxygenated* blood to the right atrium

*When parts of the heart **contract** they are said to be in a state of **systole**.
When parts of the heart **relax** they are said to be in a state of **diastole**.

6.5 Differences between arteries and veins

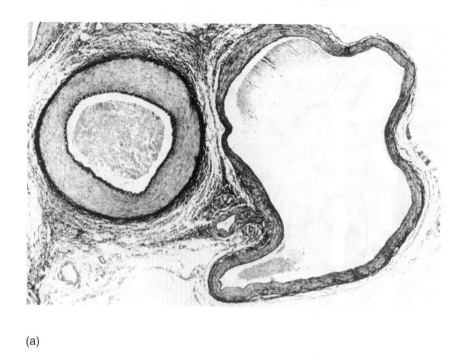

(a)

Fig. 6.3(a) Photomicrograph of a transverse section though an artery and a vein

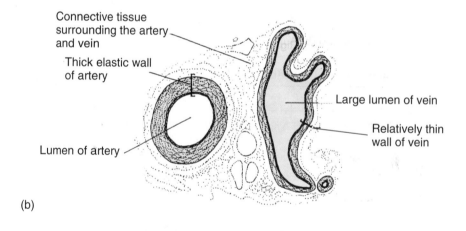

Connective tissue surrounding the artery and vein

Thick elastic wall of artery

Lumen of artery

Large lumen of vein

Relatively thin wall of vein

(b)

Fig. 6.3(b) Drawing of the photomicrograph

Functional differences

Table 6.2 Functional differences between arteries and veins

Arteries	Veins
1 All arteries carry blood **away** from the heart	All veins carry blood **towards** the heart
2 With the exception of the pulmonary arteries, all arteries carry **oxygenated** blood	With the exception of the pulmonary veins, all veins carry **deoxygenated** blood
3 They carry blood which is usually **rich in digested food material**	Apart from the hepatic portal vein, they carry blood which usually has **little digested food material**
4 They carry blood with **little waste material**	They carry blood which is usually **rich in waste material**
5 They carry blood at a **high pressure**	They carry blood at a **low pressure**

Structural differences

Table 6.3 Structural differences between arteries and veins

Arteries	Veins
(a) They have **thick, muscular** and **elastic** walls	They have **thin, inelastic** walls with little **muscular tissue**
(b) They have relatively **small lumens** (internal diameter)	They have relatively **large lumens**
(c) They **do not have valves**	**They have valves** to prevent flow of blood away from the heart

Capillaries

Capillaries link veins and arteries via **venules** (small veins) and **arterioles** (small arteries). They have walls that are *one cell thick* and are the **smallest** blood vessels of the body. It is through the walls of the capillaries that **exchange** of materials between the *blood* and *tissue fluid* (lymph) takes place.

Blood vessels

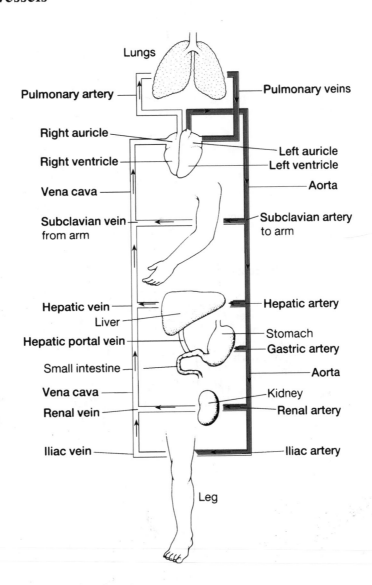

Fig. 6.4 Diagram showing the position of the main blood vessels in the body

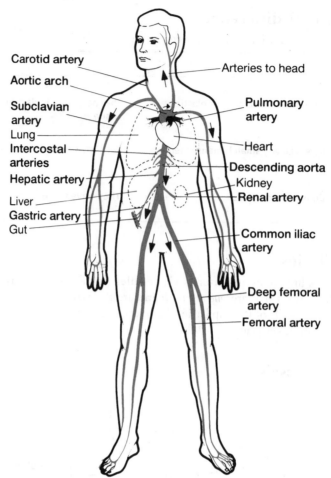

Carotid artery
Aortic arch
Subclavian artery
Lung
Intercostal arteries
Hepatic artery
Liver
Gastric artery
Gut

Arteries to head
Pulmonary artery
Heart
Descending aorta
Kidney
Renal artery
Common iliac artery
Deep femoral artery
Femoral artery

Fig. 6.5 The main arteries of the body

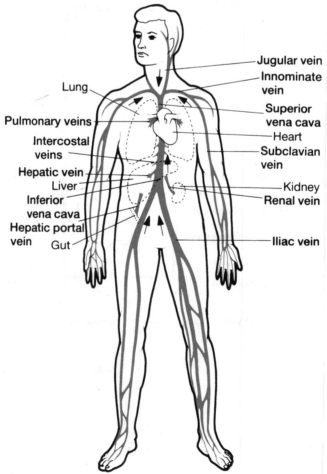

Lung
Pulmonary veins
Intercostal veins
Hepatic vein
Liver
Inferior vena cava
Hepatic portal vein
Gut

Jugular vein
Innominate vein
Superior vena cava
Heart
Subclavian vein
Kidney
Renal vein
Iliac vein

Fig. 6.6 The main veins of the body

6.6 Structure and functions of blood

Structure of blood

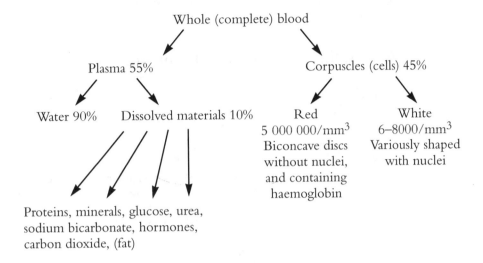

Whole (complete) blood

Plasma 55% → Water 90%, Dissolved materials 10%

Proteins, minerals, glucose, urea, sodium bicarbonate, hormones, carbon dioxide, (fat)

Corpuscles (cells) 45% → Red 5 000 000/mm^3 Biconcave discs without nuclei, and containing haemoglobin / White 6–8000/mm^3 Variously shaped with nuclei

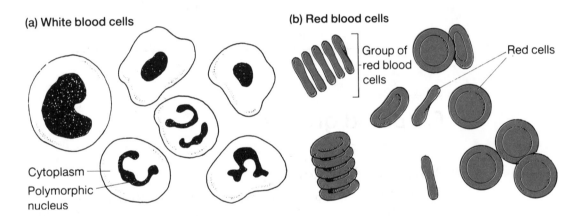

(a) White blood cells

Cytoplasm
Polymorphic nucleus

(b) Red blood cells

Group of red blood cells

Red cells

Fig. 6.7 Human blood cells

Functions of blood

1 Transport

Table 6.4 Transport of materials by blood

Materials transported	Direction of transport		Means of transport
	FROM	**TO**	
Oxygen	Lungs	All tissues	As **oxyhaemoglobin** in the red corpuscles
Carbon dioxide	All tissues	Lungs	As **bicarbonates** in solution in the plasma
Urea	Liver	Kidneys	In **solution** in the plasma
Products of digestion	Small intestine	All tissues	In **solution** in the plasma (fat in suspension)
Hormones	Ductless (endocrine) glands	All tissues	In **solution** in the plasma
Heat	Mainly liver and muscle	All tissues	**Physically**, in all parts of the blood

2 Defence against disease

- Production of **antitoxins** by white corpuscles.
- **Ingestion of bacteria** and some other harmful organisms (pathogens) by white corpuscles.
- Formation of **blood clots** which seal wounds against pathogens.
- **Antibodies** carried to sites of infection in the body. Antibodies are involved in *immunity* (see Section 12.12).

A simplified summary of clotting

Table 6.5 Blood clotting process

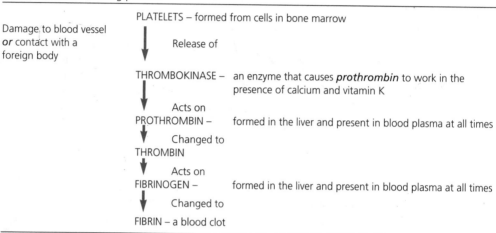

Damage to blood vessel *or* contact with a foreign body

PLATELETS – formed from cells in bone marrow

Release of

THROMBOKINASE – an enzyme that causes *prothrombin* to work in the presence of calcium and vitamin K

Acts on

PROTHROMBIN – formed in the liver and present in blood plasma at all times

Changed to

THROMBIN

Acts on

FIBRINOGEN – formed in the liver and present in blood plasma at all times

Changed to

FIBRIN – a blood clot

6.7 Blood groups

ABO blood groups

The ABO blood groups were discovered in 1900 by **Karl Landsteiner**. He found that the **antibodies** of the ABO system are naturally occurring in blood and appear consistently. The **four** main blood groups made known by his research are **A, B, AB** and **O**. Group A blood has in its red corpuscles a chemical substance (**antigen**) A; Group B has the antigen B; Group AB has both A and B antigens; while Group O has neither of them.

Table 6.6 ABO blood groups

Blood group	Antibody in plasma
A	anti-B only
B	anti-A only
AB	none
O	both anti-A and anti-B

Antigens

An **antigen** is any substance which can stimulate an **immune response** (the production of *antibodies*).

The **Karl Landsteiner Rule** states that when an *antigen* is *present* in the red cells, the corresponding *antibody* is *absent* from the serum (plasma without the clotting agents), and when the *antigen* is *absent* the corresponding *antibody* is *present*.

A, B and AB groups may be identified by their reaction with the two antibodies, anti-A and anti-B. The chief characteristic of these blood group antibodies is that they will cause the red corpuscles containing the appropriate antigen to come together in 'clumps' – **agglutination** – and if strong enough, may *destroy* the corpuscles completely. Thus anti-A will clump corpuscles containing *A antigen* (Groups A and AB), while anti-B will cause agglutination of corpuscles containing *B antigen* (Groups B and AB). Neither of them will react with Group O corpuscles. Therefore *Group O* can be identified by the *absence* of agglutination with both antibodies.

The application of Landsteiner's work is seen when **blood transfusions** are necessary. Below is a simplified summary of *dangerous* (because of agglutination) and *safe* blood transfusions, but it must be realised that it shows only the theoretical reactions of the ABO system.

Table 6.7 Blood transfusions – how the ABO system works

		Recipient's plasma		
		Group A (anti-B antibody)	Group B (anti-A antibody)	Group AB (No antibody)	Group O (anti-A and anti-B antibodies)
Donor's red cells	Group A (A antigen)	safe	clumps	safe	clumps
	Group B (B antigen)	clumps	safe	safe	clumps
	Group AB (A and B antigens)	clumps	clumps	safe	clumps
	Group O	safe	safe	safe	safe

From this table you can see that *Group A* can **be donated** to *Group AB* but *Group AB* **cannot be donated** to a recipient with *Group A*. This is because the plasma with anti-B is diluted by the recipient's AB blood. Also, *Group O* blood can be donated to a recipient with *any type* of ABO blood group; it is a **universal donor**.

6.8 The Rhesus factor

In 1940, Landsteiner and Weiner injected cells from a **Rhesus monkey** into rabbits and guinea pigs, which subsequently produced an antibody against the Rhesus monkey cells. This antibody was shown to *agglutinate* red blood cells of about 85% of humans. Landsteiner and Weiner suggested that this serum *antibody* was detecting a previously undescribed *antigen*, which may or may not be present on human red cells: they called this antigen **'Rhesus'**. People with the antigen are called **Rhesus positive (Rh+)** and those without it are called **Rhesus negative (Rh-)**. The discovery in 1941 by Levine that *anti-Rh antibodies* could cause **transfusion reactions** established their medical importance. It became apparent later that the reagent (antibody) produced by rabbits does not react in exactly the same way as the human antibody, although it detects related antigens.

The Rhesus antigen is **inherited** as a **dominant factor** and, under certain circumstances, this may lead to *agglutination* in **foetal blood**. If both parents are **Rh positive**, their offspring will be **Rh positive**. If one of the parents is **RH positive**, their offspring will probably be **Rh positive**. But if the **mother is Rh negative** and her **child is Rh positive**, in certain cases the mother then becomes *senstive* to the positive factor in the child's blood and she develops the *anti-Rh antibodies*.

Father	X	Mother
Rh+		Rh-
	Child	
	Rh+	

In future pregnancies any anti-Rh antibodies produced by the mother may affect the Rh+ red cells of the foetus should they seep through the placenta and enter the foetal circulation.

6.9 The lymphatic system

Lymph is a *colourless body fluid*, derived by *filtration* from the blood. It bathes all the tissues of the body and drains from tissue spaces into very fine vessels that join and form the main lymph vessel of the body, the **thoracic duct**. This empties into the *venous system* at the main veins coming from the arms, the **subclavian veins**.

Lymph has two main functions:

1 It acts as a **'middle-man'** between the *tissues of the body* and the *blood*. Materials needed by tissue cells pass out through the walls of the blood vessels and become *dissolved* in lymph, which is in contact with the cells' surface. Waste materials and cell products such as hormones pass from tissue cells to the lymph and then to the blood vessels. There are specialised lymph vessels in the villi of the *small intestine* that are responsible for transporting suspensions of *fat* to the blood system.

2 It is involved in **defence against disease**. Lymph contains **lymphocytes**, cells which act like some white blood corpuscles by producing **antibodies**. Lymphocytes are made in **lymph nodes** (glands), some of which are shown in Fig. 6.8. Lymphoid tissue found elsewhere in the body includes:

(a) The **tonsils**
(b) A mass on the posterior wall of the pharynx (throat), the **adenoids**
(c) Scattered patches in the small intestine, **Peyer's patches**
(d) The **spleen**
(e) The **appendix**.

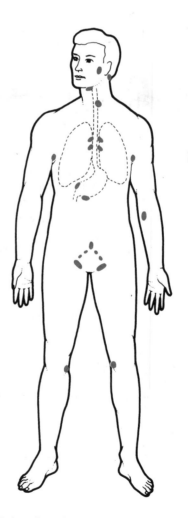

Fig. 6.8 The positions of the main lymph nodes

Examiner's tip

he most common
xamination questions on
his topic are based on:
  Heart action
  Causes of heart disease
  ABO blood grouping.

Summary

√The circulatory system

1. Our circulatory systems transport blood through our bodies.
2. Blood is a fluid tissue made of plasma, cells and platelets. Red cells carry oxygen to the body cells. They also help to transport carbon dioxide away from cells as a waste product. White cells help fight disease-causing microbes. Platelets are important in blood clotting.
3. Blood can be grouped according to types of antigens on the red blood cells. These determine the ABO system of grouping. An additional Rhesus factor is also important in the grouping of blood.
4. The heart pumps blood to all parts of the body via the arteries. The heart has to atria and two ventricles. The atria receive blood via the veins. The ventricles pump blood out through the arteries.
5. The arterial and venous systems are connected by networks of tiny capillaries. Exchanges between blood and cells takes place through the thin capillary walls.
6. Part of the blood plasma seeps into tissue spaces. From here it is collected into special tubes as lymph. The fluid is filtered at the lymph nodes and returned to the blood stream.

Quick test

(a) Universal recipients (Group AB) can receive blood from any other group because:
  A they do not suffer from anaemia
  B they receive more blood than other people
  C their blood contains no A or B antibodies
  D their blood contains no A and B antigens
(b) Most carbon dioxide is carried to the lungs:
  A dissolved in the plasma   **B** as sodium hydrogencarbonate
  C in the white blood cells   **D** in the platelets
(c) Fibrinogen is necessary for:
  A keeping the colour of blood   **B** the formation of haemoglobin
  C the clotting of blood   **D** removing carbon dioxide from blood
(d) Some babies are born with a hole between the right and left atria (auricles) of the heart. These babies often have a bluish tinge to their lips, fingers and cheeks. This is because:
  A much of the blood by-passes the lungs
  B no blood can pass to the lungs to be oxygenated
  C blood leaks out of the heart through the hole and causes bruises
  D the blood only circulates between the heart and the lungs
(e) During exercise which of the following factors is least likely to increase?
  A pulse rate   **B** stroke volume of the heart
  C digestion of food   **D** breakdown of glucose
(f) The highest concentration of oxygen in the blood is found in the small veins of the:
  A brain   **B** heart   **C** lungs   **D** liver.

Chapter 7
Regulation/ Homeostasis

7.1 Excretion

Definition: The elimination of **waste products** of the body's metabolism.
Metabolism is the sum of the chemical building up process (*anabolism*) and the breaking down process (*catabolism*) taking place in living organisms.

Table 7.1

Excretory organ	Excretory product
Lungs	Carbon dioxide and water
Kidneys	Urea, water, mineral salts, uric acid, urates
Skin	Water, mineral salts, urea

7.2 The kidneys

The kidneys have two main functions:

1 Removal of **harmful waste products**, e.g. urea, uric acid.

2 Regulation of **body fluids** by controlling the water and mineral salt content of the blood.

7.3 Formation of urine

In the kidneys two processes are involved in the formation of urine:
- **Filtration**
- **Absorption**

Urine
The average composition of urine in g per 100 cm^3 is:

Urea	2.0
Other nitrogenous substances	0.2
Sodium Chloride	1.0
Other mineral salts	0.8

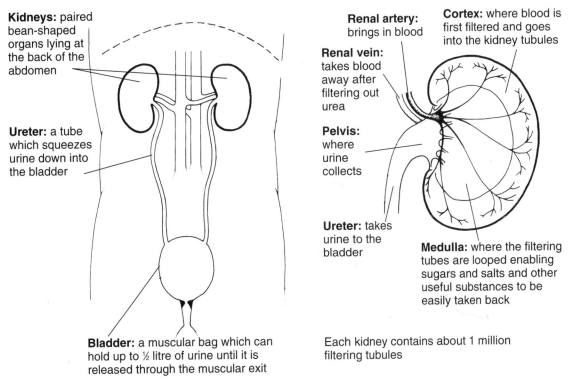

Kidneys: paired bean-shaped organs lying at the back of the abdomen

Ureter: a tube which squeezes urine down into the bladder

Renal artery: brings in blood

Cortex: where blood is first filtered and goes into the kidney tubules

Renal vein: takes blood away after filtering out urea

Pelvis: where urine collects

Ureter: takes urine to the bladder

Medulla: where the filtering tubes are looped enabling sugars and salts and other useful substances to be easily taken back

Bladder: a muscular bag which can hold up to ½ litre of urine until it is released through the muscular exit

Each kidney contains about 1 million filtering tubes

Fig. 7.1 Diagram of the human urinary system

Fig. 7.2 Section through a kidney

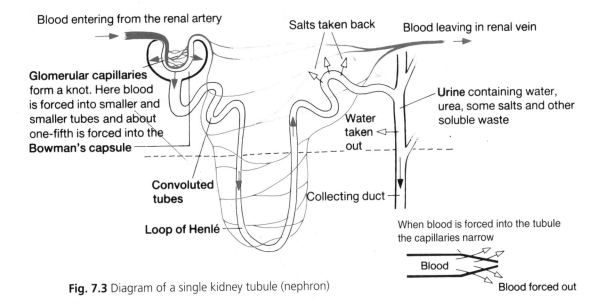

Blood entering from the renal artery

Salts taken back

Blood leaving in renal vein

Glomerular capillaries form a knot. Here blood is forced into smaller and smaller tubes and about one-fifth is forced into the **Bowman's capsule**

Water taken out

Urine containing water, urea, some salts and other soluble waste

Convoluted tubes

Collecting duct

Loop of Henlé

When blood is forced into the tubule the capillaries narrow

Blood

Blood forced out

Fig. 7.3 Diagram of a single kidney tubule (nephron)

Filtration

This is a physical process which takes place through the **glomeruli** (about 1 million per kidney). *Water, salts, urea* and *glucose* are the main substances that are filtered from blood in the glomeruli and pass into the **convoluted tubules**.

Every day 180 litres of blood are put into the tubules but only 1–1.5 litres of urine are formed. All the blood passes through the kidneys every hour but only one-fifth is filtered.

Absorption

All the *glucose* and some *mineral salts* and *water* are **actively pumped** by the cells of the convoluted tubules back into the associated blood capillaries. The amount of *water* absorbed in this way depends on the state of **dehydration** of the body. The amount of water in the blood, influences the production of **anti-diuretic hormone (ADH)** by the **hypothalamus**, which is situated on the ventral side of the mid-brain.

7.4 An artificial kidney

An artificial kidney functions on the physical principle of **dialysis**. This is the movement of small molecules through a thin, **semi–permeable barrier** whose pores are of such a size that they prevent the passage of larger molecules. Starting with the mixture of small and large molecules on one side of the barrier and water on the other, the small molecules go through the barrier into the water while the larger ones are left behind. In the artificial kidney the **patient's blood** is on one side of the barrier, and on the other is a prepared solution of salts of approximately the same concentration as blood. **Waste products** in the patient's blood cross the barrier into the salt solution, which is continually being replaced. In this way the blood is cleaned of all the substances that the kidneys would normally remove; essential substances remain in the blood. The membrane is therefore permeable to substances such as *urea, uric acid, creatinine, sodium, potassium* and *water* – the main chemical ingredients of **urine** – but not to *proteins* or other relatively large molecules. Such membrances are usually made of *Cellophane* or *Cuprophane*. The two main types of artificial kidney in use are shown in Figs 7.4(a) and 7.4(b).

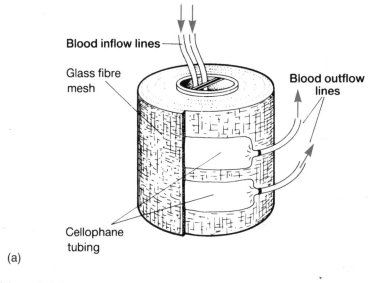

(a)

Fig. 7.4(a) A coil dialyser. Blood passes through the Cellophane tubing as the dialysing fluid permeates the glass fibre mesh

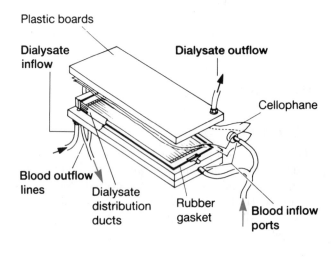

(b)

Fig. 7.4(b) A flat-bed or Kiil dialyser. Blood passes through two sheets of Cellophane which are held between plastic boards. The dialysing fluid passes in the opposite direction

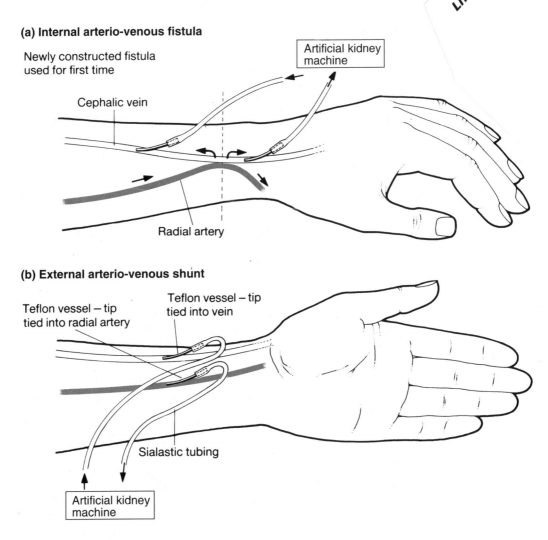

(a) Internal arterio-venous fistula

Newly constructed fistula
used for first time

Cephalic vein

Artificial kidney
machine

Radial artery

(b) External arterio-venous shunt

Teflon vessel – tip
tied into radial artery

Teflon vessel – tip
tied into vein

Sialastic tubing

Artificial kidney
machine

Fig. 7.5(a) and (b) Linking an artificial kidney with a patient's bloodstream. The top diagram **(a)** shows an *internal fistula*, in which the blood leaves and re-enters the body through a vein which has been joined to an artery. The bottom diagram **(b)** shows an *arterio-venous shunt*, in which an artery and vein are connected to the kidney machine by tubes.

7.5 Skin

General functions

1. Protection of tissues and organs from **mechanical damage** by providing a covering of cells replaceable from below.

2. Maintenance of **body shape**. The *elasticity* of skin restores the shape when joints are used during movement.

3. Protection against excessive **loss of water** from the body by *evaporation*.

4. Protection against entry of bacteria, fungi and other **harmful organisms**.

5. Acts as an **excretory organ** by removing excess *salts, water* and *urea* from the body.

6. Acts as a **sense organ** as it contains various tiny sensory structures that react to stimuli such as *temperature, pain* and *touch*.

7. **Temperature regulation** (See Section 7.7).

Structure

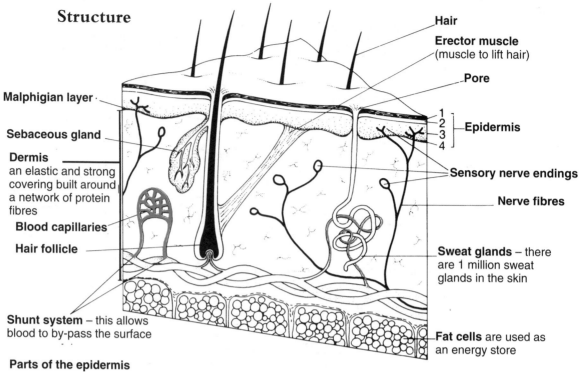

Hair

Erector muscle (muscle to lift hair)

Pore

Malphigian layer

Sebaceous gland

1
2
3
4
} **Epidermis**

Dermis
an elastic and strong covering built around a network of protein fibres

Sensory nerve endings

Nerve fibres

Blood capillaries

Hair follicle

Sweat glands – there are 1 million sweat glands in the skin

Shunt system – this allows blood to by-pass the surface

Fat cells are used as an energy store

Parts of the epidermis
(1) Waterproof layer of flattened dead cells
(2) Thinner layer of nondividing living cells
(3) Pigmented layer – protective, absorbs harmful ultraviolet light
(4) Inner layer of dividing cells to replace those worn away

Fig. 7.6 Diagram of a wedge of skin showing its internal structure

Table 7.2 Structure and function of the skin

Part of skin	Function
Epidermis	Mainly as a protective layer; it is thickest on the soles of the feet and palms of the hands
Dermis	Contains most of the important structures found in skin (see below); the link between the epidermis and surface muscle layers of the body
Malpighian layer	A layer of actively dividing cells between the epidermis and dermis which replaces cells that become worn away
Sebaceous gland	Secretes oily sebum to lubricate the hair
Blood capillaries	Regulate temperature by controlling the flow of blood through the dermis (see Section 7.7)
Sweat gland	Produce sweat for temperature regulation and excretion (see Section 7.7)
Sensory nerve endings	Detect extremes of temperature and pressure on the skin; particularly numerous in the finger tips and lips
Hair	Used mainly for temperature regulation
Erector muscle	Controls the erection of the hair

7.6 Organs concerned with homeostasis

Homeostasis is the maintenance of a constant environment immediately around cells. In man this concerns the **tissue fluid** (lymph), the composition of which is kept constant by the action of a variety of organs, each of which regulates particular factors in the blood (the source of tissue fluid).

Table 7.3 Organs concerned with homeostasis

Organs	Blood factors regulated	Blood levels in a healthy man
Liver and pancreas	Glucose	1 g/litre
Skin and liver	Temperature	36.8°C
Kidneys	Water Acidity/alkalinity Urea	90% pH 7.4 0.3 g/litre
Lungs	Carbon dioxide Oxygen	550 cm³/litre 193 cm³/litre

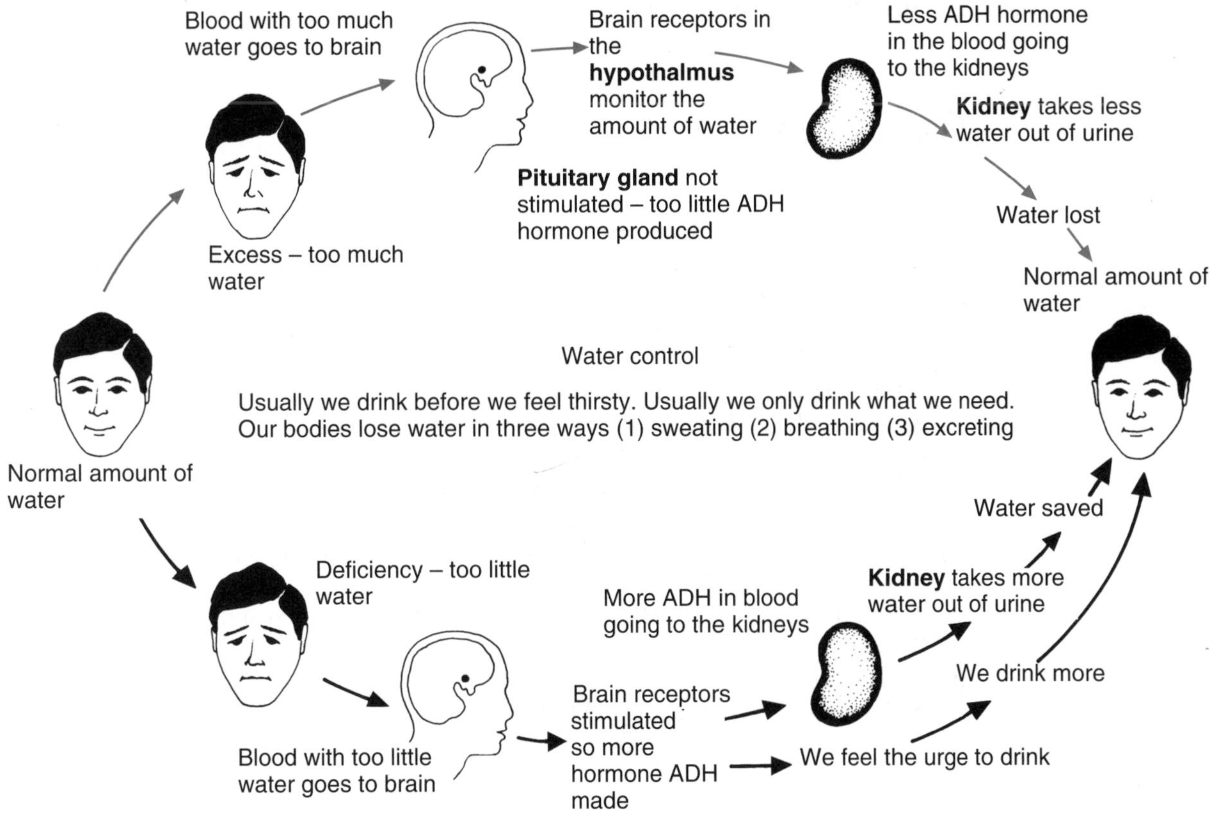

Blood with too much water goes to brain → Brain receptors in the **hypothalmus** monitor the amount of water → Less ADH hormone in the blood going to the kidneys → **Kidney** takes less water out of urine

Pituitary gland not stimulated – too little ADH hormone produced

Excess – too much water

Water lost

Normal amount of water

Normal amount of water

Water control

Usually we drink before we feel thirsty. Usually we only drink what we need. Our bodies lose water in three ways (1) sweating (2) breathing (3) excreting

Deficiency – too little water

More ADH in blood going to the kidneys

Kidney takes more water out of urine

Water saved

We drink more

Blood with too little water goes to brain → Brain receptors stimulated so more hormone ADH made → We feel the urge to drink

Fig. 7.7 Water regulation

7.7 Temperature regulation

(a)

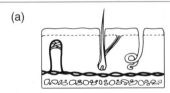

❶ Surface blood vessels contract

❷ Blood takes a path in the skin far from the surface

❸ Sweat glands stop producing sweat

❹ Hairs pulled up by erector muscles so layer of air trapped against skin surface is thicker: This provides insulation rather like double glazing

❺ Shivering occurs – rhythmic contracting of skin muscles produces heat as a by-product

Fig. 7.8(a) The skin in cold conditions

(b)

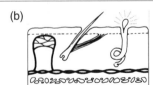

❶ Surface blood vessels relax

❷ Blood takes a path in the skin near to the surface

❸ Sweat glands produce more sweat, which cools the skin down as it evaporates from the surface (We can produce one litre of sweat per hour)

❹ Hairs drop down against skin surface as erector muscles relax – less air is trapped for insulation

❺ No shivering

Fig. 7.8(b) The skin in hot conditions

 **E** xaminer's tip

The most common
examination questions on
this topic are based on:
1 Kidney function
2 Temperature regulation
3 The artificial kidney.

Summary

Regulation and homeostasis

1. Various wastes result from the metabolism of protein, carbohydrate and fat.
2. They are removed from the body with the help of the kidneys, skin, lungs and liver.
3. The kidneys are the most important excretory organs for elimination of urea.
4. The kidneys filter all the urea from the blood and regulate water and glucose.
5. The skin also excretes wastes in sweat.
6. Sweating helps to control your body temperature.

Quick test

(a) As urine leaves the kidney and passes to the bladder:
  A its composition remains unchanged **B** glucose is removed **C** urea is added
  D water is removed
(b) When we are very hot, the capillaries in the skin:
  A dilate **B** collapse **C** constrict **D** darken
(c) A function of the human epidermis is to:
  A insulate the body with fat **B** absorb air **C** prevent entry of bacteria
  D produce sweat
(d) Which of the following controls the release of urine from the body?
  A bladder **B** ureter **C** urethra **D** sphincter muscle
(e) When you are resting, under which of the following weather conditions would sweat
  evaporate most rapidly?
  A hot, dry and windy **B** hot, dry and still **C** hot, humid and still
  D cold, dry and windy
(f) Urea is made in the:
  A skin **B** kidney **C** liver **D** bladder.

Chapter 8
Coordination

8.1 Nervous coordination

The function of the **nervous system** is to perceive **stimuli** (changes in the surroundings) and to coordinate the reaction to them in such a way that it is to the advantage of the body.

Basic organisation

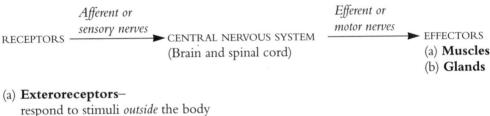

RECEPTORS ——*Afferent or sensory nerves*→ CENTRAL NERVOUS SYSTEM (Brain and spinal cord) ——*Efferent or motor nerves*→ EFFECTORS (a) **Muscles** (b) **Glands**

(a) **Exteroreceptors–**
respond to stimuli *outside* the body
  (i) Eyes
  (ii) Ears
  (iii) Taste buds
  (iv) Nose
  (v) Skin

(b) **Proprioreceptors–**
respond to stimuli *inside* the body
  (i) Stretch receptors of muscles
  (ii) Internal temperature receptors

——→ = Direction of travel of the impulse

8.2 The central nervous system

There are two main parts to the nervous system: the **spinal cord** and the **brain**.

The **spinal cord** is protected by the **vertebral column** – it passes through a canal in the centre of each vertebra – and the **brain** is protected by the **skull**. Both the spinal cord and the brain are covered by *three membranes*. Starting from the one nearest the nervous tissue, these are:

- The **pia mater** – *one cell thick*; for protection against entry of *bacteria*.

- The **arachnoid mater** – *connective tissue* containing the blood vessels supplying the nerve cells.

- The **dura mater** – a *tough, fibrous layer* continuous with the inside of the skull and the vertebral column.

The collective name for these membranes is the **meninges**. The space between the pia mater and the arachnoid mater is filled with a clear watery fluid, the **cerebrospinal fluid**, which circulates in the cavities (ventricles) of the brain and in the central canal of the spinal cord. The main function is to *cushion* the brain from contact with the skull when the head is moved vigorously.

The spinal cord

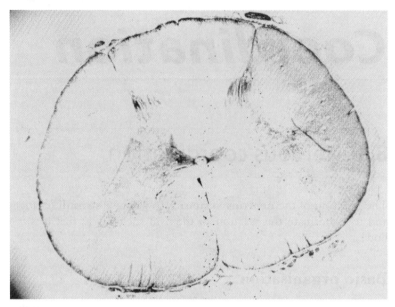

Fig. 8.1(a) Transverse section of the spinal cord

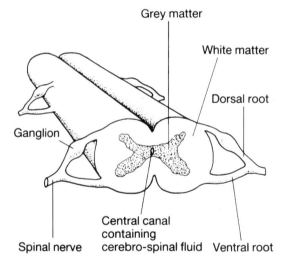

Fig. 8.1(b) A 3-D view of a transverse section of the spinal cord

The brain

Table 8.1 Structure and function of the brain

Part of the brain	Function
Olfactory bulb	Concerned with the sense of **smell**
Optic nerve	Conveys impulses to the *optic lobes* of the brain for the sense of **sight**
Cerebellum	For **balance** and **muscular coordination**
Medulla oblongata	Controls the **automatic reactions** taking place in the body, e.g. *heart beat, peristalsis, breathing*
Cerebral hemispheres	Control all **conscious activity** and act as centres for retaining past sensations (**memory**)
Pituitary body	The master gland of the **endocrine system**. It produces *hormones* which regulate the activity of all the other endocrine glands

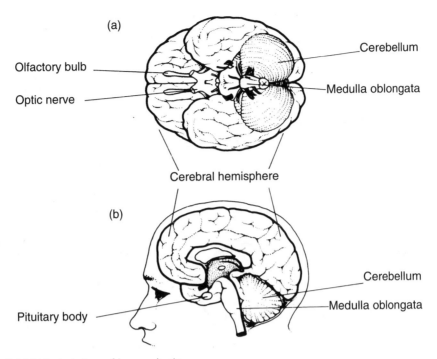

Fig. 8.2(a) Ventral view of human brain
(b) Longitudinal section through human brain

8.3 Reflex actions

These are **quick, automatic responses** to stimuli which can *by-pass* the brain. No conscious effort is needed for them to take place. They link receptors to effectors via the *spinal cord*.

Table 8.2 Examples of reflex actions

Reflex	Stimulus	Response
Coughing	Irritant in the throat	Contraction of abdominal muscles and expiratory intercostal muscles; relaxation of the diaphragm
Swallowing	Food at the back of the throat	Soft palate is raised; epiglottis is closed; peristalsis takes place
Blinking	Object coming towards the eye	Contraction of eyelid muscles
Knee-jerk (see below)	Pressure/pain on knee	Contraction of flexor muscles
Pupil contraction/dilation	Change in light intensity	Contraction of muscles of the iris

8.4 Comparison of a typical spinal reflex action and a voluntary action

Table 8.3 Comparison of a reflex and a voluntary action

Reflex action	Voluntary action
1 A very **rapid** response	The response **may be slow**
2 The nervous impulse takes the **shortest** path	The nervous impulse takes a **long** path
3 Often only the **spinal cord** is used	The **forebrain** is involved
4 Initiated by the response of a **receptor** to a **stimulus**	Initiated from the **brain** under **conscious** control
5 Effectors are **muscles** or **glands**	Effectors are **muscles only**

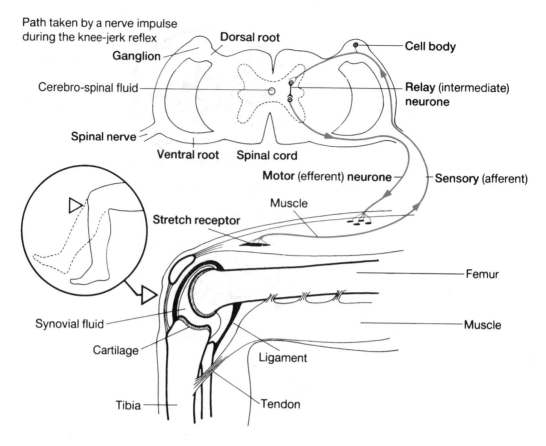

Path taken by a nerve impulse during the knee-jerk reflex

Fig. 8.3 The knee-jerk reflex

8.5 Nerves

Neurones

Nerves are made of *bundles* of nerve cells, or **neurones**, surrounded by *connective tissue*. Each neurone is a highly modified cell capable of transmitting **electrical impulses**. A neurone can act like a charged battery, converting *chemical* energy into *electrical* energy. **Afferent**, or **sensory** neurones transmit impulses **from receptors to the central nervous system**. **Efferent**, or **motor** neurones transmit impulses **to effectors from the central nervous system** (see Section 8.2). The neurones are not physically connected but are separated by minute gaps or **synapses**. When an impulse travels from one neurone to the next, the synapse is bridged by a chemical, a **neurotransmitter**, *acetylcholine*.

Structure and function of neurones

Table 8.4 Structure and function of a neurone

Part of neurone	Function and action
Receptive dendrites	Receive stimuli (at receptors) or impulses (from neighbouring neurones)
Myelin sheath	Acts as an insulator, preventing loss of electrical energy
Neurilemma	Cell membrane of the neurone
Dendron	Carries the impulse to the cell body
Node of Ranvier	Narrow, non-insulated part of the neurone which tends to boost the strength of the impulse as it passes along
Cell body	Part of the neurone containing the nucleus (the control centre)
Axon (nerve fibre)	Carries the impulse away from the cell body
Terminal dendrites	Pass on the impulse to the next neurone after secreting neurotransmitter
Schwann cells	Secrete the neurilemma
Motor end plate	Passes on the impulse to the effector

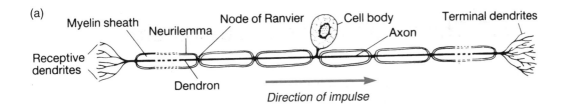

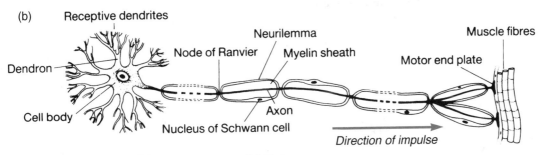

Fig. 8.4(a) Sensory neurone. **(b)** Motor neurone.

8.6 Nerve impulses

Method of impulse travel – a simplified explanation

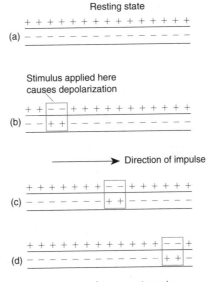

Fig. 8.5 Progressive stages in the movement of a nerve impulse

The surface of the nerve fibre is **positively** charged. Stimulating the surface *mechanically, electrically* or *chemically* causes the positive charge to be temporarily reversed. This is the process of depolarisation, and a wave of **depolarisation** sweeps over the surface, along the length of the nerve, as a **nerve impulse**. Only a small portion of the nerve fibre becomes depolarised, and it is made to **repolarise** rapidly (in 1/1000 second) so that it is ready to conduct another impulse. Depolarisation and repolarisation occur as a result of the distribution of **potassium** and **sodium** ions on either side of the membrane of an axon.

The **speed** and **strength** of a nerve impulse are **constant**. The nerve fibre obeys the 'all-or-none' rule, i.e. the strength of the stimulus is either sufficient to cause depolarisation completely or not at all. **Severe pain** depends on a **large number** of fibres being stimulated at once, whereas **mild pain** occurs if **fewer** fibres are stimulated. Human nerve fibres can transmit over **300 impulses per second** and the speed at which a nerve impulse travels can be up to **150 m/sec**.

Synapses are gaps between the endings of nerve fibres. They measure only .000002 cm wide, and the impulse bridges the gap via a **chemical transmitter** produced at the end of a nerve fibre on arrival of the impulse. One such substance is *acetylcholine*.

8.7 The autonomic nervous system

This is a system that regulates **automatic** functions of the body requiring no *conscious* effort. There are two parts:
1 The sympathetic system and
2 The parasympathetic system.
There effects are antagonistic (work in opposition to one another).

Table 8.5 Summary of actions controlled by the autonomic nervous systems

Organ under control	Effect of parasympathetic system	Effect of sympathetic system	Result
Heart	Slows down heart beat	Speeds up heart beat	Regulation of rate according to muscular activity
Sphincter muscles	Causes them to relax	Causes them to contract	Materials can pass through structures, e.g. stomach, anus, bladder, at the most suitable time
Alimentary canal	Increases peristalsis	Decreases peristalsis	Regulation of rate of passage of food
Digestive glands	Increases activity	Decreases activity	Regulation of the production of digestive enzymes
Blood vessels	Dilates those of the alimentary canal and associated glands. Constricts those of the heart	Constricts those of the alimentary canal and associated glands. Dilates those of the heart	Adjustment of blood flow to suit the demands of the body
Iris	Contracts	Dilates	Regulation of light entering the eye
Ciliary muscles	Contracts	Relaxes	Controls accommodation of the eye
Tear glands	Inhibits action	Increases action	Control of tear production, e.g. to clean the eye membranes
Bronchial muscles	Contracts muscles	Relaxes muscles	Control of air flow in and out of lungs.

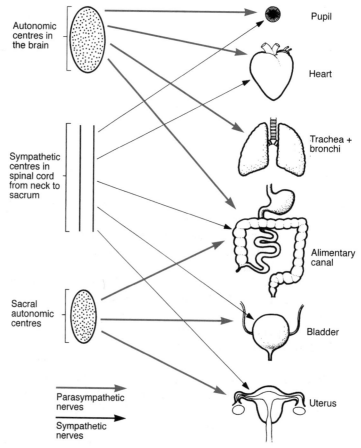

Fig. 8.6 Diagram to show the distribution of the autonomic nervous system

8.8 The eye

Structure and function

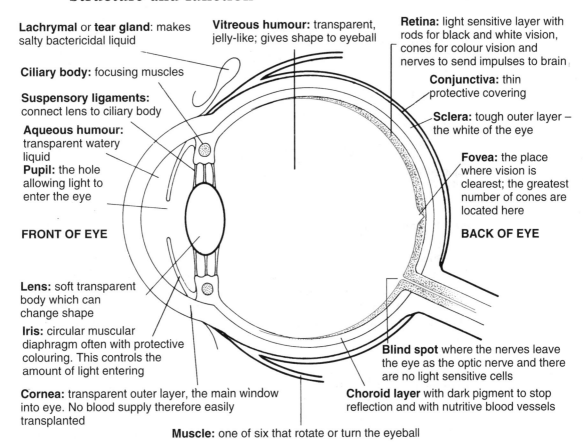

Lachrymal or **tear gland**: makes salty bactericidal liquid

Ciliary body: focusing muscles

Suspensory ligaments: connect lens to ciliary body

Aqueous humour: transparent watery liquid

Pupil: the hole allowing light to enter the eye

FRONT OF EYE

Lens: soft transparent body which can change shape

Iris: circular muscular diaphragm often with protective colouring. This controls the amount of light entering

Cornea: transparent outer layer, the main window into eye. No blood supply therefore easily transplanted

Vitreous humour: transparent, jelly-like; gives shape to eyeball

Muscle: one of six that rotate or turn the eyeball

Retina: light sensitive layer with rods for black and white vision, cones for colour vision and nerves to send impulses to brain

Conjunctiva: thin protective covering

Sclera: tough outer layer – the white of the eye

Fovea: the place where vision is clearest; the greatest number of cones are located here

BACK OF EYE

Blind spot where the nerves leave the eye as the optic nerve and there are no light sensitive cells

Choroid layer with dark pigment to stop reflection and with nutritive blood vessels

Fig. 8.7 A section through the eye

Table 8.6 Structure and function of the eye

Part of eye	Function
Sclera (sclerotic coat)	Protection and muscle attachment
Conjunctiva	Protection against entry of bacteria
Cornea	A transparent extension of the sclera which allows transmission of light
Choroid	Prevents internal reflection of light and carries blood vessels
Iris	Controls the amount of light entering the eye
Retina	A light sensitive layer made of specialised nerve cells, the **rods** (for black and white vision) and **cones** (for colour vision)
Ciliary body (muscle)	Muscles which alter the shape of the lens for focusing
Suspensory ligaments	They connect the lens to the ciliary body
Pupil	The hole through which light passes from the front to the back of the eye
Fovea centralis (yellow spot)	The region of the retina where there are most cones: the most light sensitive spot
Blind spot	The region where nerves connecting with the rods and cones leave the eye as the **optic nerve**. It is devoid of light sensitive cells
Aqueous humour	A transparent watery liquid that allows light through and helps to give the front of the eye its shape
Vitreous humour	A transparent jelly which gives the eyeball its shape
Lens	Made of layers of soft transparent material; it can become more or less biconvex (curved outwards on both sides) to focus light on the retina
Lachrymal (tear) gland	Produces a protective antibacterial liquid to lubricate the eye
Muscles (6 of these)	Allow the eye to be moved in its socket

Accommodation

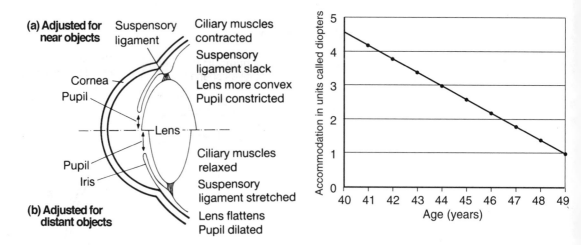

Fig. 8.8(a) and (b) Accommodation   **Fig. 8.9** A graph of accommodation against age

The **lens** of the eye is **biconvex,** the anterior (front) surface being slightly less curved than the posterior (back). It is attached at the margin to the inside of the sclerotic coat by means of the **suspensory ligaments**. The *curvature* of the lens, and thus its *focal length*, can be altered by the contraction of the **ciliary muscle**s. This change in shape of the lens – the action of **accommodation** – results from a re-arrangement of the lens' *internal fibres*, and is *automatic*, allowing the eye to focus on **near** or **distant** objects.

When the eye is accommodated for **distant** objects, the ciliary muscles are *relaxed* and the suspensory ligaments pull on the lens, *reducing* its curvature. The process of accommodation for **near** objects consists of *contraction* of the ciliary muscles, which takes the tension off the lens and allows it to become *more* curved. The range of accommodation depends on the power of the muscles and the elasticity of the lens. The muscles become less flexible with age. People notice a fairly marked deterioration from about 40 years of age. (See Fig. 8.9).

Correction of long sight and short sight

In some people the eyes are not of perfectly normal shape, e.g. the anterior–posterior axis (i.e. the distance from the front to the back of the eye) is either *shorter* or *longer* than normal. In these cases rays of light are brought to a focus *behind* or *in front of* the retina. The problem can be solved with the use of **spectacles** with either *convex* or *concave* lenses.

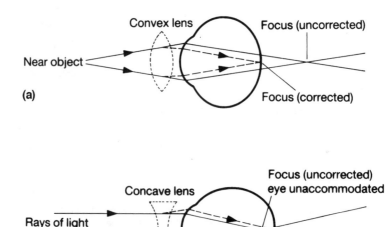

Fig. 8.10(a) Long sight and its correction. **(b)** Short sight and its correction. (The dotted lines show the rays of light after correction by each type of lens)

8.9 The ear

Structure and functions

Two functions:
1 **Perception of sound waves** (vibrations in air) – **hearing**
2 **Detection of gravity and movement of the head – balance**

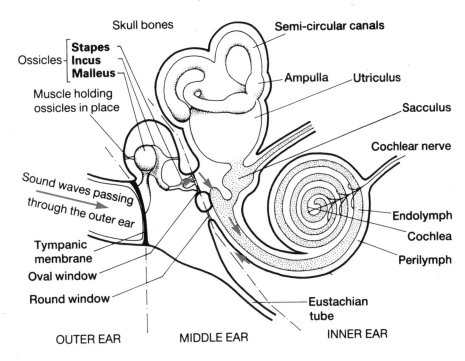

Fig. 8.11 Structure of the human ear

Table 8.7 Structure and function of the ear

Part of ear	Function
Skull bones (tympanic bulla)	For protection of the delicate structures of the middle and inner ear
Tympanic membrane (ear drum or tympanum)	It vibrates in response to sound waves striking its surface and causes the ossicles to vibrate
Ossicles (3 of these – **stapes, incus, malleus**	Transmission of vibrations across the air-filled middle ear
Oval window	It vibrates as a result of the stapes striking its surface and sets up vibrations in the perilymph of the inner ear
Round window	It bulges outwards every time the oval window bulges inwards, thus compensating for pressure changes set up in the perilymph by the oval window
Eustachian tube	Connects the middle ear to the back of the throat; equalises pressure on both sides of the ear drum and so allows it to vibrate
Perilymph	The liquid surrounding the membranous labyrinth of the inner ear (see below)
Endolymph	The liquid within the membranous labyrinth of the inner ear
Cochlea	Coiled part of the inner ear containing cells sensitive to vibrations of the perilymph
Cochlea nerve (leads to the auditory nerve)	Sends the impulse from the sensitive cells of the cochlea to the brain
Sacculus and utriculus (parts of the membranous labyrinth)	Contain sense organs which can detect gravity; filled with endolymph
Semi-circular canals and ampullae (parts of the membranous labyrinth)	Contain sense organs which can detect rotation of the head; filled with endolymph

Summary of how we hear sounds

- Sound waves are received by the **external pinna** (ear flap).
- The sound waves are directed along the **auditory (outer ear) canal** to the **tympanum**.
- The tympanum vibrates and passes the vibrations across the middle ear via the **ossicles** to the **oval window**.
- The oval window vibrates with the same frequency as the tympanum; it magnifies the vibrations 22 times.
- The vibrations of the oval window are transmitted through the liquid **perilymph** in the **cochlea** and stimulate **sensitive cells**.
- Because liquids are incompressible, the **round window** vibrates to compensate for the movement of the oval window, thus allowing for pressure changes in the perilymph.
- Stimulation of the sensitive cells causes **nerve impulses** to be sent to the brain via the **auditory nerve**. Here they are interpreted as the sensation of sound.

Balance

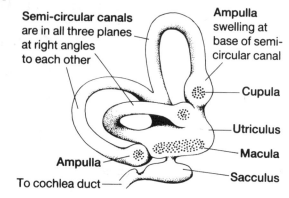

Semi-circular canals are in all three planes at right angles to each other

Ampulla swelling at base of semi-circular canal

Cupula

Utriculus

Macula

Ampulla

To cochlea duct

Sacculus

Fig. 8.12 A diagrammatic cross section of the organs of balance in the inner ear which detect the position of the head relative to gravity

The **ampullae** at the base of the semi-circular canals contain small discs of cells with sensory 'hairs' which project into the fluid **endolymph** inside. Attached to these 'hairs' is a mass of jelly-like material (**cupula**), which is made to move when the head is suddenly rotated. The wall of each ampulla moves with the head but the endolymph lags behind owing to its inertia, thus moving the cupula and bending the sensory hairs. As the hairs become bent, electrical impulses are set up which pass to the brain along the **auditory nerve**. The brain thus detects information from the ampullae about changes in **rotational** movement of the head. The **macula** in the **utriculus** (see Fig. 8.12) is similar to the **cupula**, but it is a *gravity* receptor rather than a *rotatory* receptor. From the two sets of messages, which are continuously being received by the brain, we are able to control *muscular movement* necessary to keep the body *upright*.

8.10 Taste and smell

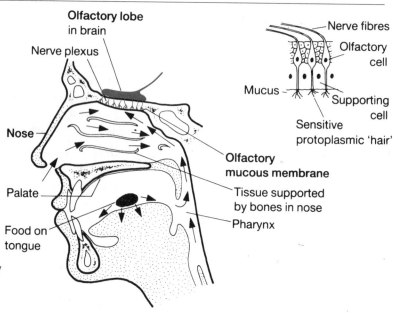

Olfactory lobe in brain

Nerve plexus

Nerve fibres

Olfactory cell

Mucus

Nose

Supporting cell

Sensitive protoplasmic 'hair'

Olfactory mucous membrane

Palate

Tissue supported by bones in nose

Food on tongue

Pharynx

Fig. 8.13 The olfactory organ showing details of the sensitive cells

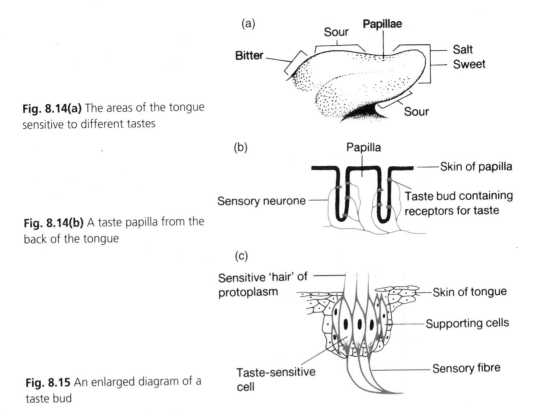

Fig. 8.14(a) The areas of the tongue sensitive to different tastes

Fig. 8.14(b) A taste papilla from the back of the tongue

Fig. 8.15 An enlarged diagram of a taste bud

8.11 Chemical coordination – the endocrine glands and their secretions

Endocrine glands, unlike *exocrine glands* (e.g. salivary glands), have no ducts. Their secretions, the **hormones**, pass directly into the **blood system** and are carried to different parts of the body where they control various aspects of metabolism. Each hormone is **specific** in its action: it affects only **one** type of tissue or organ.

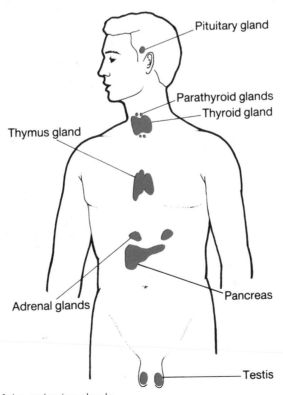

Fig. 8.16 Position of the endocrine glands

Table 8.8 The endocrine glands and their secretions

Endocrine gland	Hormone	Function
Pituitary	Prolactin	Stimulates milk production by the mammary glands
	Growth hormone	Stimulates general body growth
	Thyroid-stimulating hormone	Regulates the action of the thyroid
	Adrenal-stimulating hormone	Regulates the action of the adrenals
	Gonad-stimulating hormone	Regulates the development of the reproductive organs
	Oxytocin	Stimulates the muscles of the uterus during birth
	Vasopressin (ADH)	Regulates the amount of water excreted in urine
	Lipotropin	Increases the rate of use of stored fat
Thyroid	Thyroxine	Controls the rate of growth and the rate at which glucose is used to release energy
Parathyroids	Parathormone	Regulates the rate at which the body uses calcium
Pancreas	Insulin	Stimulates the conversion of glucose to glycogen
		Stimulates the oxidation of glucose to release energy
		Inhibits the production of glucose from amino acids in the liver
Gonads	Testosterone	Regulates the development of secondary sexual characteristics
	Oestrogen	Stimulates the thickening of the uterus wall during ovulation
	Progesterone	Prepares the uterus for pregnancy
Adrenals	Adrenaline	Raises the pulse rate and the volume of blood pumped by the heart with each beat
		Increases rate and depth of respiration
		Constricts the blood vessels in the alimentary canal and skin and dilates those in the muscles
Thymus*	(not known)	Involved in development of immunity in the newborn. May also regulate the onset of sexual maturity

*The function of the thymus gland in adults is unclear

8.12 Interaction of nervous and chemical coordination

Messages are sorted out in the brain (1). The pituitary (2) can realease hormones to affect the thyroid (3) and adrenals (4). (5), (6), (7). Nerve fibres to the eye, face muscles, and pharynx. (8). Nerves to the larynx, heart and intestines. (9). Nerves to the heart (10), blood vessels (11), adrenals (12), intestine (13), and bladder and colon (14)

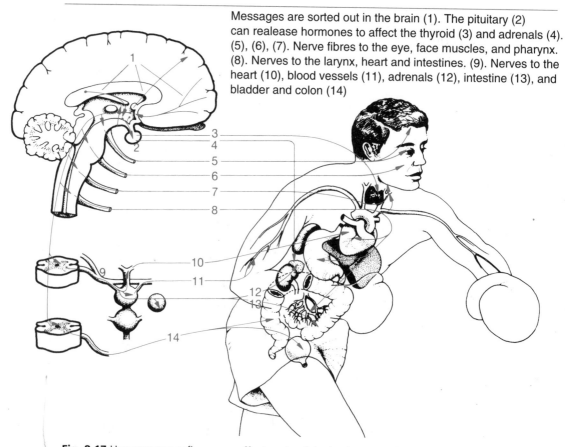

Fig. 8.17 How nervous reflexes can affect parts of the body. Messages are integrated in the brain

Summary

Coordination

1. Humans have the most complex nervous system of any animal. It is made up of the brain and spinal cord and communicates with all parts of the body via the nerves.
2. The cerebrum controls conscious activities and is the centre of intelligence. The cerebellum coordinates movement and balance. The medulla oblongata controls all the automatic actions of the body.
3. The central nervous system links receptors to effectors via sensory nerves, connecting nerves and motor nerves.
4. Receptors include cells in the skin, tongue, nose, ears and eyes.
5. Ductless glands are called endocrine glands and secrete hormones directly into the bloodstream.
6. Hormones influence metabolism, growth, mental ability and the chemical balance of body fluids.

Quick test

(a) As light rays pass through the eye they are bent by each of the following except:

    A the vitreous humour   **B** the iris   **C** the lens   **D** the cornea

(b) Conditioned reflexes differ from most other responses in that:

    A they happen much faster than other responses

    B the relationship of stimulus and response has been learned during one's lifetime

    C they need taste or smell of food to start them off

    D they do not involve nerves in their action

(c) The axons of many nerve cells are covered with a myelin (fatty) sheath which:

    A prevents impulses from going too fast

    B insulates the cell from neighbouring nerve cells

    C prevents bacterial infection   **D** keeps the cells at a constant temperature

(d) The spinal cord:

    A allows the spine to be flexible   **B** supports the weight of the back

    C allows the passage of nerve impulses to and from the brain

    D protects the spine from damage

(e) The medulla oblongata of the brain controls:

    A balance   **B** hearing   **C** learning   **D** breathing

(f) When the eye is focused on near objects:

    A the lens is thinner than normal   **B** the ciliary muscles are relaxed

    C the pupil is very small   **D** the suspensory ligaments are slack.

Chapter 9

Human reproduction and development

9.1 Sexual reproduction

Sexual reproduction is the typical method of producing **offspring** among *multicellular* animals, and though the details of the process differ in the various groups of animals, there is a general plan. The main feature of sexual reproduction is the *fusion* of two special cells, the male and female **gametes**, or more importantly, of their *nuclei*, so that the offspring receive genetic material (**chromosomes**) from both parents. This bringing together of two sets of different chromosomes allows for **genetic variation** (see Section 10.4). The female gamete is the **egg** (ovum) and the male gamete the **sperm**. Gametes are produced in special organs, the **gonads**, which in females are the ovaries and in males the **testes**.

In all mammals the *fusion* of sperm and egg, **fertilisation**, takes place inside the *female*. For this to happen, the sperm must be deposited in the female in such a position that it can swim to the egg. **Mating, intercourse** and **copulation** are all names used to describe the act in which the **penis** of the male is inserted into the **vagina** of the female and sperms are ejaculated near the neck of the womb, the **cervix**. The penis is usually soft and flaccid, but during copulation it is firm enough to penetrate the vagina. When the male becomes sexually aroused there occurs an increase in *blood flow* to the sponge-like tissues surrounding the urethra of the penis. This causes the penis to become erect. Ejaculation of **semen** (a mixture of sperms and nutritive liquid through which they swim) takes place as a *reflex action* resulting from stimulation of nerve endings in the tip of the penis. About *1.5 cm³* of semen is produced at each ejaculation. This contains about *100 million sperms*. The sperms swim through the uterus to the **fallopian tubes**, where they may come in contact with an egg (if one has been released by the ovaries). Only one sperm need reach an egg for fertilisation to take place.

9.2 The reproductive system

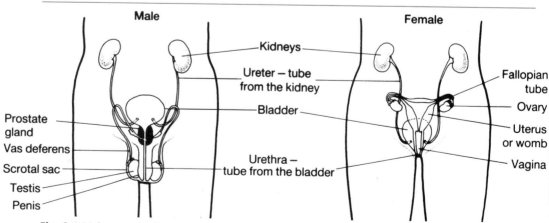

Fig. 9.1 Male reproductive organs

Fig. 9.2 Female reproductive organs

Table 9.1 Structure and function of the male reproductive organs

Structure	Function
Testes	Production of sperms
Scrotal sacs	Contain the testes; they maintain the temperature of the testes slightly below normal body temperature which is necessary for development and survival of sperm
Vas deferens	Tubes which conduct the sperms to the urethra by peristalsis
Penis	For insertion into the vagina to release sperm at the cervix of the womb
Prostate gland and seminal vesicles	Secretion of seminal fluid, which acts as a lubricant and nutritive medium for the sperms
Urethra	A tube running through the penis which both carries sperms (during copulation) and urine (during urination)

Table 9.2 Structure and function of the female reproductive organs

Structure	Function
Ovaries	Production of eggs (ova)
Uterus	Plays a part in development of the embryo and formation of the placenta
Cervix	The opening to the uterus for the passage of sperm during copulation. The baby emerges through the cervix during birth
Vagina	For the reception of the penis during copulation For the passage of the baby during birth
Fallopian tubes (oviducts)	Provide the ideal environment for fertilisation to take place Conduct the fertilised egg to the uterus
Urethra	For the passage of urine from the bladder

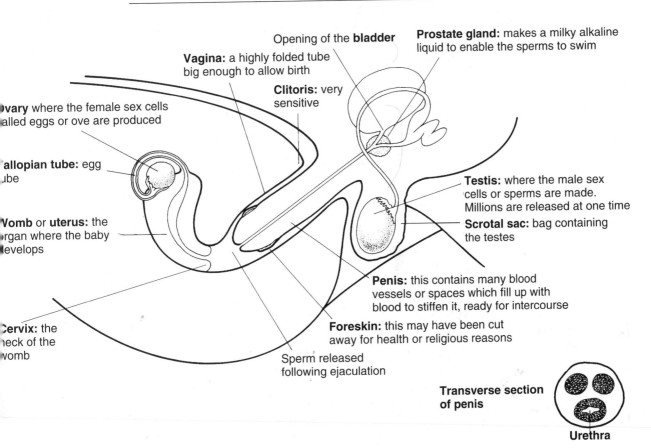

Ovary where the female sex cells called eggs or ove are produced

Fallopian tube: egg tube

Womb or **uterus:** the organ where the baby develops

Cervix: the neck of the womb

Opening of the **bladder**

Vagina: a highly folded tube big enough to allow birth

Clitoris: very sensitive

Prostate gland: makes a milky alkaline liquid to enable the sperms to swim

Testis: where the male sex cells or sperms are made. Millions are released at one time

Scrotal sac: bag containing the testes

Penis: this contains many blood vessels or spaces which fill up with blood to stiffen it, ready for intercourse

Foreskin: this may have been cut away for health or religious reasons

Sperm released following ejaculation

Transverse section of penis

Urethra

Fig. 9.3 Copulation – the discharge of male gametes near the cervix

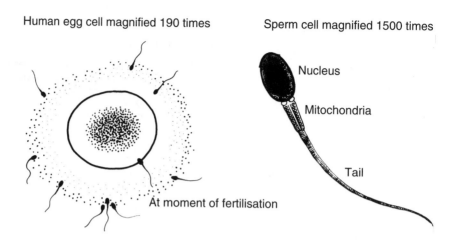

Human egg cell magnified 190 times

Sperm cell magnified 1500 times

Nucleus

Mitochondria

Tail

At moment of fertilisation

Fig. 9.4 Fertilisation – the fusion of sex cells (gametes)

9.3 The fate of an egg

Females are born with ovaries containing thousands of special sex cells, **oogonia**, each of which has the potential of developing into an egg. However, only a small proportion of the oogonia will be used as gamete-forming cells during the reproductive life of a woman. Development of eggs depends on the production of **hormones** by the **pituitary** gland and the **ovaries**. When the female becomes sexually mature these hormones control the production and release of eggs from the ovaries at regular **monthly** intervals. This continues until she is pregnant or until the age of about 45 years, when egg production ceases. Most of the eggs produced are never fertilised and, at monthly intervals, are discharged with part of the *lining of the uterus* via the vagina. This discharge is called the **menstrual flow** and it continues to pass from the vagina for about five days. After this, the uterus gradually develops a new lining so that it can accommodate an embryo should fertilisation occur.

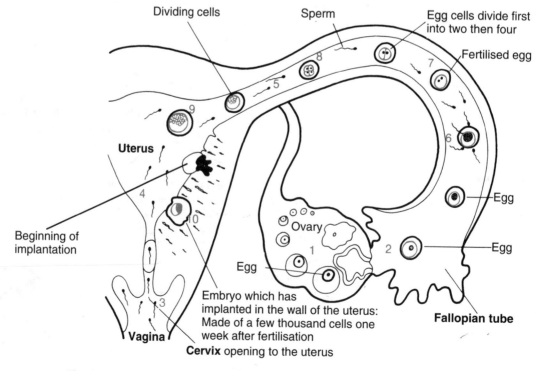

Dividing cells

Sperm

Egg cells divide first into two then four

Fertilised egg

Uterus

Egg

Egg

Beginning of implantation

Ovary

Egg

Egg

Embryo which has implanted in the wall of the uterus: Made of a few thousand cells one week after fertilisation

Fallopian tube

Vagina

Cervix opening to the uterus

Fig. 9.5 How a baby begins. Fertilisation and implantation inside the mother

1. Ovary produces egg.

2. Egg released into fallopian tube.

3. At about the same time, sperms enter vagina.

4. Sperms swim up through uterus.

5. Sperms swim along fallopian tube.

6. Sperms make contact with the egg.

7. Single sperm and egg fuse – fertilisation.

8. Fertilised egg, now divided into four cells, is conducted towards uterus.

9. Fertilised egg about to implant in wall of uterus.

10. Implantation is now complete, the placenta starts to develop.

Summary of the hormonal control of the female reproductive cycle

- **Pituitary gland** secretes **follicle-stimulating hormone (FSH)** which causes the eggs to grow inside **Graafian follicles** within the ovaries.

- **Graafian follicles** secrete the hormone **oestrogen**.

- **Oestrogen** causes the lining of the **uterus** to become *thick* and *glandular*. It also *stops FSH production* and causes the production of another pituitary hormone, **luteinising hormone (LH)**.

- **LH** causes an **egg** to be shed from an ovary and causes the corresponding Graafian follicle to grow from the corpus luteum (yellow body).

- The **corpus luteum** is an **endocrine gland**, secreting a hormone, **progesterone**. Progesterone prepares the uterus for reception and development of the embryo and *stops the secretion of LH*.

- IF NO FERTILISATION OCCURS, the corpus luteum *disintegrates* and the inability to produce progesterone causes a menstrual flow. The cycle re-starts with the production of *FSH* from the pituitary once more.

- IF FERTILISATION OCCURS, the developing **embryo** and **placenta** produce **oestrogen** and **progesterone** to maintain the uterus in a suitable state for the continued growth of the fetus.

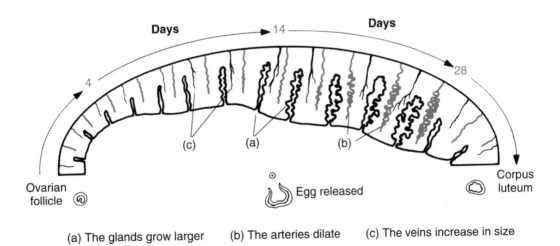

Fig. 9.6 Diagram to illustrate the gradual thickening of the lining of the womb in preparation for the nourishment of a fertilised egg

9.4 Stages in the development of an embryo

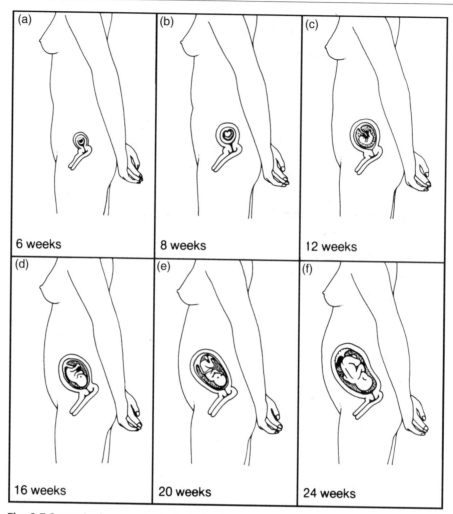

Fig. 9.7 Stages in the growth of a baby in the uterus

Table 9.3 Stages in the development of an embryo

Time after fertilisation	Description
50 hours	A ball of cells just visible to the unaided eye
10 days	The ball becomes completely embedded in the wall of the uterus
10–14 days	With rapid growth and division of cells in the ball, a lump about 0.25 cm across forms in the uterine wall
30 days	Embryo is 0.5 cm long. The head and eyes can be recognised. The spinal cord is forming
1½ months	Embryo is 1.25 cm long. The limb buds are visible. Bones are beginning to develop. The heart has two chambers. Some blood vessels are formed. The embryo is enclosed by the amnion
2 months	Placenta has formed. Note that the maternal and fetal circulations are separate
3 months	The fetus weighs 14 g. All the body organs are formed
4 months	The fetus weighs 113 g and increases rapidly in weight from this stage
5 months	Limb movements can be felt in the womb. The embryo (fetus) is covered in a fine hair, lanugo, and a thin film of fat (sebum) coats the skin
6 months	Air sacs (alveoli) develop in the lungs. The nostrils open. Weight is about 1 kg
7 months	The fetus has turned so that its head is above the cervix
8 months	Weight is about 2 kg. Fingernails have formed
9th–10th month	Lanugo disappears. Weight about 3.5 kg. Length about 50 cm at birth

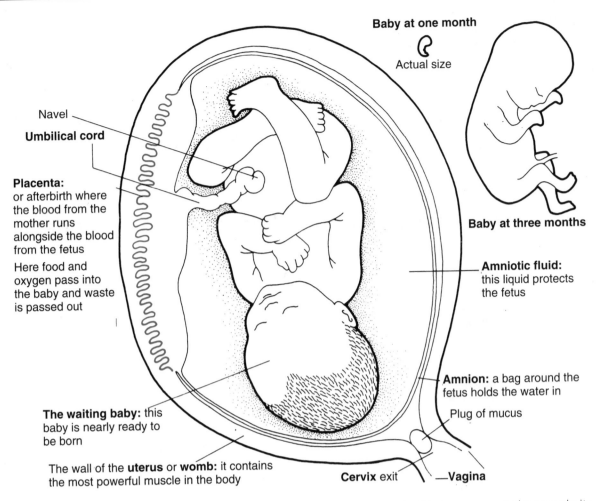

Baby at one month

Actual size

Navel

Umbilical cord

Placenta:
or afterbirth where
the blood from the
mother runs
alongside the blood
from the fetus

Here food and
oxygen pass into
the baby and waste
is passed out

Baby at three months

Amniotic fluid:
this liquid protects
the fetus

Amnion: a bag around the
fetus holds the water in

Plug of mucus

The waiting baby: this
baby is nearly ready to
be born

The wall of the **uterus** or **womb:** it contains
the most powerful muscle in the body

Cervix exit

Vagina

Fig. 9.8 The waiting baby. The baby lies curled up to protect itself but can move, and even sucks its thumb

9.5 Care of the mother during pregnancy

Pregnant women should pay particular attention to **diet, rest, smoking habits** and **alcohol intake**.

Diet

The growing embryo requires large quantities of **calcium**, for *skeletal* growth, **iron**, for the manufacture of *red blood cells*, and **vitamins**, which help the various *enzymes* in the processes which lead to growth and development.

Rest

During the later stages of pregnancy, the fetus becomes so large that it causes *crowding* and pressure on the **abdominal organs**, such as the *bladder*, and on major blood vessels and nerves. The weight of the fetus makes any exertion difficult and the woman becomes out of breath more readily than usual. She therefore requires longer rests to recover. Increased internal pressure may cause **muscular cramp, varicose veins** and the **need to pass urine more frequently**. These symptoms cause inconvenience but disappear after the birth of the baby.

Smoking

Tobacco smoke and the effects of inhaling it **reduce the efficiency of the blood to carry oxygen**. During the development of the fetus – particularly in the later stages when the rate of growth of the *brain* and *nervous system* is at its maximum – a considerable amount of oxygen must be supplied to the placenta. The effects of smoking on the fetus may be to **reduce the normal growth rate**, leading to stunting of *physical* and *mental* development.

Alcohol

If alcohol is taken in *excess* by the mother, its concentration in her bloodstream will reach a level that is dangerous to the fetus. Alcohol can pass across the **placenta** and damage the **nervous system** and the **liver** of the developing baby.

9.6 Use and abuse of drugs during pregnancy

Table 9.4 Drugs which should not be taken

Drug	Use	Effect on fetus
Chloroquine	Malaria	Eye abnormalities
Heroin	Drug abuse	Depressed respiration and withdrawal symptoms after birth
Live vaccines, e.g. smallpox, rubella	Immunisation	Viral infection
LSD	Drug abuse	Chromosome damage
Nicotine	Smoking	Poor growth

Table 9.5 Drugs best avoided if possible

Drug	Use	Effect on fetus
Streptomycin (an antibiotic)	To combat bacterial infections	Possible deafness
Sulphurazole	To combat bacterial infections	Anaemia
Tetracycline (an antibiotic)	To combat bacterial infections	Yellowing of the teeth

9.7 Birth

At the end of pregnancy the fetus moves so that its head points **downwards** at the cervix. **The muscular wall of the uterus** undergoes a series of *powerful contractions* and the baby is forced, head first, through the dilated cervix and vagina. Shortly after birth, the **placenta** is forced out in a similar manner. The **umbilical cord** is cut and tied off as soon as possible, and the part remaining on the baby withers and falls off within a few days, leaving the **navel** as a permanent scar.

9.8 Parental care

For the first months of a baby's life its food consists of **milk** secreted by its mother's **mammary glands** (breasts). During the first three days following birth, the mammary glands produce **colostrum,** which is a yellowish fluid containing antibodies (see Section 12.12) that protect the baby from many diseases during its early development. Colostrum also contains nutritive proteins, but in different proportions to those found in normal mother's milk. **Bottle-fed babies** are usually given food based on **cow's milk**.

Table 9.6 Comparison of the composition of cow's milk and human milk

Constituent	Cow's milk (per litre)	Human milk (per litre)
Water	860 g	876 g
Protein	34 g	12 g
Fat	42 g	36 g
Carbohydrate	48 g	70 g
Vitamin C	15 mg	52 mg
Vitamin A	0.4 mg	4.5 mg
Vitamin D	0.0002 mg	0.0003 mg
Sodium	0.6 g	0.15 g
Potassium	1.4 g	0.6 g
Magnesium	1.3 g	0.35 g
Calcium	1.2 g	0.3 g
Phosphorus	1.0 g	0.15 g
Energy	2730 kJ	2739 kJ
pH	6.8	7.3

Some advantages of breast feeding

- **A special relationship builds up between mother and baby** because of close physical contact lasting up to three hours per day.
- The *sucking* action of the baby stimulates **contraction of the uterus wall** and helps to bring the mother's shape back to normal following birth.
- There are **nutritional advantages** of human milk over cow's milk. **Antibodies** in the mother's colostrum are very important for the health of the newborn. Some babies become *allergic* to cow's milk, and others suffer because of an unsuitable balance of necessary minerals in cow's milk. The high protein of cow's milk can absorb too much acid from the baby's stomach. The acid normally helps digestion and kills certain harmful bacteria.

9.9 Growth of the individual

Growth is an **irreversible increase in size** of an organism involving the synthesis of **protoplasm**. It begins at the moment of *fertilisation*, continues through *gestation* (the period spent in the womb), and goes on until the end of *adolescence*. After that time, all parts of the body change and develop in significant ways. In many cases there is no further growth. Some parts of the body, such as the brain, *regress* until the end of life. The importance of growth before birth is illustrated by the fact that the fertilised egg divides *44 times* between conception and its appearance as a baby. From then until adulthood only *four* more divisions occur. The whole process is continuous: birth is merely a landmark. Indeed, **growth rate** starts to get *slower* from about the *fourth month* in the womb and, apart from a spurt in *adolescence*, gets steadily slower until it eventually stops.

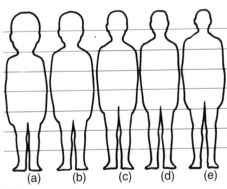

Fig. 9.9 How body proportions change during growth.
(a) Newborn baby: head is about ¼ of total body length;
(b) Infant; (c) Approaching puberty; (d) Adolescent;
(e) Adult. The rest of the body has now grown more than the head, which accounts for one-eighth of the body length

Fig. 9.10 Growth from birth to adulthood occurs as a curve, not a straight line

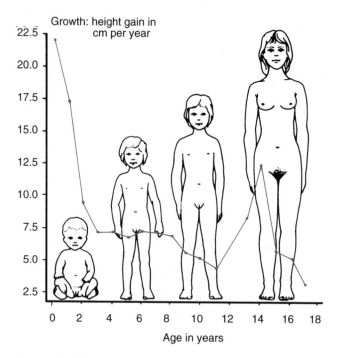

Fig. 9.11 A graph showing the number of centimetres the average girl grows in a year. After a rapid start, the rate declines until the adolescent growth spurt

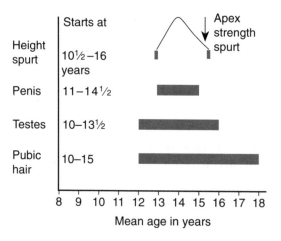

Fig. 9.12 The age range at which various systems start to grow in boys at puberty and the average period of growth

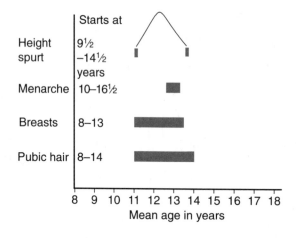

Fig. 9.13 The age range at which various systems start to grow in girls at puberty and the average period of growth

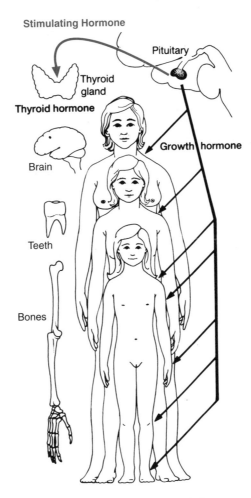

Fig. 9.14 Hormones and growth. Two important hormones influence growth. *Thyroid hormone*, released under stimulus from the pituitary, acts on the brain, teeth, bones and metabolism. *Growth hormone* secreted by the pituitary exerts an effect on the growth of all body systems

Summary

Human reproduction and development

1. Fertilisation takes place internally, the testes of the male producing games called sperms, which are released in semen during intercourse.

2. The egg is very large compared to sperms and contains all the food for the early stages of the zygote.

3. The production of several hormones by the female coordinates the development of the egg and the wall of the uterus.

4. If fertilisation does not occur, the uterus sheds its lining during menstruation. If fertilisation does not occur, the zygote travels down the Fallopian tube to the uterus.

5. The fetus is totally dependent on the mother for the exchange of materials at the placenta. During the early stages of growth of a baby, all of its food is provided by the mother in the form of milk which has several nutritional advantages compared to cow's milk.

6. Puberty is due to a marked increase in testosterone and oestrogen production. At puberty, secondary sexual characteristics become apparent.

Quick test

(a) Sperms are produced in greater numbers than eggs because:
   A they are small in size
   B they are viable for only a few days
   C more than one sperm fertilises an egg
   D the chance of a sperm reaching an egg is very small

(b) Human ovulation normally occurs approximately every:
   A 14 days   **B** 28 days   **C** 9 months   **D** 40 days

(c) Fertilisation occurs usually in the:
   A uterus   **B** vagina   **C** fallopian tube   **D** ovary

(d) During the development of the fetus it is protected by all the following *except* the:
   A uterus wall   **B** amniotic fluid   **C** muscles of the abdomen   **D** diaphragm

(e) Which of the following is *not* transported from the mother across the placenta to the fetus?
   A urea   **B** oxygen   **C** glucose   **D** amino acids

(f) The fusion of an egg and a sperm is called:
   A copulation   **B** implantation   **C** fertilisation   **D** ovulation.

Chapter 10
Genetics

10.1 Mendel's first law – the law of segregation

'Of a pair of contrasted characters, only one can be represented in the gamete (sperm or egg) by its germinal unit'.

Definitions

Gene This corresponds to Mendel's *germinal unit* and is the genetic factor present in a gamete which may lead to the appearance of the character in the adult.

Allele A gene can exist in two or more forms but only one of these is present in a chromosome. Two of the forms, or *alleles*, occupy the same relative positions on a pair of associated (homologous) chromosomes. One allele may be *dominant, recessive* or *equal* to the other in the pair of chromosomes, this determining the outward expression of the genes.

Heterozygote An individual receiving *unlike* genes from its parents.

Dominant character One of a pair of contrasted characters which expresses itself in the outward appearance of a heterozygote.

Recessive character One of a pair of contrasted characters which does not express itself in the outward appearance of the heterozygote but which is transmitted to later generations *without change*.

Phenotype The outward *expression of the genes*, i.e. an organism with certain observable characters, such as blonde hair and blue eyes.

Genotype The genetic constitution of an individual.

The formation of Mendel's first law

Gregor Mendel was the first to carry out scientifically controlled and statistically significant genetic experiments. He worked with the common garden pea plant, *Pisum sativum*. This plant is suitable for genetic experiments because it is self-pollinating, thus eliminating the possibility of outside genetic influence, and it shows pairs of contrasting characters. Mendel was able to select pea strains which bred true through many generations to several particular variations, e.g. *round or wrinkled* seeds; *yellow* or *green* seeds; *tall* or *short* stems. Although these examples may seem to be unrelated to human biology, the results and conclusions of Mendel's work have formed the basis for subsequent work in every aspect of genetics.

Concerning himself with *one* pair of contrasted characters at a time, and knowing that the parent stock was breeding true to type, Mendel crossed pairs of plants showing these contrasts. He grew the seeds resulting from the cross and noted the form of the characters in the offspring, which are designated the **first filial generation** (the F_1). The F_1 plants were allowed to self-pollinate. The resulting seeds were grown, giving the **second filial generation**, the F_2. Further generations were investigated in the same way but the behaviour of these particular characters was sufficiently revealed by the **third filial generation**, the F_3.

Let us consider the pair of contrasted characters, *yellow* and *green* seeds: Mendel's results showed that *all* the plants of the F₁ had yellow seeds but in the F₂, both yellow and green seeds were present in a ratio of 3 yellow to 1 green. As *green* seeds did not appear again until the F₂, the *yellow* character can be called **dominant** and the *green* character **recessive**. The actual numbers in the F₂ were 6022 yellow : 2001 green, almost exactly 3 : 1.

The same proportional result was obtained irrespective of whether pollen from a *yellow-seeded plant* was used to pollinate a *green-seeded plant* or vice-versa. The larger the number of plants used in the cross, the more accurate is the ratio of 3 : 1.

P (Parents)	Yellow	×		Green
F₁		Yellow (self-pollinated)		
F₂	3 Yellow	:		1 Green

Assume character for **yellow** = **Y** (dominant)
Assume character for **green** = **y** (recessive)

Genes present in the adults are shown by **two symbols** because each develops from a *zygote* (the result of fusion of two gametes).

Parents: **YY** (yellow) × **yy** (green)

gametes	**Y**	**Y**
y	**Yy**	**Yy**
y	**Yy**	**Yy**

F₁
All yellow (**Yy**) as effect of
Y dominant over **y**

F₁ selfed (Yy × Yy):

gametes	**Y**	**y**
Y	**YY**	**Yy**
y	**yY**	**yy**

F₂
3 yellow : 1 green
(**YY, Yy, yY**) (**yy**)

Human examples

Many *human* characteristics follow this simple Mendelian pattern of inheritance, with some characters being **dominant** and the others **recessive**. The study of human genetics is difficult because even the largest family is small compared with the thousands of pea plants which were used by Mendel for his statistical analyses. The *larger* the numbers used for genetical studies, the closer the agreement with the expected ratios.

Dominant human characters include *hare lip, negroid hair, the ability to taste phenylthiourea* and *the ability to roll one's tongue*. **Recessive characters** include *red hair, colour blindness* and *left handedness*. However, dominance is not always so clear cut. In some cases it is **incomplete**, for example the character for *eye colour* or for some *blood groups*. If each parent is **homozygous** for *brown eyes*, all the children will have *brown eyes*, but if the parents are **heterozygous** for *brown eye colour*, their children may have various shades such as *hazel* and *light brown*. The character for *blue eyes* is recessive so that if both parents have blue eyes, their children will also have blue eyes.

Another problem in studying human genetics is the impossibility of distinguishing people *homozygous* for some genes from those who are *heterozygous* for the same genes. It is impossible to tell if a brown-eyed man is a *pure strain* or a *hybrid* for the character merely by looking at the colour of his eyes. If a *brown-eyed man* and a *blue-eyed woman* have children, provided both parents are *homozygous, all* the children will have *brown eyes*, but if the parents are *heterozygous, one in four* children are likely to have *blue eyes*.

Let **B** = brown eyes and **b** = blue eyes

Brown eye colour is **dominant** to blue eye colour
The heterozygous parents are each **Bb**
From the cross **Bb** × **Bb** the **F₁** will be

gametes	**B**	**b**
B	**BB**	**Bb**
b	**bB**	**bb**

The blue-eyed child is **bb**.

Sometimes a particular character in an individual is controlled by more than two genes. **The ABO blood group system** (see Section 6.7) is controlled by three genes, **A, B** and **O**. An individual will inherit only two of these genes, one from each parent. **A** and **B** have the *same degree of dominance* and each is dominant to **O**. Therefore, people with **AA** or **AO** genotypes belong to group **A**. Those with **BB** or **BO** belong to group **B**. Where **A** and **B** are present, the person is group **AB**, and persons of genotype **OO** belong to group **O**. The genes are inherited according to Mendel's laws. That is, if parents have the genotypes **AA** and **BO**, they will be group **A** and group **B**, respectively. Their children's possible genotypes could be predicted thus:

Parents **AA** × **BO**

gametes	A	A	
B	AB	AB	50% group **AB**
O	AO	AO	50% group **A**

F₁

10.2 Sex determination

The sex of humans and other mammals is determined by **X** and **Y chromosomes**. These **sex chromosomes** can be distinguished from other chromosomes, **autosomes**, because the **Y chromosome** is much *shorter* than the **X chromosome** with which it is paired. A **man** has both **X** and **Y** chromosomes. A **woman** has two **X** chromosomes.

Male **XY**

gametes	X	Y
X	XX	XY
X	XX	XY

Female **XX**

F₁ 50% female 50% male

10.3 Sex linkage

Certain genes are associated with the sex of an individual because they happen to occur on the **X** chromosome. **Males (XY)** only have one **X** chromosome and therefore any *recessive* genes carried on the region that does not pair up with the **Y** chromosome cannot be masked. In **females (XX)**, a *recessive* gene on one **X** chromosome can be masked by a corresponding *dominant* gene on the other **X**. For a recessive character to appear in a female, she would have to be *homozygous* (double recessive) for that gene. Recessive forms of the sex-linked genes therefore express themselves more frequently in males than in females. **Colour blindness** and **haemophilia** (see Section 12.7) are examples of sex-linked genes.

10.4 Variation

There are two types of variation: **continuous** and **discontinuous.**

Continuous variations show an *even gradation* within a population. **Height** in humans is a good example. If in a population the height of each adult is measured, and a **histogram** constructed of the number of individuals whose height falls within a given range, each range decided upon being equal, it will show a curve of **normal distribution** (Gaussian curve) (see Fig. 10.1(a)).

Variation is **inheritable** only if it is due to **genes** (see Section 10.5). Height in man is only *partially* genetically controlled; any effects caused by the **environment** cannot be inherited. In the case of height many genes contribute to the character, for example, those controlling the production of *growth hormones* and those controlling the rate of *protein metabolism*. The environmental factors involved may be equally diverse, for example, the effects of *starvation, malnutrition, disease*, and *lack of exercise*.

Discontinuous variation within populations can be seen where the individuals fall into two or more *distinct* groups with respect to a particular character. It usually occurs where there is a completely dominant and recessive character within a pair of contrasted genes. Height in pea plants, investigated by Gregor Mendel (see Section 10.1), is an example of discontinuous variation. This particular plant character is controlled by a single pair of genes and the environment has very little overall effect on it within a large population.

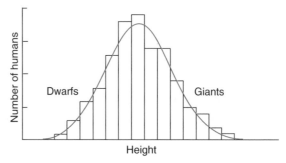

Fig. 10.1(a) Continuous variation (curve drawn from histogram)

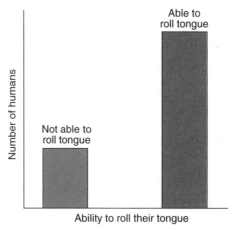

Fig. 10.1(b) Dicontinuous variation

10.5 Chromosomes as carriers of hereditary factors – DNA

When a cell is not undergoing division (and the vast majority of cells do not divide again once they have been formed), the **nucleus** appears, under the microscope, as a uniformly **greyish dot**. However, during **cell division**, the contents of the nucleus take on a very different appearance. They become organised into a number of *rod-shaped threads*. These are called **chromosomes** (from *chromos*, meaning coloured, and *soma*, meaning body, because they can be stained with dyes and show up within the cells as discrete units). Each species of animal and plant has a *fixed* number of chromosomes in each nucleus of each of its cells. Between species chromosomes differ in *number* and *shape*: the closer the relation between species, the more similar are the chromosomes. Man has **46 chromosomes** in each of his cells, except the **gametes**, which have **23** (see section on Meiosis, p. 101). In the nucleus of a cell that is not dividing, the chromosomes are still present, even though they do not stain. They are actually dispersed as a very fine network throughout the nucleus.

Chromosomes carry **genes** along their length. Genes are made of a unique chemical, **deoxyribonucleic acid**, or **DNA.** The DNA molecule is extremely large. It is roughly the shape of a long *ladder* that has been twisted into a *spiral*. It has been estimated that a molecule of DNA is 2000 to 3000 times longer than it is thick and is made of well over 10 000 smaller molecules. It is built in the following way: There are essentially identical halves, each comprising a twisted chain of sugar (**deoxyribose**) molecules linked together by phosphate molecules – this forms the backbone of the ladder – and each carrying a particular chemical base. Links between neighbouring bases hold the two chains together (and form the rungs of the ladder). The only difference between each half of the DNA molecule is the particular assortment of chemical bases.

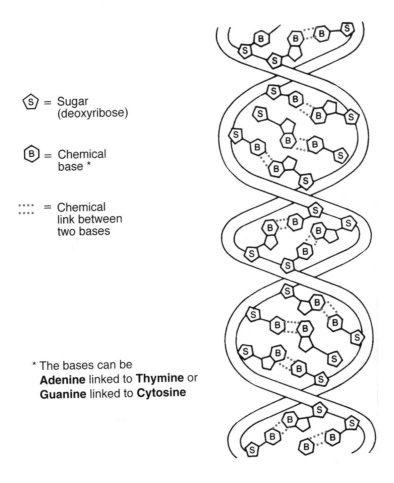

Ⓢ = Sugar
(deoxyribose)

Ⓑ = Chemical
base *

⋯⋯ = Chemical
link between
two bases

* The bases can be
Adenine linked to **Thymine** or
Guanine linked to **Cytosine**

Fig. 10.2 DNA structure

Each gene is composed of a DNA molecule with its own characteristic *arrangement of bases*. It takes only *one* base to be altered to change the particular gene. There is an almost *unlimited* number of possible arrangements if you consider that a strand of DNA can be over 10 000 base units long. Therefore, there is an almost unlimited number of possible genes in plants and animals.

The function of DNA

DNA determines which *chemical reactions* take place in a cell and at what speeds. It does this by dictating which *proteins* are manufactured in the cell. About 2000 proteins are known from living cells, and many of them are able to act as *catalysts* in the chemical activity of the cell: these proteins are the **enzymes**. Chemical reactions cannot occur at any appreciable rate in cells unless they are catalysed. Therefore, by controlling *protein synthesis*, DNA controls the life of the cell.

10.6 How proteins are made in cells

Proteins are made up of building blocks (molecules) known as **amino acids**, which consist of *carbon, nitrogen* and *hydrogen* atoms arranged such that there are *basic* and *acidic* portions of the molecules. In proteins, amino acids are linked together in chains, the acid group of one amino acid attaching to the basic group of the next. DNA is able to regulate how the amino acids are arranged. There are about *20* different amino acids and each protein has its own characteristic *types* and *arrangement* of amino acids. Similarly, the types and arrangement of the *bases* in the DNA molecule act as a code that determines which amino acids are linked together.

Link   Link

Amino acid ———— Amino acid ———— Amino acid

A   B   C

Simplified account of how DNA is used for making protein:

❶ The long molecule of DNA (remember it is like a twisted ladder) **unwinds** and **splits** along its length between the bases.

❷ One *half* of the molecule now acts as a *template* for the formation of a **messenger molecule**, which is made by new bases from the nucleus lining up opposite their *complementary* partners in the original half of the DNA, e.g. Cytosine (C) with Guanine (G), and forming a single strand. The result is that the **code** present in DNA is reproduced in the messenger molecule. (The sugar molecules forming the backbone of the larger messenger molecule consists of **ribose** not deoxyribose, and in ribonucleic acid (**RNA**) the base thymine is replace by **uracil**.)

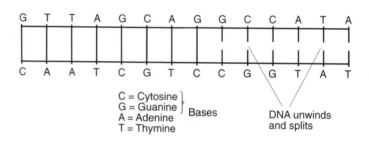

Fig. 10.3 The base pairing of a DNA molecule

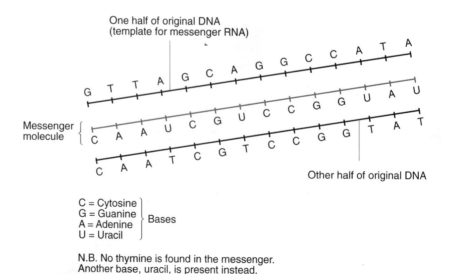

N.B. No thymine is found in the messenger.
Another base, uracil, is present instead.

Fig. 10.4 The 'transcription' of the DNA code onto a messenger molecule

③ The messenger molecule then passes through the *nuclear membrane* to the **ribosomes** (see Section 1.1).

④ The *code* on the messenger molecule then determines which *amino acids* from the *cytoplasm* of the cell become linked together and therefore the type of protein produced.

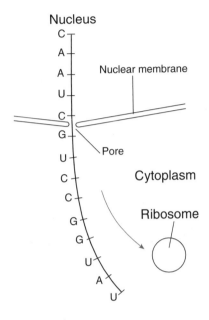

Fig. 10.5 Messenger RNA passes to ribosome

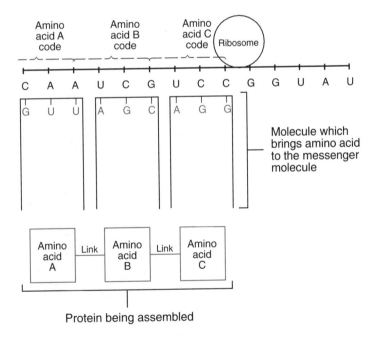

Fig. 10.6 DNA code transcribed into amino acid chain

10.7 Cell division

Mitosis

Chromosomes are made of many DNA molecules lying side by side. Any division of a cell into two must include a division of the chromosomes and if the resulting *daughter cells* are to be identical, then the division of the chromosomes must be precise. This is achieved in **mitosis**, which occurs in all cells within growing tissues.

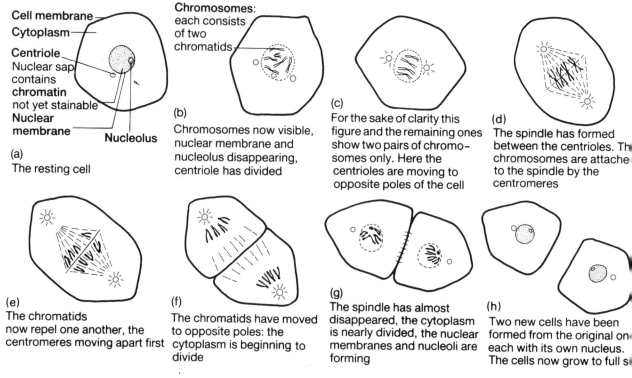

Cell membrane
Cytoplasm
Centriole
Nuclear sap contains chromatin not yet stainable
Nuclear membrane
Nucleolus

(a)
The resting cell

Chromosomes: each consists of two chromatids

(b)
Chromosomes now visible, nuclear membrane and nucleolus disappearing, centriole has divided

(c)
For the sake of clarity this figure and the remaining ones show two pairs of chromo-somes only. Here the centrioles are moving to opposite poles of the cell

(d)
The spindle has formed between the centrioles. Th chromosomes are attache to the spindle by the centromeres

(e)
The chromatids now repel one another, the centromeres moving apart first

(f)
The chromatids have moved to opposite poles: the cytoplasm is beginning to divide

(g)
The spindle has almost disappeared, the cytoplasm is nearly divided, the nuclear membranes and nucleoli are forming

(h)
Two new cells have been formed from the original on each with its own nucleus. The cells now grow to full si

Fig. 10.7 Stages in mitosis

❶ The DNA molecules *unwind* along their length between the bases. On to each of the resultant halves, a new *complementary* second half is added from the pool of molecules in the nucleus.

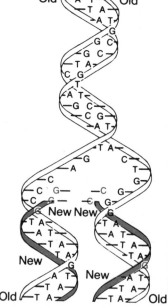

Fig. 10.8 Division of DNA. During the division of a cell to form two daughter cells, the double helix of DNA divides and forms two daughter helices. This it does by unwinding itself; each strand then acts as the template for the formation of a new strand

The outcome is the **doubling** of the chromosomes into two strands, the **chromatids**, which lie side by side. There is one part of the chromosome that does *not* become duplicated in this way; it is the **centromere**.

❷ Their duplication having been completed, the chromosomes *shorten* and *increase in thickness*.

❸ The **nucleolus** and **nuclear membrane** disintegrate and the chromosomes spread throughout the *cytoplasm*. The **centriole** divides and the two halves move to opposite ends of the cell. These first 3 stages comprise the **prophase** of mitosis (stages (a)–(c) in Fig. 10.7).

4 The chromosomes move together and arrange themselves in a *single plane* in the *centre* of the cell. As a result, the centromeres of the different chromosomes are at an equal distance from either end of the cell (d). In plant cells, *fibrous threads* appear in the cytoplasm, radiating out from the two halves of the centriole, or **poles**, which are present, one on each side of the chromosomes. This forms the **spindle**. The fibrous threads are not obvious in animal cells undergoing mitosis.

This stage is often called the **metaphase**.

5 The centromeres *divide* and one *complete set* of chromatids is pulled back towards each pole. This is the **anaphase** ((e)–(f)).

6 The two sets of chromatids organise themselves as *two nuclei*. In each case, a *nuclear membrane* re-forms and then the *nucleolus* appears. Next the cytoplasm separates into two equal parts to complete the division ((g)–(h)).

The *significance* of mitosis is the formation of *two new cells* which are *identical* to one another, and to their parent cell, in every respect except in the amount of cytoplasm.

Meiosis

During **sexual reproduction**, if the egg had 46 chromosomes and the sperm had 46 chromosomes the zygote (produced by fusion of the gametes) would have 92 chromosomes, double the normal number. When the zygote grew into an adult via the embryo and fetus stages, then it would produce gametes with 92 chromosomes. So there would be a *progressive doubling* from one generation to another. But we know that the number of chromosomes in a species remains *constant*. This is called the **diploid** number, and for this number to remain unaltered there must be a **reduction** of the diploid number by a *half* every time gametes are formed by cell division. The 'half' diploid number of chromosomes is the **haploid** number and *gametes* acquire this as a result of meiosis (reduction division).

Meiosis occurs *only* in *diploid* cells that give rise to gametes. Apart from sperm and egg cells all human cells are diploid. Human diploid cells have 46 chromosomes – 23 from the mother's egg and 23 from the father's sperm – that are arranged as 23 pairs.

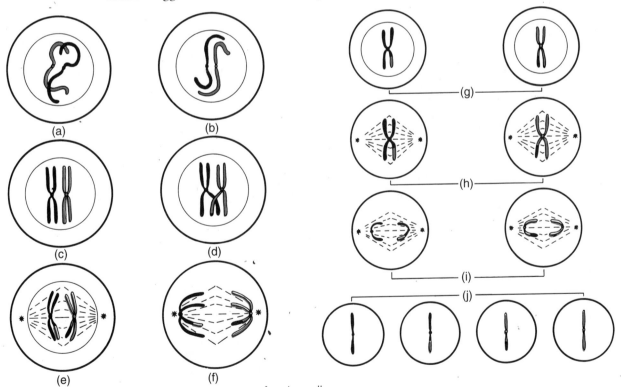

Fig. 10.9 Meiosis in a gamete-forming cell

1 Each *chromosome* moves towards, and begins to pair with, its partner. The pairing process results in a very *close contact* along the whole of the length of the chromosomes (b). Thus the first stage of *meiosis* differs from that in mitosis. At the start of mitosis the chromosomes consist of two chromatids which are formed by duplication, but in meiosis whole *pairs* of chromosomes come together.

2 While in this close union, the chromosomes *shorten* and *thicken*, and each becomes *duplicated* into **two chromatids** (c). At this stage the *nuclear membrane* begins to disintegrate.

3 Along the length of the pairs of chromosomes, individual **chromatids cross** one another in complex ways. As a result of this, chromatids **exchange** various sections (d). The force of attraction that up to this point has held the pairs of chromosomes together now ceases to operate fully, and the pairs of chromosomes begin to *separate* (e). (In Fig 10.9 for simplicity only one cross-over is shown.)

4 The *chromosomes separate completely* and move to *opposite* poles of the cell (f). The *cytoplasm divides* (g). At this point, each daughter cell still has the *diploid* number of chromosomes, but because of *crossing over* of sections of the chromatids, **genes** from one partner have been mixed with genes from the other partner.

5 Each new cell undergoes a *mitotic* division. The chromosomes, each consisting of *two complete chromatids* (even though parts have been exchanged), line up along the centre of the new cell (h). One set of chromatids passes to each pole of the cell. Each new set of chromosomes starts to form a nucleus (i).

6 A division of the cytoplasm occurs and nuclear membranes re-appear. As a result, **four gametes**, each with the *haploid* number of chromosomes, have been formed from an original *diploid* cell (j).

The significance of meiosis is:
- The formation of cells with **half** the normal number of chromosomes.
- **Mixing of genes** between pairs of chromosomes contributing to **variation** within the chromosomes.

E xaminer's tip

The most common examination questions on this topic are based on:
1 Genetics of human disorders (see pp.130–131)
2 The role of DNA (Higher Tier)
3 The significance of mitosis and meiosis.

Summary

Genetics

1 Gregor Mendel's experiments with garden peas lead to the formulation of the basic laws of genetics.

2 Plants and animals show continuous and discontinuous variations which can be expressed graphically.

3 DNA controls protein synthesis through a code of bases. By transcription, this code is passed on to messenger RNA.

4 Messenger RNA carries the code into the cytoplasm where it acts as a template for the building of proteins. Transfer RNA brings amino acids to be template where proteins are assembled.

5 Body cells divide by a process of mitosis which results in the formation of cells which are identical to one another and to the parent cell from which they arose.

6 Sperms and eggs are produced by meiosis in which the diploid number of chromosomes is reduced to half.

Quick test

(a)

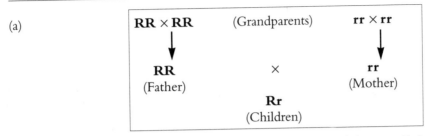

The diagram shows the inheritance of a gene **R** (giving the ability to roll the sides of the tongue) and a gene **r** (the inability to do so), on the opposite sides of the family. If **R** is dominant to **r**, the children able to roll their tongues will be:
   A only the boys **B** only the girls **C** all of them **D** half of them

(b) Mitosis occurs:
   A in gametes **B** in males only **C** when there are too many chromosomes in a cell
   D whenever new body cells are produced

(c) A chromosome:
   A is found only in gametes **B** carries genetic information
   C is present at all times in cells **D** can migrate across the nuclear membrane

(d) The sex of a baby is determined by:
   A the mother's ovum **B** the number of ova produced **C** the father's sperm
   D the age of the father

(e) A gene is:
   A a unit of heredity **B** made up of chromosomes
   C found only in male gametes **D** produced after fertilisation.

Chapter 11
Interdependence

11.1 The interdependence of plants and animals

People feed at the end of food chains

e.g. grass → grasshopper → frog → trout → man

If man were to live on trout alone, to survive, he would have to eat approximately one every day, and he would require about *300 trout* to support him for a year. Each trout would similarly require a frog every day. Therefore the 300 trout needed to support the man for a year would themselves have to eat *90 000 frogs* annually. In turn, each frog would require a grasshopper every day, so the frog population would eat *27 million grasshoppers* in a year. A herd of grasshoppers that large would require *1000 tons of grass*. So we can draw a food pyramid that looks like this:

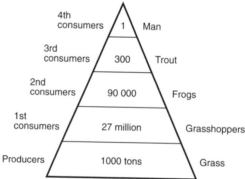

4th consumers	1	Man
3rd consumers	300	Trout
2nd consumers	90 000	Frogs
1st consumers	27 million	Grasshoppers
Producers	1000 tons	Grass

Fig. 11.1 A theoretical food chain

The large numbers of organisms towards the base of the pyramid are required to support the smaller numbers of organisms near the apex because none of the organisms is very efficient at *converting food into body tissue*. Only about **1%** of the solar energy striking the field is converted into grass via photosynthesis. The grasshoppers are able to convert only about **10%** of the grass into grasshopper tissue: most of the grass is uneaten, undigested, or used to provide energy for hopping, chewing and other activities. Similarly, the man, trout and frogs are able to convert only about **10%** of their food into man, trout, and frog tissue, respectively. It is apparent that the *number of animals* that can be supported at the top of the pyramid is directly related to the *number of layers within the pyramid*.

We can support more people on this food chain simply by *shortening* it. Eliminate the trout and the land will yield 90 000 frogs for human consumption. Assuming each person could survive on 10 frogs per day, the frogs would support *30 people for a year*. (Fig. 11.2)

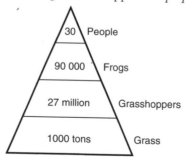

30	People
90 000	Frogs
27 million	Grasshoppers
1000 tons	Grass

Fig. 11.2 A shorter food chain

But who likes frogs? Let us consider grasshoppers instead and assume that 100 a day would satisfy you. Now the 27 million grasshoppers would support *900 people for a year*.

Fig. 11.3 A still-shorter food chain

Fig. 11.4 The simplest food chain

If we eliminate the grasshoppers and eat the grass ourselves, the land would support even more people. In fact, about 2000 people, each eating about 1 kg of grass per day, could live on the land that supported the one fish-eating man we met at the beginning of this argument.

The conclusion is that, theoretically, the *shorter* the food chain, the *more efficient* it is at energy conversion. In practice, however, the anatomy, physiology and behaviour of man make it impossible for him to be a primary consumer of grass, apart from cereal crops. The feeding relationships of man and plants are rarely, if ever, as simple as the food chain quoted. Usually, several food chains are interconnected forming **food webs**. A complete food web for any habitat is impossible to illustrate because of the vast variety of feeders and their food. Here is a simplified version of a food web which incorporates the food chain mentioned above:

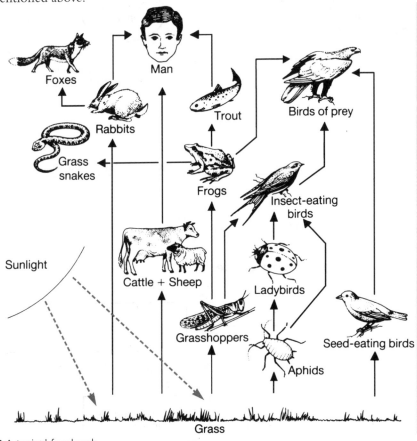

Fig. 11.5 A typical food web

11.2 Decomposition cycles

The nitrogen cycle

The cycle can be divided into a 'building up' part and a 'breaking down' part. Each part uses a different set of bacteria.

'Building up' bacteria
- **Nitrifying**: These build up molecules of nitrates from nitrites and ammonium salts.
- **Nitrogen fixing**: These take nitrogen from the air and change it into a form which can be used by plants to make proteins. They are found in the soil and inside the roots of pod-bearing plants (legumes), e.g. peas, beans, clover.

'Breaking down' bacteria
- **Denitrifying**: These break down nitrates into nitrogen and oxygen which then pass back into the air.
- **Putrefying**: These cause the decay of dead things. They break them down into carbon dioxide and ammonia. Ammonia quickly reacts to form ammonium salts in the soil.

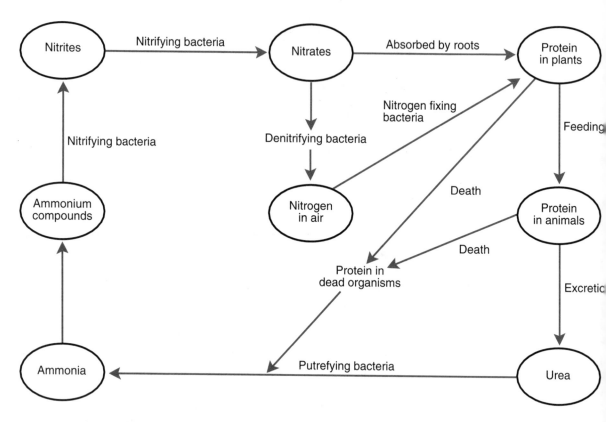

Fig. 11.6(a) Circulation of nitrogen

The carbon cycle

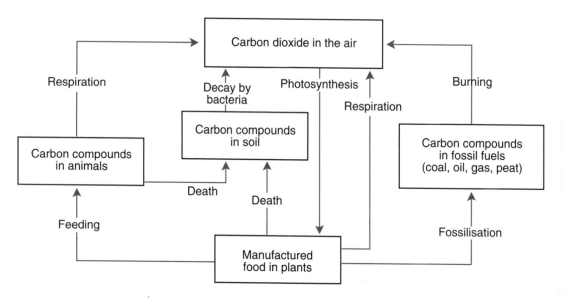

Fig. 11.6(b) The carbon cycle

The carbon cycle ensures a constant supply of carbon dioxide to plants and relies on animals putting it into the air during respiration. Plants take it out of the air during photosynthesis. It is added to the air during respiration, decay, and burning fossil fuels.

11.3 Plants as the ultimate source of man's food

Plants (and some bacteria) are the only organisms that can *make food*. Animals either *eat plants* or they *eat other animals* which themselves have eaten plants. The process by which plants make food is called **photosynthesis**. Plants use inorganic materials, in particular *carbon dioxide* from the atmosphere and *water* from the soil, and in the presence of **chlorophyll** and *energy* (in the form of sunlight) they manufacture carbohydrates.

Photosynthesis

This can be divided into *two* basic stages:

1. **Splitting water** using energy from the sun.
2. **Reduction of carbon dioxide** by the addition of hydrogen.

Stage 1

Energy from sunlight, trapped by the green pigment, *chlorophyll*, splits water molecules into *oxygen* and *hydrogen*, the process of **photolysis**.

$$4H_2O \xrightarrow[\text{Chlorophyll}]{\text{Sunlight}} 4[OH]+4[H] \qquad 4[OH] \longrightarrow 2H_2O+O_2 \text{ (by-products)}$$

Stage 2

The hydrogen is combined with carbon dioxide in a complex series of **reduction** reactions. The product acts as a starting point for the manufacture of all carbohydrates, proteins, fats and most vitamins. The significance of photosynthesis to *animals* is thus:

(a) It provides the source of their dietary requirements.
(b) It provides them with oxygen (given off in Stage 1).
(c) It uses the carbon dioxide that animals produce as waste during respiration and releases oxygen into the atmosphere.

11.4 The world food problem

There is a growing fear of a **world food crisis**. More than half the human population suffers from *hunger* or *malnutrition*, and worldwide the number of people is increasing faster than the food supply. Some authorities have produced statistics of food and population growth which show that a *food crisis* is imminent. But throughout history there has been insufficient food for all the people of the world; *population size* has always tended to *increase faster* than the *food supply*. Periodic **famines**, reducing the population of a region to what the available food could support, have occurred in every part of the world, including Europe. However, starting in the 17th century, developments took place which eventually freed Europe from recurring famines. First, from about 1650 to 1900 more than 60 million people left Europe for the sparsely populated continents of America and Australasia, and then these regions exported food back to Europe. By 1900, two-thirds of the food consumed in Britain was imported. A second, and an even more important development, was the **application of science to agriculture**. In the past 300 years this has produced nearly a tenfold increase in the yield per hectare on the best farmed lands. At times, food has been produced in such abundance that unmarketable surpluses have arisen. In the 1930s Britain and the United States took measures to control production to adjust the supply to economic demand.

In less economically developed countries, in most areas agriculture continues to be largely primitive (except where production of crops such as *sugar* is concerned, which is exported to western industrialised nations), and famines continue to occur. Since 1800, there have been more than 400 famines in China and in India today there is an acute shortage of food in several provinces. In recent years, hunger has been a problem in most of the poorer countries of the world, while a surplus of food has caused economic problems in both Europe and the United States. These surpluses have now disappeared: the Soviet Union and China have bought the grain and dairy product 'mountains' of Canada and Australia. The United States has sent its surplus food to a variety of Third World countries. From 1951 to 1966 it sent 52 million tons of food products to India alone.

The **food stocks** of the world are relatively small. In spite of the efforts of some nations, food production is not increasing as fast as world population. A **world food plan** needs estimates of the world population in the foreseeable future, of the amount of food needed to support it, and of the measures which could be taken to produce this. Modern science can increase production enormously only if the following are taken into account:

1. All human food ultimately comes from **green plants** which survive and grow by fixing the energy of sunlight. There is a vast difference between the theoretical rate of plant food production and the best rates achieved by present-day agriculture.

2. We can only generalise about **human dietary requirements**; even the amounts of different foods required to *prevent crippling disease* or *produce optimal health* are very imprecisely known. Yet such knowledge is vital if malnutrition is to be prevented.

3. **Farm animals** sometimes compete directly with man for food, but more often they provide the most practical means – and occasionally the only way – of providing **essential protein**. In the future, more animals, husbanded more efficiently, will be needed to improve the quality of human diets throughout the world.

4. We know technically, or can find out, **how to produce enough food for mankind**, but to actually achieve this cannot be done without far-reaching changes in the social, economic and agricultural structure of the hungry nations. To learn how to bring about these changes is more urgent than any technical discovery.

5. **Plant protein** in oil-seeded meal until recently was not normally used for human consumption, but it is now available commercially for use in foods, often being mixed with other proteins. If fully expanded, this development could meet almost the entire present world protein deficit.

6. **Salt water** has been used successfully to irrigate plants grown on sand. Such experiments indicate that very large *desert areas* can be reclaimed for food reproduction.

7. Management of commercial **marine fish stocks** and an increasing exploitation of the less known varieties of fish can yield vast quantities of food.

8. The world shortage of protein could be alleviated by new foods obtained from cultivated **bacteria**, **algae**, **yeasts**, **protozoans** and **fungi**. Protein from these single-celled organisms is now being produced in many countries of the world.

11.5 Growth of populations

The population of the world as a whole has been *growing steadily*, though in individual countries there have been *fluctuations* in population size as people have migrated to newly discovered territories or have gone off in search of new food and mineral sources. Malthus, in 1798, suggested that because the population *increases faster* than food production there should be some sort of **birth control**. The growth of the world's population is now much faster than it has been in the past for the following reasons:

1. The **increased effectiveness of medical science in saving lives** and virtually wiping out many formerly fatal diseases, such as *diphtheria*, *smallpox* and *tuberculosis*.

2. Practically all mothers and babies survive childbirth because of **improved pre- and post-natal medical care**.

3 Increased lifespan in the Western industrial countries due to a **better diet** than that enjoyed by our ancestors.

4 **Agricultural development** (see Section 11.4).

5 **Industrial development** due to technological advances leading to greater potential for trade and greater affluence.

Consequences of an increasing population growth rate

● **Shortage of food** (see Section 11.4).
● **Pollution** (see Section 14.4).

Methods used to calculate population growth

1 **Crude birth rate**: This is the number of *births per 1000 of the population per year* and is calculated as follows:

$$\frac{\text{Number of births in a year}}{\text{Total population of that year}} \times 1000$$

2 **Fertility rate**: This is the number of *live births per 1000 women of child-bearing age per year*. It is used for forecasting population trends and is calculated as follows

$$\frac{\text{Number of births in a year}}{\text{Number of women aged between 15 and 45 in that year}} \times 1000$$

3 **Infant mortality rate**: This is the number of *deaths of children under 1 year of age per 1000 live births per year*. It is an indication of standards of hygiene and medical care in a community and is calculated as follows

$$\frac{\text{Number of infant deaths in a year}}{\text{Number of live births in that year}} \times 1000$$

4 **Crude death rate**: This is the number of *deaths per 1000 of the population per year*. It is an indication of the relative health of a community and can be calculated as follows

$$\frac{\text{Number of deaths in a year}}{\text{Total population of that year}} \times 1000$$

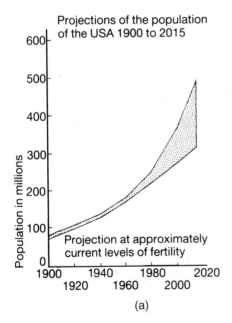

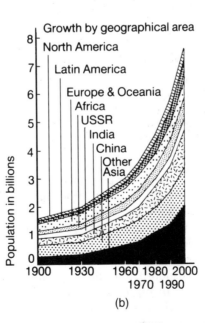

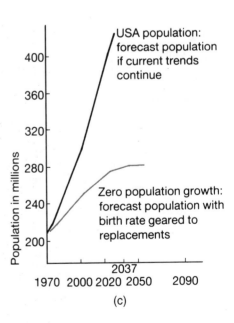

Fig. 11.7 Within 70 years the population of the world has doubled and it is expected to double again by the end of the century. The graphs illustrate the problem of the population explosions.
(a) The population of the USA with a projection to AD 2015 based on current fertility rate data.
(b) The rise in population up to the year AD 2000 for the major areas of the world.
(c) A comparison between the anticipated population growth of the USA and what it would be if kept in check by birth control.

11.6 Population control – contraception

Table 11.1 Methods of contraception

Method	How it is used	Reasons why it might fail
1 **Contraceptive pills** taken by women	As prescribed by a doctor; usually taken orally, one every day	Not following the instructions or forgetting to take the pill at the prescribed time
2 A **contraceptive sheath** (condom, Durex, French letter, rubber)	Put on the erect penis before intercourse	Not put on before any contact with the vagina. Not carefully removed after intercourse.
3 The **intra-uterine device** (IUD) (coil or loop) worn by women	Put inside the womb by a doctor	Fails in a proportion of women. Reasons not understood. Can cause pain and heavy bleeding
4 The **diaphragm** (Dutch cap) worn by women	Inserted by the woman at the cervix prior to intercourse. Removed eight hours later	Not put in place properly. Not used with a spermicide
5 **Spermicides** (sperm killers). As a cream; used by men and women	The woman put the spermicide high up in the vagina. The man puts the cream inside a contraceptive sheath before use	Impossible for the cream to reach every part of the folded inner wall of the vagina
6 The **'safe' period** calculated by the woman	No sexual intercourse after the egg is shed and is in the oviduct	Very difficult to be accurate with the timing of egg release (ovulation). Woman vary in the length of their menstrual cycles. Sperms can remain active in the female reproductive tracts for some time after intercourse
7 **Withdrawal of penis** by man (coitus interruptus)	The man removes his penis from the vagina before ejaculation	A very high risk of pregnancy as any sperms left in the reproductive tract can swim to the egg
8 **Sterilisation** of men and women	In men, the vas deferens are cut and tied. In women, the oviducts are cut and tied	This never fails if the operation has been carried out properly

E xaminer's tip

The most common examination questions on this topic are based on:
1 Food webs
2 The nitrogen cycle and
- the carbon cycle
3 Population growth.
Note that questions on contraception will be found only in the *Human Physiology and Health* examination

Summary

Interdependence

1 Food chains begin with plants and represent energy flow from one feeding level to the next.

2 Feeding relationships can be shown in the form of pyramids which demonstrate the rule that the biomass decreases from the base of the pyramid to the apex because of the energy loss between feeding levels.

3 Essential microbes enable materials to be recycled and are involved in the carbon and nitrogen cycles.

4 Almost all forms of life depend on photosynthesis which only occurs in green plants.

5 A stable population density depends on a balance between birth rate and death rate. Present trends in human populations suggest that future generations may have difficulty in providing themselves with enough food.

6 Methods of contraception include barriers, prevention of implantation of the egg, prevention of gamete production and regulation of the times of sexual intercourse.

Quick test

(a) The feeding relationship in a pond can be represented by Fig. 1(a) below.

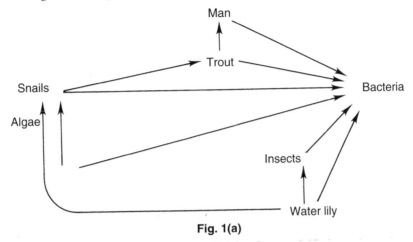

Fig. 1(a)

What is the name given to this feeding relationship?
A food web   **B** food pyramid   **C** consumer chain   **D** food chain

(b) Consider the feeding relationship represented in Fig. 1(b) below.

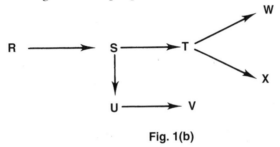

Fig. 1(b)

The letters represent organisms. Which of the following population changes in the other organisms would be most likely to directly result in an increase in the population of T?
A a decrease in the population of S   **B** a decrease in the population of U
C a decrease in the population of V   **D** a decrease in the population of W

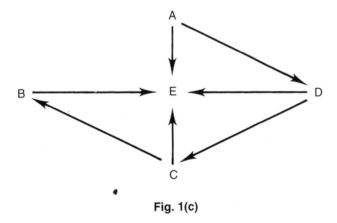

Fig. 1(c)

(c) Fig. 1(c) represents the passage of energy through a biological community. The arrows show the direction of movement of energy from one group of organisms to another.
  (i) Green plants would be represented by:
      A B C D
  (ii) A collective name for the organisms represented by E is
  A producer   **B** primary carnivore   **C** decomposer   **D** herbivore

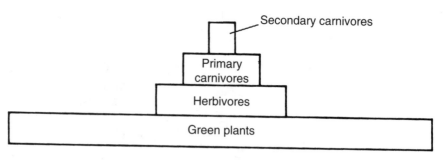

Fig. 1(d)

(d) Fig. 1(d) can be used to represent the numbers, per unit area in a community. It shows that:
  A there are fewer herbivores than carnivores
  B as food chains progress, fewer organisms are involved
  C there are more animals than plants
  D food chains always have four organisms in the chain

(e) The destruction of all bacteria would be catastrophic for all life on earth because:
  A bacteria are the hardest organisms to kill
  B the organisms that feed on bacteria would starve
  C soil nutrients would remain in undecayed organisms
  D evolution begins with bacteria

(f) Energy absorbed by a grassland community enters as:
  A light and is lost as light   **B** light and is lost as heat
  C heat and is lost as light   **D** heat and is lost as heat

(g) The most important way to help relieve world food shortages is by:
  A trying to kill all insects with sprays
  B controlling the size of cities
  C giving more education about balanced diets
  D developing adequate birth control schemes

(h) What is the biological reason for producing protein-rich vegetables in preference to rearing animals for human food?
  A it is much cheaper to produce vegetables than meat
  B there is more roughage in vegetables than in meat
  C vegetables contain less fat than meat does
  D less energy and fixed nitrogen is lost in producing vegetables.

Chapter 12
Disease

12.1 Bacteria

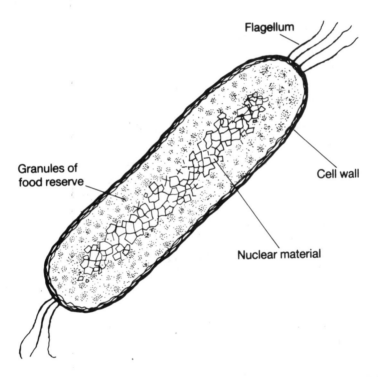

Fig. 12.1 A single bacterium magnified under the electron microscope (approx. × 107 000)

Labels: Flagellum, Cell wall, Nuclear material, Granules of food reserve

Minute *acellular* organisms that lack both mitochondria and a distinct nucleus. They can be **saprophytic** (feeding on dead material), **parasitic** (feeding on living organisms), **photosynthetic** (capable of using light energy and inorganic materials to make food) or **chemo-autotrophic** (capable of using energy from chemical compounds to manufacture food). Their shape can be: spherical – **coccus**; rod-like – **bacillus**; spiral – **spirillum**; comma-like – **vibrio**; **filamentous**; or corkscrew-like – **spirochaete**.

Those which infect humans are parasitic and feed using *extracellular digestion*. Their life cycle involves:

- Secretion of digestive enzymes
- Extracellular digestion
- Absorption
- Metabolism
- Excretion
- Growth

Most bacteria are killed by temperatures above 70°C. However, certain species can form resistant spores which can remain alive in boiling water for periods varying from a few minutes to several hours. Reproduction in bacteria involves simple cell division and in ideal conditions can occur every half hour.

12.2 Culture of bacteria

The streak plate method is one of many methods which is useful for isolating *pure colonies* of bacteria from a *mixed culture*. The materials needed are: source of bacteria (e.g. mixed culture of soil bacteria); nutrient agar plate; wire loop; and a Bunsen burner.

Procedure (for results within 24 hours)

Taking the bacterial sample
Hold the tube of bacterial culture in the left hand, the wire loop in the right hand. Flame the loop and allow to cool. Remove the cotton wool plug of the tube with the little finger of the right hand. Flame the mouth of the tube. Insert the loop and remove one loopful of culture. Flame the mouth of the tube, replace the plug and return the tube to its rack.

Streaking the plate

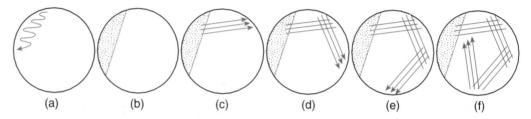

(a)   (b)   (c)   (d)   (e)   (f)

Fig. 12.2 Diagrammatic representation of the stages of streaking an agar plate

(a) Raise the lid of the Petri dish enough to insert the wire loop. Spread the loop of culture evenly over an area of the agar surface using light sweeping movements to avoid tearing the agar surface. To achieve an even distribution of bacteria, using zig-zag strokes.
(b) and (c) Flame the loop and allow to cool. Place the cooled loop on the well and draw across the agar in a straight line. Repeat twice to make three parallel streaks in all. *Do not flame the loop between these strokes.*
(d) Flame the loop and allow to cool. Place the cooled loop on the agar surface and streak across previous streaks three times.
(e) Flame the loop and allow to cool. Streak as shown in the diagram.
(f) Flame the loop and allow to cool. Streak for the last time as shown in the diagram.
During the entire streaking operation, the lid must be kept only very slightly ajar to reduce *aerial contamination*.

Incubation
On completion of streaking, label the plate, and place it upside down in an incubator at 37°C for 24 hours. Examine the plate.

Result
In the *first* streaking, a small fraction of the total number of bacteria is spread across the plate. In the *second* and *third* streakings, the numbers spread over the agar are very much reduced. With the *fourth* streakings, only a few individual bacteria are drawn across the plate. Each of these reproduces to form a pure colony or a **clone**.

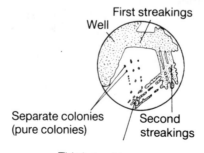

Fig. 12.3 Typical appearance of a streaked plate after incubation

12.3 Bacteria and disease – pathogens

If a *parasitic* bacterium gets into human tissue, establishes itself, reproduces and produces a *disease*, it is classed as a **pathogen**.

Body defences

1 **Skin** – acts as a barrier, preventing entry into the body of micro-organisms, dust particles and most chemicals.

2 **Lachrymal glands** – secrete tears containing a bacterial chemical.

3 **Blood clotting** – provides a temporary barrier before a wound heals.

4 **Phagocytes** – special white blood cells which ingest micro-organisms that have invaded the body.

5 **Antibodies and antitoxins** – produced by lymphocytes (see Section 6.9).

6 **Stomach** – produces hydrochloric acid which sterilises food.

Important terms to understand when studying all infectious diseases are:

- **Incubation period** During this early stage of an infection the pathogen multiplies rapidly and the person begins to show symptoms of the disease.
- **Isolation period** The length of time that a sick person is infectious and should be kept away from other people.
- **Quarantine period** The length of time that people who have been in contact with an infected person and who may therefore carry and spread the pathogen should avoid mixing with other people.
- **Mode of transmission** How organisms causing disease are spread from one person to another. The main methods are: (a) air-borne droplets; (b) by infected food and water; (c) by insect vectors; (d) by objects contaminated by micro-organisms; (e) by human carriers; (f) by direct contact with the infected person.
- **Prevention of spread** How to stop or reduce the spread of micro-organisms to healthy people.

How bacteria cause disease

Like all living organisms, bacteria produce *waste products*. Unfortunately for the infected host, these act like **poisons** and are harmful to its cells. If the bacteria are able to establish themselves and thrive within the hosts, overcoming its *defence mechanisms* (even if only temporarily), there occurs a rapid increase in the amount of bacterial waste products in the host's tissues. This produces the symptoms of a disease. The nature of the disease depends on the particular kind of bacterium: some bacteria thrive in blood, some in nerve tissue, and some in bone tissue, etc. The following is a summary of the effects of some types of harmful bacteria.

12.4 Some diseases caused by bacteria

Table 12.1 Characteristics of some bacterial diseases

Disease	Incubation period	Isolation period	Quarantine period	Mode of transmission	Prevention of spread	Symptoms and course of disease	Treatment
Diphtheria	4 days	Until tests show the patient is free from infection	No definite period, but all contacts should be tested for immunity and immunised if necessary	By airborne droplets and by carriers	Isolation of infected person and contacts. Used handkerchiefs should be burned because the mucous fluid from the nose contains bacteria. Immunisation of contacts	Bacteria infect membranes of the respiratory system, releasing a poison. Fever and sore throats are followed by damage to the heart and the nervous system	Injection of antitoxin. Antibiotics
Tuberculosis	Variable	Until all evidence of infection has disappeared	None	By airborne droplets; in milk	Vaccination. Mass X-ray programme to detect carriers	Many organs may be infected by the bacteria but lungs are the prime targets. General weight loss occurs. Sputum often contains blood. A persistent cough develops	Antibiotics
Pneumonia	Variable	None	None	By airborne droplets	Avoid low temperatures. Treat infections following from colds and influenza with antibiotics for a year after an attack of pneumonia	Coughing, fever, chest pains. Fluid in the lungs	Antibiotics and sulphonamide drugs
Typhoid	7–21 days	Until tests show faeces and urine free from the bacteria	21 days	By contaminated water and food	Vaccination lasts up to 1 year	Fever, abdominal pains, constipation followed by diarrhoea. Ulceration of the intestine often occurs	Antibiotics
Dysentery	1–7 days	Until tests show the person is free from infection	14 days	By contaminated water and food. Insects can carry bacteria	Strict hygienic handling of food	Fever, abdominal pains, vomiting and diarrhoea	Antibiotics, also fluids to replace loss

Table 12.1 (continued)

Disease	Incubation period	Isolation period	Quarantine period	Mode of transmission	Prevention of spread	Symptoms and course of disease	Treatment
Food poisoning	1 day	1–2 days	1–2 days	By contaminated water and food	Strict hygienic handling of food	Abdominal pains, vomiting diarrhoea and possibly fever	Antibiotics, also fluids to replace loss
Scarlet fever	5 days	28 days	10 days	By airborne droplets, food, or insect vectors	Isolation of infected person and contacts. Strict hygiene. Contaminated handkerchiefs should be burned and bedding and utensils disinfected	Scarlet rash– white around mouth. Skin peels	Antibiotics
Cholera	5 hours to 3 days	Until tests show the person is free from infection	21 days	Contaminated water	Purification of water supply and treatment of sewage. Vaccination gives protection for 3–12 months	Inflamed intestine. Severe diarrhoea. Massive loss of fluids which may prove fatal	Injection of saline. Antibiotics and sulphonamide drugs
Whooping cough	8–14 days	42 days	21 days	Airborne droplets	Vaccination	Severe coughing with a 'whoop' sound as air is inspired	Antibiotics
Bubonic plague	36 hours to 10 days	As for typhoid	As for typhoid	Rat flea	Eradication of rats. Storage of food in rat-proof containers	High fever. Swollen lymph nodes in groin and armpits. Haemorrhages in capillaries leading to a darkening of the skin (hence the name, Black Death)	Antibiotics
Yaws	3–4 weeks	21 days	21 days	Direct contact with infected sores	Strict hygiene. Prevention of overcrowding	Open sores spread over the body, particularly in children under 16. Bones become affected	Antibiotics

Venereal (sexually transmitted) diseases

- **Gonorrhoea** (caused by a coccal bacterium)

Symptoms: Itching and burning sensation when passing urine. Pus may occur in the urine. The untreated condition leads to eventual arthritis, heart disease and blindness.

Incubation: Normally 2–3 days but can be up to 10 days.

Mode of transmission: As a result of direct contact between sex organs during intercourse. It can also be passed from mother to baby during birth via the mother's vagina.

Treatment: Sulphonamide drugs and antibiotics.

Prevention: Avoiding sexual intercourse with infected persons and identification and treatment of carriers.

- **Syphilis** (caused by a spirochaete bacterium)

Symptoms: A sore appears where the infection has taken place. It may appear as a blister or as an open sore. After 3–6 weeks a body rash, sore throat and fever usually occur. The hair may fall out in patches. Ulcers develop on the lips or in the mouth and, in the female, in the vulva. If the disease remains untreated it may attack the heart, blood vessels and brain.

Incubation: 10–90 days.

Mode of transmission: Sexual contact, as with gonorrhoea, but also through skin wounds and scratches. The bacterium can also pass from an infected pregnant woman to her foetus across the placenta, resulting in the disease being present in the newborn.

Treatment: Antibiotics or arsenical drugs.

Prevention: As for gonorrhoea.

12.5 Food preservation

In order to prevent the decay of food, one must provide and maintain conditions that are unsuitable for the growth of bacteria, i.e. dryness or a temperature which either kills the bacteria or prevents their reproduction.

Table 12.2 Methods of preserving food from bacterial attack

Technique	Preparation of food	Effect on bacteria	Foods preserved
Deep freezing	Reduction of temperature below 0°C	Low temperature prevents reproduction or is fatal	All types, but certain fruits have their flavour altered
Salting	Addition of salt	Removes water by osmosis thereby preventing growth	Meat and fish
Bottling	Food sealed in airtight jars then boiled	High temperature and pressure kills them	Fruits
Freeze-drying	In a desiccator at very low temperature	Removes water and lowers the temperature so that reproduction is impossible	Most foods
Pickling	Pre-soak in strong salt solution, then store in vinegar	Vinegar, which is an acid, kills or prevents the growth of most bacteria	Vegetables
Curing	Hang the food over charcoal fires	Formaldehyde in smoke kills most bacteria	Meat and fish
Canning	Strongly heat the food to drive out air from the can which is then sealed	Kills them in a similar fashion to bottling	Most foods
Sterilisation	Very high temperatures or exposure to gamma rays	High temperature or radiation kills them	Milk and cream (high temperature), fish and pork products (radiation)
Vacuum packing	Air is sucked out of containers by a vacuum pump. The container is then sealed completely	Bacteria and their spores cannot survive in the absence of oxygen	Meat and cheese

12.6 Hygienic preserving, handling and distribution of milk

Milk is an excellent, highly nutritious food for *bacteria* as well as for *humans* and so it is essential to prevent its *contamination* at all stages in its production. The bacterium which causes **tuberculosis** can spread in milk taken from an infected cow. Milk can also be contaminated with those bacteria responsible for *diphtheria, scarlet fever, food poisoning* and *epidemic diarrhoea*, those being introduced when present on the hands and clothing of anyone concerned with the collection and transport of milk.

Collection

Laws governing the hygiene of milking methods are strict. *Udders* and *hind legs* must be washed before the animal is attached to the milking machine. The machine and the building itself must be regularly *disinfected*. Cows must be regularly *inspected* for disease (especially bovine tuberculosis). After being collected from cows, milk is cooled, filtered, tested for contamination, then collected in sterilised stainless steel tankers. It is pasteurised before bottling.

Pasteurisation

This is a process that kills pathogenic bacteria. There are two methods:

1 The high temperature, short time (HTST) method in which milk is heated to 72°C, held at that temperature for 15 seconds, then cooled to about 10°C.

2 The milk is heated to a temperature between 63°C and 66°C, held at that temperature for 30 minutes, then cooled rapidly to about 10°C.

To test whether the milk has been correctly pasteurised, one of two procedures is carried out:

(a) **The phosphatase test:** Phosphatase is an enzyme produced by pathogenic bacteria. If it is found to be present in the milk, pasteurisation has not been successful.

(b) **Methylene blue test:** This dye changes colour based on the amount of oxygen in the milk. If the test proves positive, there is a danger of there being sufficient oxygen for the growth of bacteria.

Sterilisation

Milk can also be preserved by subjecting it to very high temperatures, which kills all bacteria present. Unfortunately, the flavour of the milk is altered by this treatment.

12.7 Microbial production processes

Yoghurt

Bacteria used:

Lactobacillus bulgaricus and *Streptococcus thermophilus*

Stages

❶ Milk is pasteurised and homogenised.

❷ 2.5% starter culture is added at 45°C.

❸ It is packed into containers and fermented at 45°C for four hours. Lactose is changed to glucose which in turn is changed to lactic acid.

❹ After cooling, the yoghurt will keep for up to three weeks. If fruit is added it reduces the shelf life of the yoghurt.

Cheddar cheese

Bacteria used:

Streptococcus thermophilus

Stages

1 Rennet is used to coagulate the milk.

2 Starter cultures of *S. thermophilus* are added to pasteurised milk. The rennet produces the curd.

3 After cooking for 45 minutes at 38°C the cheddaring process begins. This consists of cutting the warm curd into blocks and stacking them on each other. The pH falls to 5.2–5.3 and the harmful bacteria are killed.

4 Bacteria or fungi are added to ripen and flavour the cheese. The bacteria or fungi produce enzymes during maturation. Protein and fat are acted on by a series of enzymes to produce chemicals with the distinctive flavours of the various types of cheese available in shops.

Table 12.3 Micro-organisms used to make different types of cheese

Type of cheese	Micro-organism
Limburger and Bel Paese	*Brevibacterium linens*
Gorgonzola, Stilton, Roquefort	*Penicillium roqueforti* and *P. glaucum*
Camembert	*P. camemberti*
Brie	*Brevibacterium linens* and *P. camemberti*

Vinegar

Summary

1st reaction: glucose $\xrightarrow{\text{fermentation (yeast)}}$ ethanol + carbon dioxide

2nd reaction: ethanol + oxygen $\xrightarrow{\text{fermentation (bacteria)}}$ acetic acid (vinegar) + water

Micro-organisms involved

1st reaction: *Saccharomyces cerevisiae var elipsoides* (yeast)
Anaerobic (without oxygen)

2nd reaction: *Acetobacter* (bacterium)
Aerobic (with oxygen)

There are two methods of production: slow or quick.

Slow

- Yeast present on grapes are added to 11–13% ethanol to form a low grade wine.
- The alcoholic solution is then put in barrels and a culture of *Acetobacter* is added.
- It is left for up to three months to produce vinegar.

Quick

This relies on actively moving the liquid over a large surface for good oxygenation.
- The alcoholic solution is sprinkled over wood shavings with *Acetobacter* growing on them.
- The ethanol is changed into acetic acid.

12.8 Some diseases caused by viruses

A virus is a minute particle that is capable of reproduction only within *living cells*. Viruses are often classed as non-living. Each consists of a **nucleic acid core** and a **protein coat**.

Table 12.4 Characteristics of some viral diseases

Disease	Incubation period	Isolation period	Quarantine period	Mode of transmission	Prevention of spread	Symptoms and course of disease	Treatment
Common cold	3 days	1–2 days	1–2 days	By airborne droplets	Avoiding large gatherings, stuffy rooms especially in winter, or contact with infected persons	Irritation of the respiratory tract, coughing and sneezing	None, but aspirin may relieve discomfort
Measles	10 days	14 days	16 days	By airborne droplets	Keep young babies away from the infection because the disease can have serious consequences for those under 3 years of age. Strict hygiene. Handkerchiefs should be burned because of contamination with virus-filled mucus	Sore throat, runny nose, cough and fever. Small white spots (Koplik's spots) on the inside of mouth. Rash on scalp, neck and ears. Mainly a disease of children. Occasionally, the virus can damage the heart, kidneys and brain	Injection of gamma globulin protein
Rubella	18 days	7 days	21 days	By airborne droplets and saliva	Vaccination, particularly of girls aged 11-14 because women during the first 4 months of pregnancy can pass on the virus to the fetus: there is a 20% chance of the baby being born blind and deaf as a result of this	Fever and body rash which disappears after 3 days	None, but aspirin can relieve discomfort. Pregnant women are injected with gamma globulin
Poliomyelitis	10 days	21 days	14 days	By airborne droplets, contaminated water and food	Isolation of the infected person and contacts. Strict hygiene. Handkerchiefs must be burned and all faeces disinfected before flushing away. Bed pans should be disinfected immediately after use. Vaccination	Fever, stiffness of muscles, followed by paralysis and wasting of muscles. Respiratory movements may have to be performed by an 'iron lung' if the virus affects intercostal muscles and the diaphragm	No known successful treatment

(continued)

Table 12.4 (continued)

Disease	Incubation period	Isolation period	Quarantine period	Mode of transmission	Prevention of spread	Symptoms and course of disease	Treatment
Smallpox	14 days	Varies but should continue until scabs have gone	21 days	Direct contact or insect carriers	Vaccination	High fever, rash on the face which spreads all over the body. Secondary bacterial infection causes permanent scars. The disease is believed to have been eliminated throughout the world	None, but antibiotics to control secondary bacterial infections
Influenza	1–3 days	7 days	7 days	By air-borne droplets	Vaccination may give immunity for 1–2 years. Avoiding contact with infected persons	Fever and headache. Sore throat and muscular pains. Secondary infection by bacteria can lead to pneumonia	Aspirin to relieve discomfort. Antibiotics against secondary infections
Mumps	14–21 days	21 days	21 days	By air-borne droplets and saliva	Vaccination	Fever and swelling of paratid salivary glands lasting about 10 days. Testes and ovaries may be affected in those who have reached puberty	Aspirin to reduce fever and relieve discomfort
Chickenpox	14 days	Until all sores have disappeared	21 days	Direct contact and droplets from sores	Isolation. Strict hygiene. Disposal of any materials which have come into contact with the patient's infected blisters	Most common in young people. Fever, headache, sore throat and rash all over body. Blisters may become infected by bacteria, leading to secondary infection	Antibiotics to treat secondary infection

Acquired Immune Deficiency Syndrome (AIDS)

AIDS is a condition which interferes with the body's normal immunity to disease. The spread of the disease has become one of the most serious medical problems in recent history. The director of the World Health Organization stated, in 1986, that 100 000 people throughout the world suffer symptoms of AIDS and that a staggering 10 million carry the virus in their blood. Methods of controlling its spread depend on prevention because a cure has not yet been found.

AIDS is transmitted via blood and semen. A few weeks after infection, the virus causes an illness similar to influenza or glandular fever. Next follows a period of months or even years when no symptoms are shown, then weight loss, fever, diarrhoea and infections such as TB or pneumonia. As the white cells of the immune system have been destroyed by the virus, death follows these more serious illnesses. AIDS can also infect brain cells as well as the blood cells in the lymph nodes and spleen.

12.9 Notifiable diseases

Highly infectious diseases must be reported immediately to your local doctor who may then, if necessary, notify the local Environmental Health Officer. The aim is to trace the source of the infection and thus *minimise the spread* of the disease. Some notifiable diseases are: *cholera, diphtheria, food poisoning, malaria, measles, poliomyelitis, smallpox, tetanus, tuberculosis, typhoid, whooping cough* and *yellow fever*. Various countries have their own laws governing notifiable diseases. In Britain, gonorrhoea and syphilis, though highly infectious, are not notifiable (as they are in many other countries), neither are the common cold, influenza, pneumonia, chickenpox, German measles and mumps.

12.10 Antibiotics

These are substances produced naturally by organisms such as fungi which *prevent the growth* of bacteria, e.g. *Penicillium* is a fungus that makes the antibiotic **penicillin**. This prevents the growth of pathogenic bacteria such as *streptococci* and *staphylococci*.

Production of antibiotics

Penicillin

A mutant form of the fungus, *Penicillium*, has been developed under laboratory conditions. It produces far more of the antibiotic, penicillin (up to 100 000 units per cm^3 culture) than normal *Penicillium*. Tanks of 90 000 litre volume are used and the culture conditions are computer controlled.

Semi-synthetic penicillins are produced using enzymes. Ordinary penicillin made by fermentation is treated with an enzyme (*acylase*) which produces the starting material for semi-synthetic penicillin.

Neomycin

This is produced by *Streptomyces fradiae*. It grows best at 28°C in the presence of oxygen at a pH of 7.0–7.5.

Two growth phases occur:
- In the presence of a high concentration of oxygen, carbohydrates are broken down and this results in a drop in pH.
- In the presence of low oxygen concentration, nitrogenous compounds are released resulting in a rise in pH. The body of the fungus breaks down and neomycin is produced.

12.11 Antimicrobial methods

- **Sterilisation** is the *elimination* of live micro-organisms. Hospital clothes and equipment, for example, are sterilised in a steam-pressure chamber or autoclave at 121°C.
- **Disinfection** is the *reduction in the number* of live micro-organisms and usually involves subjecting material to chemical treatment.
- **Antisepsis** is the *prevention of the reproduction* of micro-organisms.
- **Asepsis** is the *prevention of contamination* by micro-organisms.

12.12 Immunity

Definition

The ability of the body to resist the possible dangers of invading organisms.

When micro-organisms enter the body, they stimulate the production of antibodies within certain cells, the **lymphocytes** (see page 50). Antibodies are able to counteract the effects of the invading organisms. There are two main forms of immunity, *natural* and *acquired*.

Table 12.5 Natural immunity

Form A – specific	Form B – genetic	Form C – contact
One species of animal (or plant) may be immune to diseases from which other species suffer, e.g. *myxomatosis* in rabbits does not affect man	Some people inherit immunity to a disease, e.g. many people are not affected by the *chickenpox* virus even after contact with the disease	By suffering once from a disease, e.g. with *whooping cough* the body produces antibodies during the first attack. Immune persons will resist a second invasion by the same micro-organism

Table 12.6 Acquired immunity

Form A – passive (short term protection)	Form B – active (long term protection)
Obtained by injecting **serum** (plasma without clotting agents) of an animal which has previously been subjected to a mild infection of the disease. The serum contains antibodies for that disease and these retain their effect after injection into man. The serum may be given in an emergency, e.g. a person with *diphtheria* is given antitoxin at the beginning of the infection to boost his own supply. *Antitetanus serum* works in the same way	The body makes its own antibodies over a long period. There are three methods: (i) By inoculating with a vaccine containing a **weakened** micro-organism, e.g. *smallpox* or *poliomyelitis* (ii) By inoculating with a vaccine containing **dead** micro-organisms, e.g. *whooping cough* (iii) By inoculating with **modified toxins** produced by harmful micro-organisms. This makes the body produce antitoxins which give protection against a more virulent attack

Interferon

Interferons were discovered in 1957. They are hormone-like proteins that are part of the body's defence against viruses and other disease-causing agents. Until 1970 human white blood cells were the only source of interferon and the world's supply for medical use was no more than a few milligrams. Now bacteria can be used to make more than a milligram of interferon per litre of culture.

For certain types of leukaemia, treatment with interferon has been very successful. Cancer of the breast, intestine and lungs do not generally respond to treatment with interferon. There are some side effects of its use including fever, tiredness and muscle pain. High doses may lead to hallucinations and coma. Interferons act directly on cells, not on the viruses that infect them. They limit the course of virus infection. They may not cure virus-caused diseases but they may prevent them. Hepatitis, herpes virus and shingles respond to interferon treatment.

12.13 Protozoa and disease

The malarial parasite

The organisms that cause malaria belong to the genus *Plasmodium*, which is a member of the phylum of one-celled animals, the **Protozoa**. They share a common life cycle, part of which takes place in the **mosquito** and part in **man**. If a person suffering from malaria is bitten by a mosquito of the right type, the parasite passes with the blood into the mosquito's **stomach**. Here it undergoes a series of changes and becomes capable of *sexual reproduction*, which results in the production of more individuals. These pass to the

salivary glands of the mosquito. If the mosquito bites another person, the parasites are passed into that person's **bloodstream**. The parasites then pass to the liver and undergo *asexual reproduction*, resulting in a massive increase of numbers. They then invade **red blood cells**, from which they obtain their food. At this stage, *poisons* are released into the bloodstream, causing the **fever** which is a characteristic symptom of malaria. The fever usually develops 10 days after the entry of the parasite. It may be *continuous, irregular* or occur *twice a day*, depending on the species of *Plasmodium* injected by the mosquito.

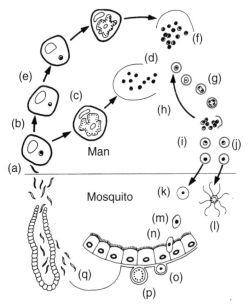

(a) The parasite is injected into the blood vessels of man by a female mosquito and passes into the liver cells.
(b) The parasite divides in the liver cells.
(c) Many thousands of individuals are formed.
(d) Some of the parasites enter red blood cells.
(e) Others remain in liver cells and invade red blood cells several months later.
(f) The parasites feed on the blood cell's cytoplasm.
(g) Asexual reproduction continues in red blood cells.
(h) A massive build up of asexual stages.

(i) Sexual stages develop.
(j) These are taken up by a mosquito when it feeds.
(k) Gametes form inside the mosquito's stomach.
(l) Fertilisation occurs.
(m) A zygote forms.
(n) The zygote bores into the gut wall.
(o) A cyst forms in which division occurs.
(p) Large numbers of parasites are formed in the cysts.
(q) These break out and move to the salivary glands of the mosquito.
(r) They are injected into a human when the mosquito feeds on blood.

Fig. 12.4 Life cycle of the malarial parasite, *Plasmodium vivax*

Control of malaria ideally should be aimed at elimination of the mosquito vector but the parasites can be killed when they are inside man using the drugs *chloroquine* and *quinine*. Other drugs, for example *paludrine* and *daraprim*, are used to prevent infection. They must be taken regularly during, and for a month after, a stay in a malarial area.

Entamoeba histolytica

This protozoan causes **amoebic dysentery**. The symptoms of the disease are *severe diarrhoea* with loss of blood, *fever* and *vomiting*, the combination of which can lead to death. The parasite can live in the human **intestine** and can pass out in the *faeces* to contaminate anything with which it comes in contact. Therefore, unhygienically prepared food may be a source of the parasite. The *housefly* and other insects may carry the parasite and spread the disease. The disease is controlled by strict hygiene, especially in the handling and storing of food. Antibiotics and sulphonamide drugs can be used as effective treatments.

12.14 Nematodes

Enterobius vermicularis (Pinworm)

This is a nematode worm which lays its eggs near the anus. They cause severe itching and the infected person, often a child, cannot resist scratching the area. The eggs on the fingers are often transferred into the mouth and are subsequently swallowed to cause a reinfection or a new infection.

Intestinal worms are killed with drugs called *anthelmintics*. Proper hygiene will prevent the spread of this species of worm. Faeces should be deposited where flies, food or bare feet cannot be contaminated.

Ascaris lumbricoides

Just like *Enterobius*, this roundworm (nematode) lives as an adult in the intestine. It is much larger than *Enterobius* and causes diarrhoea, pain in the abdomen, or even blockage of the intestine.

Life history

The egg is swallowed in food or drink. The cyst covering the egg dissolves and the larvae escape. They burrow through the wall of the small intestine and enter the blood stream, eventually reaching the lungs. These larvae are then carried up to the trachea to the throat when they are swallowed. They pass to the small intestine where they become adults. The eggs of the adults pass out in the faeces and may contaminate food or drinking water.

12.15 Diseases caused by fungi

Ringworm

Caused by several species of the fungus *Tinea*, each of which infects a different part of the body, for example, the *feet* (**Athlete's foot**), the *groin* (**Dhobies itch**), the *scalp* (**true ringworm**), the *nails* or the *trunk*.

Symptoms: Irritating blisters and reddened areas from which the skin eventually peels.

Mode of transmission: By spores carried on pets, by contact with infected people or their contaminated clothing or, with athlete's foot, via showers.

Treatment: Use of fungicidal ointments or powders. Keep infected region covered to prevent scratching and to prevent spores spreading. All combs, brushes, towels, underclothes and bedding should be discarded if they have come into contact with badly infected skin. With athlete's foot, do not use public swimming baths and gymnasia while the symptoms are present: to avoid contracting the disease, wash the feet daily and dry well between the toes. Air shoes after use and change socks, tights or stockings daily. Do not use swimming baths unless there are special disinfectant footbaths provided for use before and after bathing.

Thrush

Caused by a yeast-like organism. It affects the *mouth, intestine* and *vagina*.

Symptoms: Irritating reddened patches of tissue. The disease is particularly obvious when it occurs on the inside of the cheeks.

Mode of transmission: Spores are spread by contact with infected people. After a course of antibiotics, the disease may re-establish itself because some of the bacteria that normally defend the body from fungal attack may have been killed along with the thrush organism.

Treatment: The fungicide *Nystatin* is used as a cream. The most important point is to establish the source of the infection and eliminate it.

12.16 Vectors (carriers of disease)

Housefly

Life history

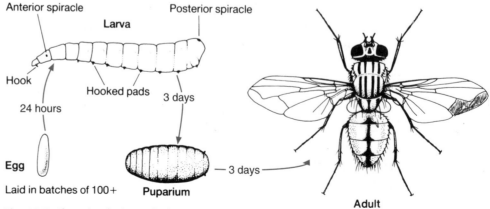

Fig. 12.5 Life cycle of a housefly (*Musca domestica*)

Habits

1 *Diet.* Decaying organic material, e.g. faeces, sweet substances, meat.

2 *Feeding.* Sucks up liquid. It releases digestive enzymes on to its food and sucks up the dissolved nutrients. It then regurgitates the food by vomiting and sucks it up again after mixing it with more digestive enzymes.

3 *Egestion.* It frequently passes out faeces on to its food.

4 *Reproduction.* A rapid rate of reproduction: several thousand eggs are laid by each female during her lifespan. The pupae can remain dormant in winter.

5 It cleans its body using a brushing action of its legs.

Factors relevant to the spread of disease

1 Has a hairy body and sticky pads on its feet to which micro-organisms readily become attached.

2 Transmits pathogenic bacteria from faeces and decaying refuse to food.

3 Its regurgitated food and its faeces contain those micro-organisms that are present in its gut.

The most common pathogenic bacteria carried by houseflies cause **dysentery** and **diarrhoea**, particularly in summer.

Control

1 Elimination of breeding places, for example, by burning refuse and using disposable polythene waste sacks inside dustbins which, when full, are sealed to prevent entry of flies.

2 Elimination of the adult insect by the use of insecticides.

3 Prevention of contamination of food (e.g. keeping foodstuffs in refrigerators or in sealed containers) and of cooking utensils, crockery and cutlery.

Mosquito

Life history

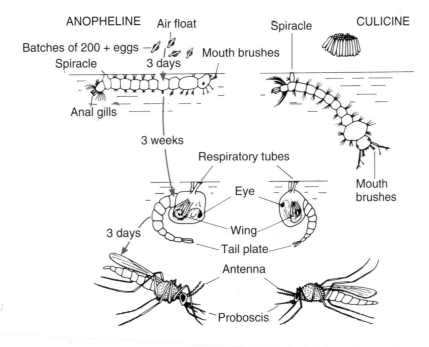

Fig. 12.6 The life history of mosquitoes. The drawings on the left show the eggs, larva, pupa and female imago of the anopheline mosquito and those on the right show the same stages of the culicine mosquito. The anopheline mosquito is responsible for carrying the single-celled animal, *Plasmodium,* which causes malaria

Habits

❶ *Diet.* The *female* mosquito requires *blood* because this contains a protein essential for the manufacture of egg cases. The *male* feeds on *plant juices*.

❷ *Feeding.* It inserts its needle-like mouth part (proboscis) into its food and sucks up the liquid. The female produces an **anti-coagulant** to stop the blood from clotting.

❸ *Reproduction.* The female lays her eggs on the surface of stagnant water. The larval and pupal stage are aquatic (see Fig. 12.6).

Control

❶ Elimination of the adult mosquito by the use of insecticides such as DDT.

❷ Prevention of reproduction by draining the insect's stagnant water breeding sites.

❸ Elimination of larvae by spraying oil on the breeding sites, which reduces the surface tension of the water, thereby interfering with larval breathing.

❹ Elimination of larvae by *biological control*, e.g. introducing to breeding waters fish that eat the larvae.

Lice

Life history

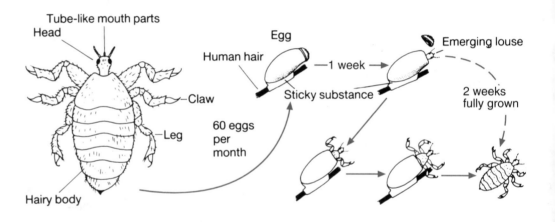

Fig. 12.7 Life history of a louse

Habits

❶ *Diet.* Blood

❷ *Feeding.* Mouthparts are adapted for piercing the skin and sucking blood.

❸ *Reproduction.* **Head lice** lay their eggs (*nits*) in the hair of the scalp. **Body lice** lay their eggs in clothing, usually around seams and buttonholes. Crab lice lay their eggs in pubic hair (see Fig. 12.7).

Factors relevant to the spread of disease

❶ Irritation caused by a bite leads to scratching and sores become infected by bacteria.

❷ The body louse can spread, in its faeces, the virus which causes *typhus*.

Control

The use of an insecticide such as *gamma benzene hexachloride* in shampoos and as a powder dusted on to clothing.

Bed bug

Life history and role in spreading disease

Similar to the body louse.

Habits

1 *Diet.* Blood.

2 *Feeding.* Mouthparts are adapted for piercing skin and sucking blood. Feeding occurs at night; during the day bed bugs remain in crevices in walls, furniture and in mattresses. A bed bug can survive several months on a single blood meal.

Control

1 Elimination of the adult using insecticides.

2 In severe cases fumigation of homes with hydrogen cyanide gas to eliminate the eggs. This gas is extremely poisonous but milder toxins are unable to kill the eggs.

Human flea

Life history

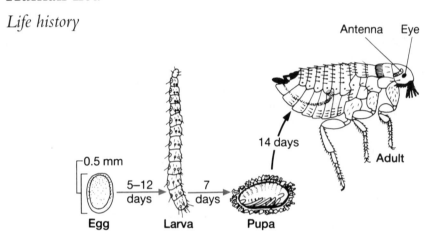

Fig. 12.8 Developmental stages of a flea

Habits and role in spreading disease

Similar to the body louse.

Control

1 Elimination of the adult using insecticides.

2 Use of insect repellants, for example *dimethyl phthallate*.

Rats

Habits

1 *Diet.* Omnivorous.

2 *Feeding.* During feeding on stored food they often contaminate foodstuffs with their urine. Many obtain their food in sewers.

3 *Reproduction.* A very high reproductive rate. A typical female starts to breed at 4–6 months old and produces 4–5 litters, each of 6–10 offspring, per year.

Factors relevant to the spread of disease

The *rat flea* can carry *bubonic plague* and *typhus*. **Scrub typhus** is spread by *rat mites*. **Salmonella food poisoning** and **Weil's disease** are caused by *bacteria* carried by rats. The latter can be contracted as a result of contact with contaminated rat urine; it is an occupational hazard of *sewage workers*. Symptoms include serious disorders of the liver and kidneys.

Control

1 Trapping and killing rats.

2 Using poisons such as *Warfarin* although some rat populations have developed immunity to this particular chemical.

12.17 Inherited diseases

Haemophilia

An inherited disease that is characterised by **uncontrolled bleeding**. It usually affects *males* although women are carriers, transmitting the disease to future generations. (A female carrier usually has blood that clots normally but she may give birth to sons in whom the condition is expressed.)

Normal people possess substances in the blood that rapidly stop bleeding by an efficient clotting mechanism. The *haemophiliac*, however, has no such mechanism and spontaneous bleeding, usually into *joints*, occurs. As a result, the joints become swollen and stiff. Internal bleeding can often be more serious than external bleeding, for example it may cause pressure on the windpipe resulting in asphyxiation. The severity of the disease is highly variable. There is no cure for haemophilia, only treatment to stop haemorrhaging.

The condition is a classic example of a **sex-linked disease** in man. (see p. 95). In the nucleus of every human cell (except sperm and eggs) there are *23 pairs* of chromosomes one of which is concerned with *sex determination* (the **X** and **Y** chromosomes). In females the sex chromosome pair consists of two **X**s, and in males, of an **X** and a **Y**. These chromosomes differ in size:

X   Y

The *inheritance of sex* can be followed:

MALE

gametes	X	Y
X	XX	XY
X	XX	XY

FEMALE

OFFSPRING
50% male, 50% female

The *gene for haemophilia* is carried on the *non-pairing segment* of the **X** chromosome and is inherited as follows:

NORMAL MALE

gametes	X	Y
X^h	XX^h	X^hY
X	XX	XY

CARRIER FEMALE

OFFSPRING
normal males   **XY**
normal females   **XX**
carrier females XX^h
haemophiliac males X^hY

Down's syndrome

An inherited disability caused by the presence of an extra chromosome in the number of cells (see Section 10.5). Affected children are of *short* stature for their age and are *mentally retarded*. The head is *smaller* than normal, the face *round*, the eyes *slanted* and there is a *fold of skin* across the inner corner of the eyes. The hands are *short* and *stubby*, often with a curved little finger. The feet have a large *gap* between the first and second toes. *Abnormal development of internal organs* such as the heart and intestine may also occur.

The internal abnormalities and an above-average tendency to catch infectious diseases used to cause early death in Down's syndrome children but survival has improved with advances in medical treatment. The *incidence of Down's syndrome* is approximately 1 in 600 births. However, the risk of giving birth to a Down's syndrome child depends on the mother's age. For women in their 20s, the chances are 1 in 2000, and the figure rises sharply at the age of about 35, reaching a maximum of 1 in 50 for women giving birth at the age of 45 or more. In rare cases, Down's syndrome is caused by **fusion** of one chromosome with another. The fused chromosome can be carried by clinically normal people, who run the risk of having further affected children. There is no cure for Down's syndrome. Parents of Down's syndrome children who are contemplating having further children should discuss the problem with a *genetic counsellor.*

Cystic fibrosis

This is possibly the most common human genetic disorder. It is an inherited condition which affects the pancreas and bronchioles of the lungs. It results in failure of the pancreas to function properly, intestinal obstruction, and sweat-gland and salivary-gland malfunction. It is inherited as a recessive gene in the following way:

Let **C** = the gene for a normal pancreas and normal bronchioles.

Let **c** = the recessive gene for cystic fibrosis.

A person suffers from the condition only if he or she has two genes for cystic fibrosis i.e. the genotype **cc**. A person with the genotype **Cc** is a *carrier* of the condition, but does not suffer from it. If two carriers have a child, there is therefore a one in four chance of the child suffering from the condition.

Parents: **Cc** × **Cc**

gametes	C	c
C	CC	Cc
c	cC	cc

The condition occurs once in about 2000 births and accounts for between 1 and 2% of admissions to children's hospitals. In people with cystic fibrosis, bronchioles become blocked with mucus and have to be cleared regularly.

Huntington's chorea

This is an inherited disease characterised by involuntary muscular movement and mental deterioration. The age of onset is about 35 years. The majority of those affected can therefore produce a family before being aware of their own condition. It is transmitted by a dominant gene and both sexes can be equally affected. An estimate of its frequency is roughly 5 in 100 000 and affected people are heterozygous.

Let **HC** = Huntington's chorea
Let **hc** = Normal

Parents: **HChc** × **hchc**

gametes	hc	hc
HC	HChc	HChc
hc	hchc	hchc

Phenylketonuria

There is an enzyme that certain people cannot make, because of a single mutant gene. This enzyme is responsible for changing a chemical called *phenylalanine* to an amino acid used by the body. Phenylalanine occurs in fish, cheese, eggs, wheat and butter. In the absence of the enzyme which acts on it, phenylalanine accumulates in the tissues of the body. Some of it is converted into a dangerous chemical which causes damage to the central nervous system. The accumulation of phenylalanine leads to a condition called *phenylketonuria.* A person with this condition is usually mentally retarded. About 1 in 15 000 babies suffers from this problem and synthetic substitutes for protein containing phenylalanine must be given in the diet.

12.18 Occupational diseases

Pneumoconiosis

A general term for a group of **lung diseases** caused by **inhalation of dust**. The diseases are occupational hazards of *miners, stone masons, quarrymen* and workers in *asbestos* and *metal-finishing factories*. Normally, the cilia of cells lining the respiratory system carry dust away from the bronchioles in mucus. Continued exposure to dust causes this natural cleansing system to become inefficient. Air flow is obstructed by blockages in the air passages. Thus less **oxygen** is delivered to the alveoli for gaseous exchange (see pp. 28–30). Furthermore, the **abrasive action** of the dust particles leads to *infection, accumulation of secretions* and *destruction of lung tissue*. The latter, in turn, leads to increased resistance to the flow of blood through the lungs at each cycle. This places a stress on the **heart**, which may fail.

Symptoms include **breathlessness** and a **dry cough**. An X-ray examination generally shows the presence of **scar tissue**, with the destruction of air spaces. **Bronchitis** often results, and further complications include *pulmonary tuberculosis* and *lung cancer*. Treatment consists of early diagnosis of lung damage and prevention of the above complications, if necessary by cessation of working in a dust-laden environment. **Smoking** should be discouraged as it heightens the symptoms. Preventive measures including the wearing of *helmets* and *face masks, damping down dust* with water sprays and the use of *ventilation systems* to remove dust from the air.

Asbestosis

A type of **pneumoconiosis** caused by continuous inhalation of the dust and fibres of **asbestos**. It often develops among workers in asbestos factories (even after only a few weeks' exposure to the dust) and used to be a hazard in the *building industry* before safety regulations restricting the use of asbestos materials in houses were introduced. In serious cases, lung cancer is a complication.

Silicosis

A type of pneumoconiosis caused by continuous inhalation of **silica dust**, generally from *fine sand* or *crushed rock*. It is a hazard of stone masonry and quarrying.

Emphysema

This is a condition of the **lungs** in which there is *overdistension* of the **air sacs**; some of which *rupture* and fuse together to form abnormally large air spaces. The efficiency of the lungs in *gaseous exchange* is greatly reduced. Symptoms include *breathlessness* and *cyanosis* (blueing of the skin). The most common cause of emphysema is **bronchitis**, which in turn is caused by *irritative particles* in the bronchial tubes leading to the invasion of *bacteria*. Destruction of the air sacs makes it more difficult for the heart to circulate blood through the lungs and this often leads to **heart failure**. There is no real cure for emphysema because it occurs as the final consequence of damage. **Smoking** must be avoided because this aggravates the condition. A certain amount of relief can be obtained by giving *antispasmodic* drugs which dilate the bronchial tubes and minimise the resistance to air flow.

12.19 Environmental diseases

Stress

Today, in overcrowded cities, people work in an atmosphere of intense competition. If this is allowed to get out of hand, it can upset the natural rhythms of life and the body's reaction shows itself in physical and mental disturbance.

Causes of stress

- Overcrowding – aggravation in commuting to and from work.
- Noise – from traffic.
- Pollution of the environment – from traffic and factories.
- Competition with others – 'Keeping up with the Joneses'.
- Crises of everyday life – having to work long hours, not having time to eat regularly and well, etc.
- Major disasters – such as death of a close relative or unemployment.

Forms that stress takes

- Mental breakdown
- Withdrawal from society
- Anxiety
- High blood pressure
- Ulcerated digestive tract
- Asthma
- Migraine
- Eczema
- Constipation
- Diarrhoea

Coping with the problem

Sympathy and understanding can help to reduce the harmful effects of stressful situations. Wherever possible, stress should be avoided. The person who is prone to high blood pressure should avoid unnecessary anxiety and control his or her *smoking, eating* and *drinking* habits. Parents of children who seem *anxious, shy* or *aggressive* should encourage the children to talk about their worries and to feel less afraid of the world outside the home environment.

Radiation sickness

The results of exposure to **radioactivity**. Chemical elements above *atomic number 83* emit subatomic particles as the nucleus of the atom disintegrates. The emissions damage molecules in cells, including those from which *genes* are composed. The genes can become altered (mutations) and if they are in gametes can give rise to abnormalities in future generations.

When a human is exposed to large doses of radiation (above 1000 roentgen units) death is inevitable. Doses over 200 roentgen units can produce symptoms of radiation sickness. The body starts to show disturbances in its most rapidly dividing tissues. The first tissue to be affected is the **gut lining**. Within 24 hours, there is *nausea, vomiting* and *diarrhoea*, and these symptoms may prove fatal. Intravenous fluid replacement is essential at this stage. On about the sixth day there is failure to produce the normal number of *white blood cells*. *Gamete production* can be affected by doses of 400 roentgen units, leading to temporary or permanent *sterility*.

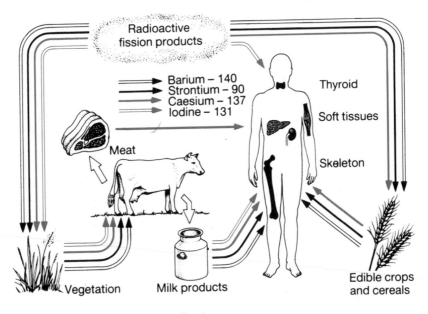

Fig. 12.9 Routes to radioactive substances affecting man

Leukaemia (inability to produce blood cells in the correct proportions) and other forms of **cancer** have been linked with the effects of radiation. **Radioactive fall-out** from nuclear reactions has an indirect as well as direct effect on man. The indirect effect may be more widespread and longer-lasting. Figure 12.9 shows how some radioactive materials get into plants, then via food into man.

Hypothermia

Low body temperature generally resulting from prolonged exposure to cold. The initial effects of cooling are to stimulate *shivering, increased pulse rate, constriction of the blood vessels in the skin* and a *rise in blood pressure*. When the body temperature falls below **32°C** these compensatory mechanisms begin to fail, the nervous system becomes less efficient and consciousness is impaired. Death normally occurs at body temperatures of **26°C**. *Babies* and the *elderly* are particularly susceptible to cold, and deaths from hypothermia are not uncommon where old people live alone with inadequate heating. It is also the main cause of death in cases of **exposure** in mountainous regions where, in addition to cold, *high winds* and *wet clothes* contribute to a very rapid loss of heat.

Arthritis

This is a name given to several diseases of the **joints**. There are those due to *degeneration* and *inflammation* (the latter of which may be due to infection); *reaction to an organism* (**rheumatic fever**); *non-infective inflammation* (**rheumatoid arthritis** and similar diseases); and the presence of *crystals of uric acid* in the joints (**gout**). In some of these diseases symptoms may also occur elsewhere in the body. Arthritis is one of the most painful and crippling diseases in the Western world, severely affecting older people and making a normal active life impossible for them.

There is no overall cure available. Arthritis caused by *bacteria* is treated with *antibiotics*. **Physiotherapy** keeps affected joints as flexible as possible, while a thin film of *hot wax* applied to arthritic hands has soothing properties, but is not a cure. Pain relief can be obtained with *aspirin* and inflammation can be suppressed with *chloroquine* compounds, *gold* salts and *cortisone* derivatives.

Rheumatism

A frequently mis-used name for a variety of disorders which involve pains in the body. It is strictly a disease or set of symptoms related to the joints. It is more or less synonymous with arthritis.

Heart disease

- **Congenital.** 1% of the population suffers from some sort of heart *structural* abnormality. The majority of these abnormalities involve defects of heart *valves* or *abnormal links* between the two normally separate circulations (see Section 6.4) leading to the mixing of *oxygenated* and *deoxygenated* blood. The defect may be a symptom of chromosome abnormality, e.g. in **Down's syndrome** a hole between the ventricles occurs (see Section 12.17). Heart defects are also common in children born to mothers who contract **rubella** (German measles) in the first three months of pregnancy. All of these defects can usually be cured by surgery.
- **Acquired.**
- **Coronary ischaemia.** More common in *males* than in females and most often caused by **atheroma** (fatty deposits in blood vessels). Factors which contribute to this disease are *smoking, obesity, hypertension* (high blood pressure) and *lack of exercise*. The person is limited in exertion by *breathlessness* and *pain in the chest* (angina pectoris). The heart may *stop beating gradually* or there may be a *sudden blockage of an artery* supplying the heart, in which case part of the heart muscle dies (**myocardial infarction**). Angina can be controlled with drugs which dilate arteries or those which diminish the work rate of the heart. Surgery to clear diseased arteries may be possible.
- **Rheumatic fever.** Affects *joints*, the *heart*, and possibly the *skin*. It is due to **toxins** produced by a group of *streptococcal bacteria*. The *valves* of the heart may be permanently damaged, leading to **heart failure** in middle age. This is particularly liable to happen if the patient suffers recurrent attacks of rheumatic fever. The initial infection can be treated effectively with *antibiotics*.

12.20 Deficiency diseases

Diabetes mellitus – deficiency of insulin

A condition which gives rise to a **high blood sugar level** and **loss of blood sugar** in urine. It is a common disorder, with more than 200 million sufferers in the world. In the western hemisphere, about 1–2% of the population are affected.

Types of diabetes:

- **Juvenile.** Either insulin is not produced or the body does not react to insulin in the normal way.
- **Maturity onset.** Confined mainly to overweight, middle-aged women and occurs when there is too little insulin to meet the demands of the body.
- **Stress.** May occur during pregnancy or under physical stress. The body fails to respond to insulin at its normal levels in the blood.

Several diseases of the **endocrine glands** can cause diabetes, and it can also be caused as a side-effect when patients are on *steroid hormones* or *diuretic drugs* (those which increase urine production). In order to understand diabetes, it is necessary to know how the normal person uses carbohydrates.

Carbohydrates are digested to form **glucose**, which is absorbed into the bloodstream. The increased concentration of blood sugar is detected by special **beta cells** of the **islets of Langerhans** of the *pancreas*. These cells secrete the hormone **insulin**; the higher the glucose concentration, the greater the secretion. Insulin causes the glucose to be used for **energy release** or stored as **glycogen** or **fat** in the *liver*. The stored material can be reconverted to glucose when the body requires it. This is under the control of hormones produced by the **adrenal glands** and by **glucagon** made by the **pancreas**. In this way, a **balance** is set up between *regulators* which remove glucose from the circulation, and those which put it back. A relatively *constant* blood sugar concentration of *0.1%* is controlled in this way and can be regarded as a form of **homeostasis** (see Section 7.6).

In a *diabetic,* this fine regulation is lost. The blood sugar concentration rises to a very high level and the **kidneys**, which normally reabsorb glucose back into the bloodstream, fail to cope. Glucose is lost in **urine**, and this is a symptom of the disease. If glucose continues to be lost in this way, then the patient often suffers *unconsciousness*. Long-term treatment to control the problem consists of regular injections of carefully controlled doses of *insulin* and dietary regulation to *reduce carbohydrate intake*. **Emergency treatment** for a patient who has accidentally injected too much insulin is the administration of an immediate glucose supply to make up for the shortage of it in the body.

Scurvy – deficiency of vitamin C

A disease produced by an inadequate dietary intake of vitamin C (ascorbic acid), which is involved in the manufacture of **connective tissue** that acts like a sort of *cement* between cells of the body. Symptoms include *swollen, bleeding gums, loss of teeth, weakness in the legs and knees*, disorders of the skin such as prominence of hair follicles over the back and thighs, *coiling of hair* and *bleeding under the skin*. Old scars become tender and new ones heal slowly. There may be bleeding into the walls of the *heart, lungs and intestine*. Scurvy is rare in economically developed countries but still not totally eliminated. It is seen in elderly people who eat meals lacking in **fresh fruit** and **vegetables** and also in young children who are not given plenty of fruit juice or vitamin supplements. It is almost unknown in *breastfed babies*. Treatment consists of daily administration of adequate amounts of ascorbic acid, either in the form of tablets or citrus fruits and blackcurrants.

12.21 Cancer

A disease of *multicellular* organisms, characterised by **uncontrolled multiplication** and spread within the body of **abnormal** forms of the organisms' cells.

There are three principal characteristics of the disease:

1. Increase in size resulting from the rapid multiplication of cells.

2. Invasion and destruction of surrounding normal structures by cancer cells.

3. Seemingly spontaneous development and independent nature of abnormal cells.

How a cancer cell may arise

A normal cell has the following features:

1. It is immobilised because of contact with neighbouring cells.

2. It only divides if triggered by various regulator chemicals.

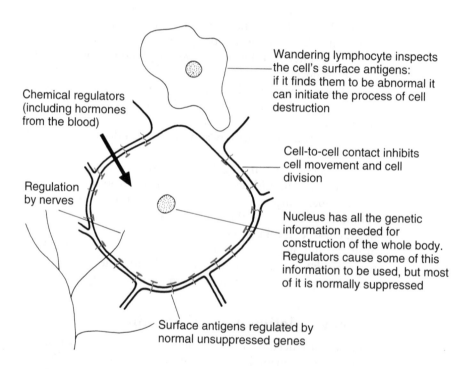

Fig 12.10 How a normal cell is prevented from becoming a cancer cell

3. Has only normal surface antigens (chemicals that trigger an immune response). Under certain circumstances there occurs either a **breakdown in cell regulation**:
   (a) by expression of information that is normally suppressed,
   (b) by failure in cell contact, hormone or nervous control,
   (c) by failure of lymphocyte action after abnormal antigens have developed, and/or an **abnormality in genetic information**:
   (a) because of the presence of a virus,
   (b) because of mutation altering the cell's genes,
   (c) by loss of genetic information and therefore of normal surface antigens.

The result may be a cancer cell which *moves freely* around the body and has *few or no contact with other cells; divides in an uncontrolled way*; and has *abnormal surface antigens* or has lost some of its normal ones.

Common forms of cancer

Table 12.7 lists the most commonly occurring types of cancer found in men and women in the UK.

Table 12.7 Common sites of cancer in males and females

Males	Females
Lung	**Breast**
Colon and rectum	**Cervix**
Prostate gland	**Colon and rectum**
Blood (leukaemia)	**Lung**

Examiner's tip

The most common examination questions on this topic are based on:
Human genetic disorders
Microbial food production processes
Diseases caused by parasites.

Summary

Disease

1. Disease-causing microbes are called pathogens and can be transmitted through the air, by direct contact, through food and water and by vectors (carriers).
2. Control of disease depends on hygiene, including handling and storage of food.
3. We use many microbes to make useful products. They include types involved in the production of yoghurt, cheese, vinegar and antibiotics.
4. Some disorders are inherited, including haemophilia, cystic fibrosis, Huntingdon's chorea and phenylketonuria.
5. Some diseases may result from occupational hazards and include pneumoconiosis, asbestosis, silicosis and emphysema.
6. Environmental disorders may include stress, radiation sickness, forms of cancer and heart disease.

Quick test

(a) After having a disease such as mumps, a person is likely to have acquired:
   A artificial immunity   **B** passive immunity
   C natural immunity   **D** active immunity

(b) The use of an insecticide is most likely to reduce the number of people suffering from:
   A athlete's food   **B** rabies   **C** diabetes   **D** malaria

(c) Penicillin is no longer effective against some infectious diseases caused by bacteria because:
   A these diseases have been totally eliminated
   B some people are allergic to penicillin
   C the bacteria have developed resistant strains
   D there are new antibiotics to combat these diseases

(d) The incubation period of an infectious illness follows soon after:
   A the formation of antibodies in the blood   **B** the quarantine period of the illness
   C development of a high temperature
   D entry of the infective organism into the body

(e) Dysentery and food poisoning may be spread by houseflies that land on food after they have:
   A walked over open wounds on the body   **B** been sprayed with insecticides
   C settled on human faeces   **D** sucked blood from an infected person

(f) The antibiotic effect of penicillin was first discovered by
   A Jenner   **B** Lister   **C** Pasteur   **D** Fleming.

Chapter 13
Personal health and hygiene

13.1 Care of the skin, hair and teeth

Skin

Reasons
- Prevention of infection by micro-organisms via sweat pores.
- Prevention of accumulation of oil, sweat and mico-organisms which will encourage insect parasites.

Treatment

1. Bathe frequently or take a shower in hot water using soap, which will remove the oil and bacteria contained in it.
2. Wash your feet every night and dry them thoroughly between the toes to prevent skin diseases developing.
3. Wash your hands before meals, before handling food and after using the toilet.
4. Keep your nails short, smooth edged, and clean.
5. Treat any open cuts with an antiseptic cream. They should be covered with a light bandage to prevent entry of micro-organisms.

Hair

Reasons
- As for **skin**.

Treatment

1. Wash the hair at least once a week to remove dirt and micro-organisms.
2. Brush and comb hair daily. This removes dirt, micro-organisms and loose skin. It also increases the circulation of blood in the scalp, improving the growth of hair.

Mouth

Reasons
- Prevention of tooth decay (see Section 5.2).

Treatment: Rules for healthy teeth

1. A pregnant woman must have a well-balanced diet so that her baby's teeth will develop properly.
2. Visit the dentist every six months for a check-up from an early age.
3. Always brush teeth after meals and last thing at night.

4 Eat tooth-cleaning foods such as celery.

5 Renew old, worn out toothbrushes with new soft-bristled ones.

6 Use toothpaste containing fluoride.

7 Brush teeth with a circular motion around the necks and in-between.

8 Brush the backs of the front teeth and the biting surfaces of the back teeth.

9 Avoid chewing gum, sweets and other sugar-rich foods. Do not use teeth to crack nuts or remove bottle-tops.

13.2 Characteristics of good posture

- **Good posture**. The vertical *axis of the body* and the *axial skeleton should nearly coincide*. In Fig. 13.1 note that the ear, hand and foot are on the same axis.
- **Round shoulders**. The *head is pushed forward*, resulting in a *tilted pelvis* to maintain balance. Shoulders become very rounded, back muscles are strained and correct breathing is impossible.
- **Hollow back**. The *shoulders are held back* and the person may think that he is standing well. However, the *abdomen is pushed forward* and the abdominal muscles have become slack. This may result in *digestive* and *respiratory* problems.

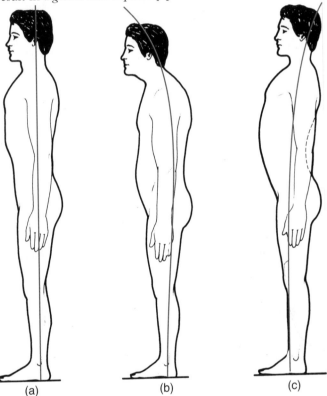

(a)   (b)   (c)

Fig. 13.1 Posture

13.3 Need for exercise

During exercise, the **heart** beats *faster* and there is an *increase* in its stroke volume (the volume of blood pumped per beat) (see Section 6.3). The *rate* and *depth* of **respiration** also increase so that the lungs completely fill and almost completely empty of air. **Lymph** flows out *faster* as body muscles contract and relax. (see Section 2.11). Further effects of exercise and training programmes include increased *power* and *endurance* of muscles and *enhanced motor skills* by repeated practice of complex movement patterns. In general, all organs of the body function optimally.

13.4 Need for sleep

Sleep is required for the following:

❶ To allow the brain and body to rest.

❷ To provide a period of inactivity so that waste material, accumulated during activity, can be removed from cells.

❸ To allow replacement and repair of damaged cells.

❹ To allow long bones to regain their correct length after being compressed during exercise. This is particularly important in young children.

The **amount of sleep** needed varies with *age* and with *the individual*. A graph of the average number of hours of sleep needed by an individual per 24 hours against age shows a decline from birth to adolescence (see Fig. 13.2).

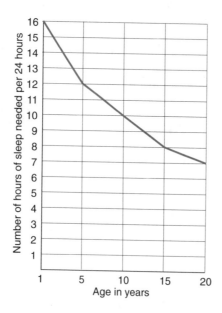

Fig. 13.2 Graph of the number of hours' sleep needed per 24 hours against age

13.5 Drugs and the nervous system

Sedatives

These are drugs which promote *relaxation* and *relief of anxiety*. **Barbituates** and **morphine** are the most commonly used sedatives. There are two main disadvantages with this group of drugs:
- There is a danger of people becoming **addicted**.
- The drugs cause **drowsiness** even in moderate doses.

The first disadvantage is true of most drugs, but the second is partially overcome by **tranquillisers** such as *chlordiazepoxide, diazepam, medazepam* and *meprobromate*. These have considerable *calming* qualities with relatively little tendency to cause drowsiness.

Stimulants

These are drugs which *quicken responses*. The main disadvantage with this group of drugs is that they can be *addictive*. **Caffeine** is the most readily available being present in drinks such as coffee, tea and cola. *Drinamyl* in tablet form was the basis of '*pep pills*', which due to their addictive properties are now not available.

Narcotics

These have a very powerful effect on the nervous system and are only prescribed under very *strict supervision* and in *small doses*. **Overdoses** cause states of unconsciousness, or *comas*, and can be *fatal*. **Drug addiction** caused by narcotics is one of the most serious social problems in the world, leading to complete loss of *psychological* and *physiological* independence of the drug. Consequently, addicts will resort to all methods – particularly crime – to obtain narcotics. The most well-known narcotics are *cannabis, cocaine, opiates, heroin* and *LSD*. The preparation and sale of these is *illegal*.

Cannabis is a drug which produces *hallucinations*. It is a resin obtained from the leaves and flowering tops of the tropical **hemp plant**. In Europe and the Middle East, the resin is also known as *hashish*, and in India as *charas, bhang* and *dagga*. A crude preparation of the whole flowering top and upper leaves is known as **marijuana**. The resin contains a complex mixture of chemicals. Due to the lipid (fat-like) nature of one of these, the active ingredient in cannabis is rapidly passed from the blood to the brain. *Lung cancer* and a condition leading to the birth of *deformed children* are possible consequences of chronic cannabis addiction.

Cocaine was the first drug to be used as a *local anaesthetic*. It comes from the coca plant, which is native to Peru, Bolivia and Chile and is cultivated in other tropical countries. Cocaine is **toxic**: in *high dosage* it gives rise to excitement, then depression, loss of co-ordination, convulsions, respiratory paralysis and death. In 1905 it was superseded by a synthetic substitute, *Novocaine*, which is still in general use.

Opiates are derivatives of the dried latex seed capsule of the *opium poppy*, which is cultivated mainly in Turkey, Iran and India. The *narcotic* action of opiates is mainly due to their **morphine** content. Addiction to opium is very common in the Far East, where opium smoking is prevalent.

Heroin is a semi-synthetic drug obtained from *morphine*. It is more readily addictive than morphine and produces *side-effects* of nausea, vomiting and constipation. Addiction leads to *mental* and *moral* deterioration. Heroin is a drug of increasing abuse and its addiction is much harder to cure than addiction to morphine.

LSD is the abbreviation of *lysergic acid diethylamide*, the most potent of a group of drugs which affect a person's powers of *perception*. LSD itself is synthetic but many of the substances of this group of drugs are present in extracts of *fungi* and *wild plants*. LSD produces **hallucinations** and *emotional reactions* which may include anything from *euphoria* to *depression* and *panic*. Self-injury, suicide and murder have been known to have been committed under the influence of this drug. Chronic use may cause organic brain damage and fetal malformities.

13.6 Alcohol

Harmful effects:

1. Impairment of the nervous system, resulting in slower conduction of nerve impulses, slow reaction to stimuli, loss of accurate judgement and poor muscle co-ordination.

2. Dilation of skin blood vessels causing dissipation of excess body heat. This can lead to chilling.

3. A reduction in the volume of blood (and therefore heat) reaching organs. The liver and the kidneys, in particular, are seriously affected.

4. More water is passed out in sweat. The kidneys may be damaged from the lack of water passing through them.

5. Addiction produces permanent damage to brain and liver cells.

For **smoking** see Sections 3.6 and 9.5.

 **xaminer's tip**

The most common
examination questions on
this topic are based on:
1 The harmful effects of
   alcohol
2 The harmful effects of
   drugs.

Summary

Personal health and hygiene

1 Our health depends on basic standards of personal cleanliness which include dental care, skin care, exercise and diet.

2 Correct oral hygiene prevents tooth decay and gum disease.

3 Attention to a well-balanced diet and regular exercise prevents obesity and the health problems related to it.

4 Tobacco poses serious health problems by contributing to many diseases.

5 Alcohol, used excessively, leads to health and social problems of addiction and alcoholism.

6 Misuse of drugs is harmful, leading to psychological and physical addiction and may directly or indirectly cause the death of the user.

Quick test

(a) Regular drinking of large quantities of alcohol is most likely to damage
   A the lungs   **B** the liver   **C** the teeth   **D** the bone marrow

(b) Which of the following is a stimulant drug?
   A opium   **B** morphine   **C** aspirin   **D** amphetamine.

Chapter 14
Public health

14.1 The water supply

Origin of surface water

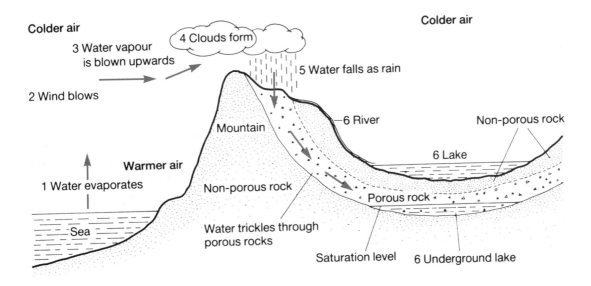

Fig. 14.1 Diagram to show the cycle of events that leads to the formation of rain, rivers and lakes

Stages in the supply of water for domestic purposes

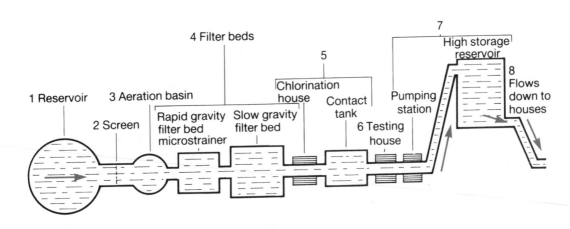

Fig. 14.2 Simple plan to show the order in which water is treated during purification

1. **Storage** in reservoirs.

2. **Screening.** Water passes through channels, partly blocked by metal screens: floating matter is trapped and raked away.

3. **Aeration.** Water is sprayed as fountains to facilitate oxygen in the air to dissolve in the water. The oxygen destroys many harmful anaerobic (thrive in the absence of oxygen) micro-organisms present in the water.

4. **Filtration.** Water passes through gravity filter beds.

Water trickles slowly through the sand and then more rapidly through the gravel and stones until it collects in pipes. All its *floating* matter, some of its *suspended* matter, and *micro-organisms* are left behind in the spaces between sand and gravel.

In all gravity filter beds, sand and the smallest stones are at the top and the largest stones are at the bottom so that particles are not carried along to the pipes but become trapped by the layers of progressively larger particles. Beds which use coarse sand as the top layer permit rapid filtration. These **primary filters** must be washed daily to remove the impurities from the sand and gravel. Clean water and air are blown upwards through the bed and then the water is allowed to flow away from the top carrying the dislodged impurities.

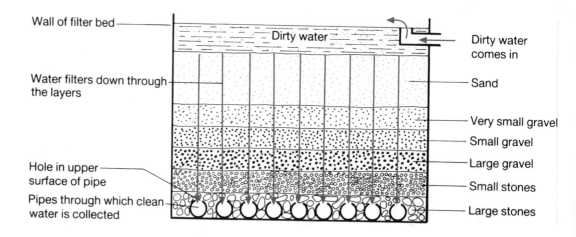

Fig. 14.3 Diagram to show the structure of a gravity filter bed

Those beds which have a top layer of very fine sand permit only *slow* filtration. They are **secondary filters**. In these, the impurities form a jelly-like film, the **zoogloea layer**, on the surface. This prevents rapid filtration but, more important, the micro-organisms in the film help to reduce the numbers of harmful bacteria in untreated water by eating them. Secondary filters are cleaned only once every few weeks and then by scraping off the top layer of dirty sand, washing it and adding clean sand.

Modern waterworks often filter water using *micro-strainers*. These are cylinders bearing a fine mesh. Dirty water is channelled through the cylinders and is forced through the mesh, which traps all the impurities. The mesh is washed continuously. Rapid and slow filter beds are also being replaced by *pressure filters*. These make use of a layer of sand for filtering but water is forced through them instead, rather than relying on gravity to produce a flow of water.

5. **Chlorination.** The filtered water is passed through a tank where *chlorine* is added (in carefully monitored minute quantities), approximately one part chlorine to two million parts water, to kill any remaining harmful micro-organisms. *Fluoride* may be added at this point.

6. The water is tested regularly through the day for *impurities* and *taste*.

7. The water is pumped to high level *storage reservoirs* for distribution to houses, offices and factories, etc.

14.2 Sewage disposal

Collection – domestic

● **Pipes**

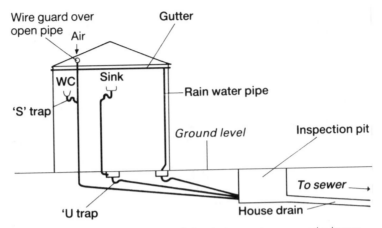

Fig. 14.4 Diagram to show the arrangement of the drainage pipes around a house

● **Traps.** These are U- or S-shaped bends in pipes in which water collects. They prevent unpleasant smells getting back from the sewers into the house. The water in the traps acts as a seal. U-bends tend to be in pipes leading away from rainwater and kitchen drains and S-bends tend to be under baths, washbasins and toilets.

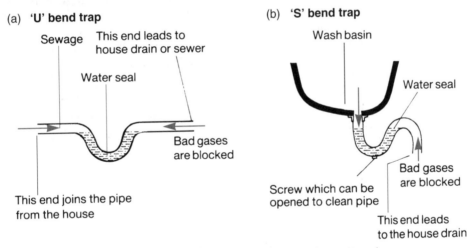

Fig. 14.5(a) and (b) Diagrams to show the structure of traps in sewage pipes

● **Inspection pits.** These are necessary to provide access points to blockages in the pipes and are sealed with gas–proof, heavy metal lids.

Treatment

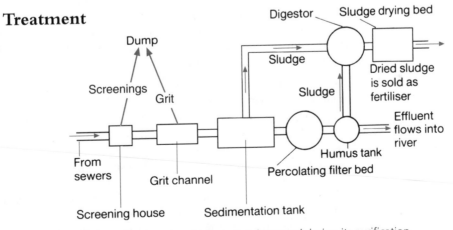

Fig. 14.6 Plan to show the order in which sewage is treated during its purification

❶ **Screening.** In underground channels, sewage passes through *iron screens* that trap solid coarse material. The material is regularly scraped away, dumped on waste ground and covered with a layer of soil.

❷ **Settlement.** Sewage is made to flow slowly through narrow *grit channels* so that any heavy solid particles settle to the bottom. The deposits are removed and dumped with the screenings. The sewage then passes into *sedimentation tanks*, where fine sand and organic matter settle in the form of sludge. The floor of each sedimentation tank is shaped like a funnel, sloping to a central exit pipe. This pipe is kept closed until the tank is ready to be emptied. Liquid emerging from the tanks is known as *effluent*. The sludge remaining on the floor of the tanks is periodically removed and pumped into a *digestor* building, where it is dried. Having a rich nutrient content, the dried sludge can be used as a fertiliser.

❸ **Aeration.** Air is made to come in contact with as much of the effluent as possible. There are three methods of achieving this:
(a) *Percolating filtration.* This takes place in a round shallow filter bed filled with coke, clinker and small stones. The effluent is forced up through a vertical pipe in the centre of the bed and out through two or more horizontal side tubes which are perforated with many holes. The side tubes radiate from the vertical pipe like spokes on a wheel and constantly rotate about it, spraying jets of effluent onto the stones. Anaerobic micro-organisms in the effluent are killed by aeration or by being eaten by useful micro-organisms that grow on the surface of the filter bed stones. The clean effluent passes out of pipes at the base of the beds.
(b) *Activated sludge.* Streams of air are passed through aeration tanks containing the effluent. Harmful anaerobic micro-organisms are again killed by the oxygen or by the action of beneficial micro-organisms. The cleaner effluent is drawn off and some of the settled sludge is removed and dumped with the screenings. A thin layer of activated sludge is allowed to remain in the tanks to be mixed with the next flow of effluent and to act as a source of new colonies of useful micro-organisms.
(c) *Land filtration.* (Not often used in Britain.) On the basis that soil acts as a natural filter, the effluent is poured over any large area of flat land. Solid material eventually becomes dry, killing the micro-organisms, and is removed, the liquid part filters through the land and becomes trapped within a depression in impervious rock.

❹ **Settlement of humus.** Effluent is sent to humus tanks where any suspended material settles to form more activated sludge and this in turn increases the destruction of any remaining harmful micro-organisms. The sludge is sent to the digestor.

❺ **Discharge** of the effluent – now harmless – into the sea or a convenient river.

14.3 Refuse disposal

❶ **Incineration.** This is the best way to dispose of dry refuse contaminated with harmful micro-organisms, e.g. a hospital's used wound dressings. Most modern methods reduce to a minimum contact between the refuse collectors' hands and the refuse. The resultant ash or clinker is dumped on local tips. The smoke and other potential air pollutants are filtered before being passed out through tall chimneys. The main problem of this method of disposal is expense.

❷ **Tipping.** Special selected sites are used according to rules suggested by the Department of the Environment. These rules are:
(a) Refuse must not be allowed to reach rivers, ponds or reservoirs.
(b) Waste metal should be at the bottom of the tip as it takes a long time to deteriorate.
(c) Refuse should be spread not more than 2 m in depth if deterioration and decay are to proceed sufficiently quickly.
(d) Each layer of refuse should be covered by 50 cm of soil: micro-organisms in the soil will help in the breakdown of refuse materials.
(e) Screens should be used to stop waste paper from blowing about.

(f) Insecticides should be regularly sprayed on the tips.

(g) Each layer of refuse should be given sufficient time to settle before the next layer is added.

14.4 Pollution

Pollution can be described as anything which when added to the environment destroys its purity.

Pollution and society

Many people used to take natural resources for granted. We now know that people have wasted many of these resources. Without realising the widespread effects of their activities, people have caused thousands of hectares of land to become useless.

As science, technology, and industry have developed, they have speeded up the destruction of our environment. Huge cities have been built. Rapid methods of transportation have made it possible for people to reach all places quickly and begin to change them. As populations increased creating a demand for more food, crop yields have increased. Then farmers began to look at what was happening to the fields and the harm being done. Fertilisers are now used to replace organic matter and minerals. Crop rotation is valuable in putting nitrogen back into the soil. Erosion, caused by wind and water, is prevented by contour farming and terracing.

Water, also, has been wasted. We now know the value of storing it behind dams. Watersheds are protected and planted to prevent water from scouring out channels and washing away valuable soil as it runs over the land on its way to the rivers.

The huge numbers of people, as well as industry, cause pollution problems due to the waste materials they create. *Biodegradable* substances can be broken down by bacteria. This releases minerals for recycling. However, there is a limit to how much material can be treated in this way. The remainder, non-biodegradable substances that are not broken down, may be toxic to organisms in the environment.

Even our air is being polluted with many kinds of chemicals. Many of these chemicals are poisonous to plants and animals and some have caused people to die. Radioactive particles can also pollute the atmosphere. Radioactivity may be carried to all parts of the earth and can cause tissue damage and death. It is important to realise that pollution is a dangerous two-way process. Humans are affected by the biological and physical factors of the environment and these factors may be the effects of human actions. Finding a solution to pollution problems is essential. Every person needs to take part in restoring the soil, cleaning the water, and purifying the air.

Pollution and the environment

Air

Table 14.1 Air pollution

Pollutant	Source	Effect	Control
Sulphur dioxide and oxides of nitrogen	Industrial combustion particularly from power stations. Also from traffic	Acid rain which kills plants due to release of aluminium ions from soil. ph of water is also affected. This kills fish by affecting their eggs and gills	Alternative sources of energy which do not use fossil fuel. Catalytic converters on cars. Electrostatic precipitators in power stations.
Carbon monixide	Internal combustion engines	Prevents oxygen from combining with haemoglobin in blood	Exhaust after-burners which change carbon monoxide to carbon dioxide.
Lead	Leaded petrol	Poisons the nervous system as it prevents enzymes working	Use lead free petrol

(continued overleaf)

Chloro-fluoromethane (CFC gas)	Aerosols Refrigerators	Breaks down ozone in the stratosphere and allows more ultraviolet light through the atmosphere which can cause skin cancer.	Use substitute chemicals in aerosols and refrigerants
Carbon dioxide (When in excess)	Combustion of fossil fuels	The **greenhouse effect**: Radiant energy from the Sun warms up the Earth but the heat cannot escape, leading to **global warming**	Use alternative methods of generating electricity

Water

Table 14.2 Water pollution

Pollutant	Source	Effect	Control
Sewage	Human waste	Spread of disease-causing organisms. Reduction of oxygen by increased bacterial activity	Proper sewage treatment to remove or reduce bacteria.
Fertilisers	Agriculture	Nitrates and phosphates make water over-fertile which increases plant growth.When plants die, putrefying bacteria increase and use up oxygen	Limit use of fertilisers. Use crop rotation with leguminous plants
Oil	Oil spillages (accidental and deliberate)	Destruction of marine life, directly and indirectly	Effective laws banning dumping of oil and restricting transport routes.
Heavy metals (mercury, lead cadmium, zinc)	Industrial effluent	Build up in food chains to toxic levels which prevent enzymes of the nervous system working.	Extraction of metals from effluent
Detergents	Domestic and industrial cleaning	Phosphates cause water to be over-fertile. This causes plants to grow excessively. They die and putrefying bacteria take oxygen from water	Use substitutes for phosphates. e.g. zeolite

Land

Table 14.3 Land pollution

Pollutant	Source	Effect	Control
Insecticides, fungicides, herbicides	Agriculture	Build up in food chains to toxic levels, killing wildlife.	Use biological control. (Natural predators). Collect harmful gases (biogas) and use as a fuel.
Refuse	Domestic and industrial waste	May break down in land-fill dumps to harmful substances e.g. methane or dioxin	Incinerate chemical waste at very high temperatures
Radioactive waste	Nuclear reactors	Mutation rates are increased which increases chances of foetal abnormalities and cancer	NO SATISFACTORY SOLUTION

14.5 Conservation

Man has helped to create an imbalance in nature by destroying forests and wildlife, damaging and depleting soil and wasting and polluting water. An active concentrated programme of conservation of resources will help resotre the balance of nature, which is vital to the successful living of man.

Resources

- **Nonrenewable.** Minerals and fossil fuels such as coal, oil and gas.
- **Renewable.** Foods such as marine fish, wildlife such as tigers and whales, and vegetation, primarily trees.

Possible solutions to depletion of these resources

Minerals. Recycling of metals and reversing the policy of producing disposable (throw-away) items such as tin cans.

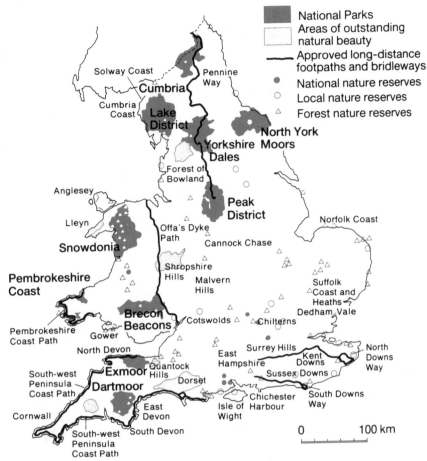

National Parks
Areas of outstanding natural beauty
Approved long-distance footpaths and bridleways
● National nature reserves
○ Local nature reserves
△ Forest nature reserves

Solway Coast
Pennine Way
Cumbria
Cumbria Coast
Lake District
North York
Yorkshire Moors
Dales
Forest of Bowland
Anglesey
Peak District
Norfolk Coast
Lleyn
Offa's Dyke Path
Cannock Chase
Snowdonia
Shropshire Hills
Malvern Hills
Suffolk Coast and Heaths
Pembrokeshire Coast
Dedham Vale
Cotswolds
Chilterns
Pembrokeshire Coast Path
Gower
Brecon Beacons
North Devon
East Hampshire
Surrey Hills
Kent Downs
North Downs Way
South-west Peninsula Coast Path
Exmoor Quantock Hills
Dorset
Sussex Downs
Dartmoor
Chichester Harbour
South Downs Way
Cornwall
East Devon
Isle of Wight
South Devon
South-west Peninsula Coast Path

0   100 km

Fig. 14.7 Map to show the pattern of parks, paths, beauty spots and protected areas of biological interest in England and Wales

Fossil fuels Use of other methods of energy conversion, e.g. tidal energy (Severn Estuary Project) and solar power. The public must be made to reduce fossil fuel consumption.
Foods Expansion of fish farming projects. New sources of food in the form of micro-organisms. More use of primary producers as a source of protein, e.g. soya beans.
Wildlife Stricter laws against destruction of endangered species. Education of the public to show the futility of hunting for sport, ivory, skins, aphrodisiacs. Use substitutes for whale oil and animal hides.
Trees Continuous re-afforestation.

The conservation of wildlife and natural vegetation may, in the long term, be of more importance to man than its destruction for more immediate use. The public should be made aware of access to national parks and areas of outstanding beauty for recreation and enjoyment of nature.

14.6 International health control

World Health Organisation (WHO)

This was established in 1948. Its headquarters are in Geneva, Switzerland, and there are regional offices in Egypt, The Republic of the Congo, Denmark, India, Philippines and the USA. The WHO is responsible for:

● Coordinating health information and research services on such topics as **nutrition**, **vaccines**, **drug addiction** and **radiation hazards**.

- Control of diseases such as *malaria, tuberculosis, venereal* (sexually transmitted) *disease* and *smallpox*. It sponsors the control of epidemic and endemic diseases via **vaccination programmes, purification of drinking water** and **health education**. *Cholera, yaws* and *yellow fever* are some diseases which are being fought on an international level. It also organises *quarantine* measures.
- The administration of health policies by giving technical advice and conducting field surveys. It helps to set up *health centres* and aids the *training of medical staff*.

Food and Agriculture Organisation (FAO)

This has its headquarters in Rome. It is responsible for increasing the efficiency of agriculture, fisheries and forestries. It provides the expert help necessary in these fields in the developing countries of the Third World.

United Nations International Children's Emergency Fund (UNICEF)

This has its headquarters in London and provides aid for the needs of children suffering from the effects of wars or of major disasters.

Examiner's tip

The most common examination questions on this topic are based on:
1 Sewage disposal
2 The effects of humans on the environment.

Summary

Public health

1. Microbes are used in sewage treatment.
2. The large numbers of people living in limited space, with the consequences of industrial demands, cause pollution problems.
3. Air is polluted with many harmful gases, mainly from industrial combustion and traffic.
4. Water is polluted by chemicals including those produced as by-products of industry, fertilisers, detergents and oil.
5. Land is being used and polluted by the disposal of both biodegradable and non-biodegradable wastes.
6. There are attempts being made to redress the balance between the excessive negative effects of humans on the environment and the positive effects. These are based mainly on conservation of renewable and non-renewable resources.

Quick test

(a) Which of the following processes is not necessary in the purification of water for drinking purposes?
   A filtration   **B** sedimentation   **C** fluoridation   **D** chlorination
(b) Which of the following breaks down organic matter in sewage?
   A chlorine   **B** viruses   **C** oxygen   **D** bacteria
(c) The purpose of the U-bend in a toilet is:
   A to prevent rats climbing up from the sewers
   B to prevent bacteria from entering the sewers
   C to stop unpleasant smells rising from the sewers
   D to keep the pipes lubricated
(d) Which of the following does the National Health Service provide free to *all* adults?
   A spectacles·   **B** false teeth   **C** vaccination against influenza
   D hospital treatment for illness
(e) If you wanted to reduce the long-term unsightliness of a refuse dump, which of the following would you be most keen to prevent being dumped?
   A wooden and cardboard boxes   **B** tins and plastic containers
   C sheets of newspaper and magazines   **D** tree prunings and hedge trimmings
(f) The activated sludge process is a method of:
   A sewage treatment   **B** water purification   **C** refuse disposal   **D** land drainage.

Questions

Introduction

There now follows a series of questions, some of which are taken from actual GCSE papers, and others which have been prepared in the style appropriate to GCSE Human Biology. The questions have been selected to assess a variety of skills including:

- Knowledge with understanding
- Skills and processes
- Application of knowledge
- Interpretation of data
- Observation

The questions are divided into groups that correspond to the headings of the sections previously covered. These questions usually require short answers or ask you to label diagrams. At the end of each question, there is an indication of the mark you can expect from answering the questions correctly.

Advice on answering questions

If the questions are multiple choice

1. Remember that, unless otherwise stated in the beginning of the question, there will only be one correct answer.

2. If you are asked to underline the correct answer or tick an appropriate box, never underline or tick more than one of the alternatives.

3. Read the stem (beginning of the question) very carefully.

4. Try to form an answer in your mind.

5. Look for the alternative in the multiple choice which matches your answer.

6. Check the other alternatives to make sure that they are wrong.

7. If another alternative appears to be correct, check your original idea.

If the questions require very short answers

- If you are not sure how much information to supply, give more rather than less.
- Keep your answer as concise as possible. An examiner may not be able to see that you have the right idea if your answer is written in an overcomplicated way.

Finally, while using this Test Yourself section, do not consult the answers at the end until you are certain that you have done your very best to complete the questions on your own.

1 Man's position in the living world

1   (a) Draw a typical animal cell. Label **three** cell parts on your drawing.   **(3)**
       (Choose the labels from the box below.)

cell surface membrane	chloroplast	nucleus
cell wall	cytoplasm	vacuole

   (b) **On your drawing**, label with an **X** the part which controls movement of
       substances in and out of the cell.   **(1)**

SEG 1995

2   (a) The diagram shows some cells from the epithelium inside a human cheek. The
       cells are shown as they appeared when examined with a microscope.

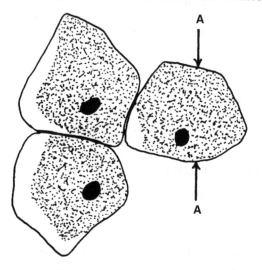

       (i) Write a description of these cells.   **(3)**
       (ii) The actual distance between points **A** and **A** was 0.025 mm. What was the
            magnification of these cells as they are shown in the drawing?   **(1)**
   (b) The diagram shows some other cells.

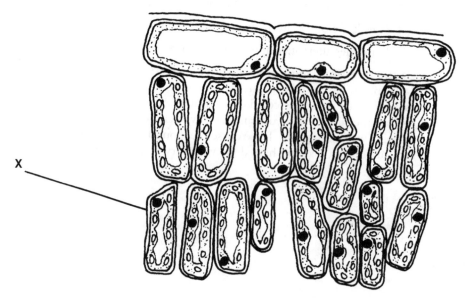

       (i) Give **three** features of these cells which show that they were part of a plant.   **(3)**
       (ii) Make a drawing of cell **X**. Your drawing must be **four** times larger than cell **X**
            in the diagram.   **(3)**

SEG 1993

3 (a) The box gives the names of nine structures likely to be found in cells.

cell membrane	cell wall	chloroplasts	cytoplasm
genes	mitochondria	nucleus	starch grains	vacuole

Complete the table by writing in the names of the structures you would expect to find in each of the cells mentioned. Each name must be used **only once**. **(9)**

Structure found in

Plant cells only	Animal and plant cells

(b) The drawing shows two views of a red blood cell.

One important job of the red blood cells is to carry oxygen from our lungs to where it is needed. Describe and explain **two** features of a red blood cell that help it to do this job. **(4)**

SEG 1995

4 A student noticed that the flesh of an apple turned brown shortly after the apple was cut open and exposed to the air.

(a) Suggest the parts played by the air and enzymes in causing this brown appearance. **(2)**

(b) The student was told that the addition of lemon juice to the apple flesh as soon as possible after cutting prevented this browning. She thought that this effect could be due to either the citric acid or the vitamin C present in the lemon juice.

Describe a controlled experiment she could do to find if one or both of these substances had such an effect on the apple. Use materials and apparatus normally present in a laboratory. **(6)**

SEG 1993

2 The skeleton and movement

1 (a) Give **three** functions of the human skeleton. **(3)**

(b) The diagram shows part of the **left** arm and shoulder of the human body.

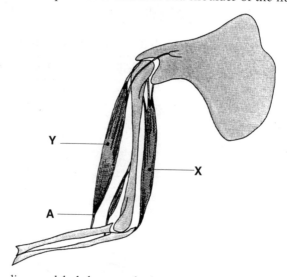

(i) On the diagram label the scapula, humerus, ulna and radius. **(3)**

(ii) The arm bones are held in a synovial joint at the elbow. Give **two** functions of a synovial joint. **(2)**

(iii) Name the muscles labelled X and Y. **(2)**

(iv) Suggest why the structure labelled A, which attaches muscle Y to the bone, is non-elastic. **(1)**

(v) Describe what happens to the lower arm and muscle Y when muscle X contracts. **(2)**

(c) The diagram shows the legs of an athlete starting a sprint race. Some of the muscles of the right leg are labelled A, B, C, D and E.

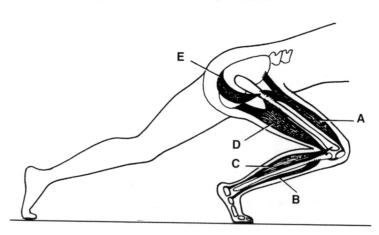

Use the diagram to help you select the muscles which contract when the right leg is straightened forcing the athlete forward. **(3)**

NICCEA 1995

2 (a) The photograph shows an X-ray of a hip which has had an artifical replacement to the joint.

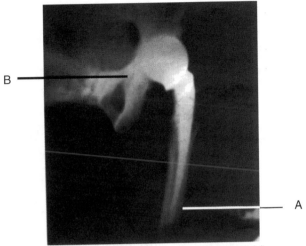

(Photo. A. Brinded)

    (i) Name bones **A** and **B**. (2)

    (ii) State **one** of the functions of bone **A**. (1)

    (iii) What **two** substances are usually present at the hip joint to reduce friction and allow easy movement? (2)

    (iv) Suggest a reason why a person's hip joint may need to be replaced in old age. (1)

(b) The diagram shows the artifical hip (ball and socket) in detail.

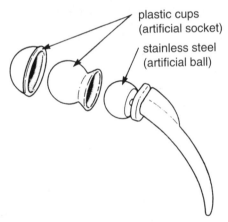

plastic cups
(artificial socket)

stainless steel
(artificial ball)

    (i) Suggest **three** reasons why the ball and socket are made from materials such as metal and plastic. (3)

    (ii) How is the degree of movement allowed by the ball and socket at the hip different to movement at the elbow? (2)

(c) Read the passage carefully and then answer the questions that follow:

> "Kim was a very active 12-year old when her hip problem was discovered. She had inherited a condition which causes the ends of the bones in her hips to be shaped abnormally. This means that the ball does not move smoothly in the socket. It is a painful condition and will probably get worse. Her doctors decided that a hip replacement was necessary but they did not want to operate immediately."

    (i) Give **two** reasons why hip replacement was felt to be necessary. (2)

    (ii) Using your biological knowledge, explain why the operation needs to be delayed. (2)

SEG 1993

3 The respiratory system

1 (a) The diagram shows a vertical section through the chest.

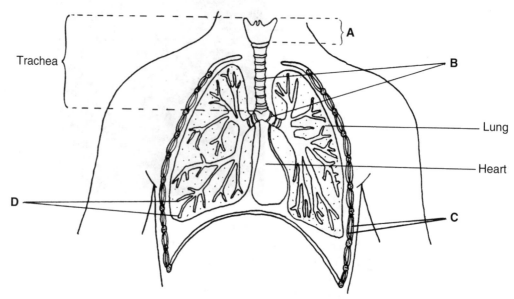

   (i) Give **one** different function for each of the parts labelled **A**, **B** and **C**. (3)
   (ii) The branches labelled **D** end in a very large number of alveoli (air-sacs). Give **three** features of these alveoli which help them in their function of allowing oxygen to enter the blood. (3)

(b) The table shows a comparison for two athletes who ran in races of different distances.

Athlete	Distance of race (m)	Oxygen needed in the race (dm³)	Oxygen entering blood in the race (dm³)
A	100	10	0.5
B	10 000	150	134.0

   (i) The difference between the oxygen needed and the oxygen actually entering the blood during the race is known as the oxygen debt.
       What is the oxygen debt for each of the athletes **A** and **B**? (1)
   (ii) When a race is over both athletes continue to breathe more rapidly and more deeply than normal for some time as they rest. Suggest the reason for this. (2)

   (iii) Both of the athletes obtained some of their energy from anaerobic respiration. What is meant by the term *anaerobic respiration*? (1)

SEG, 1993

3 The diagram below shows a section through the human breathing system.

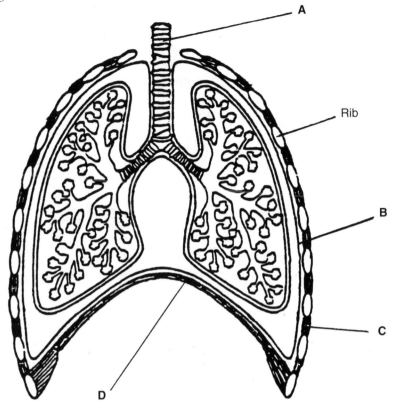

(a) Name the parts labelled **A, B, C** and **D**. (4)

(b) The graph below shows the effects of different amounts of carbon dioxide on the rate of breathing.

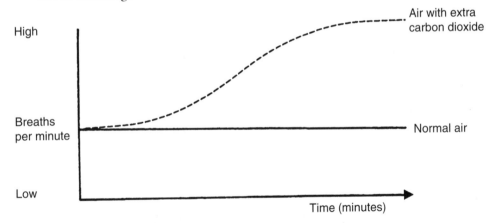

(i) Describe the effect of extra carbon dioxide on breathing rate. (1)

(ii) In the "kiss of life" method of artificial respiration air is blown into the lungs of the person who has stopped breathing.
Use information from the graph to suggest why the "kiss of life" may cause the person to start breathing again. (2)

(c) The diagram below shows a section through part of a human lung.

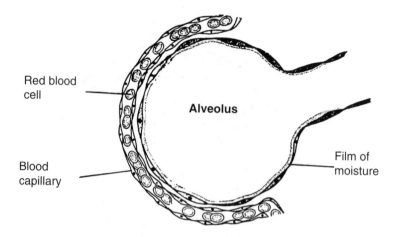

Describe how oxygen passes from the air in the lungs into the blood. **(3)**
(d) Give **two** effects of cigarette smoking on human lungs. **(2)**

NEAB 1993

4 Food and nutrition

1 The table shows a person's diet on one day.

Meal	Foods
Breakfast	cereal with milk, coffee, beans on toast
Lunch	chips, peas and meat pie, apple pie with cream
Tea	cake and sandwiches, chocolate bar, tea
Evening meal	sausage with vegetables and potatoes
Supper	cheese sandwich and crisps, tea

The food eaten on other days was very similar to this day's diet.
The pie charts show an analysis of this diet and the recommended healthy diet for this person. (Vitamins, minerals, fibre and water are not shown.)

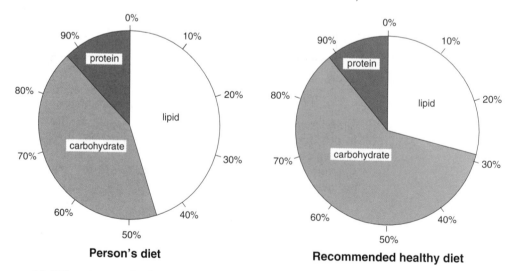

(a) What do you think is most seriously wrong with the diet of this person, as shown by the pie charts? **(1)**
(b) Suggest **three** changes which could be made to the diet shown in the table so that the recommended diet was eaten. **(3)**

SEG 1993

5 The digestive system

1   In an experiment to find the effect of pH on the activity of the enzyme amylase, three test tubes were labelled **A, B** or **C**. The same quantity of amylase solution was put in each. The solution in test tube **A** was left neutral, in test tube **B** it was made acidic and in test tube **C** it was made alkaline. The same quantity of starch suspension was than added to each test tube and the contents well shaken to mix them.

At intervals, recorded using a clock, a few drops of the mixture were removed from each test tube. The drops were placed in cavities on a tile and iodine solution was added to each sample to test for starch.

When the testing with iodine solution was finished, the remaining contents of each test tube were heated with Benedict's reagent.

The diagram shows the results obtained when testing with iodine solution. The diagram of the clock shows the time of each test. The clock is shown recording minutes.

On testing with Benedict's reagent the contents of test tube **A** turned red, as did the contents of test tube **B**. The contents of test tube **C** did not change when heated with Benedict's reagent.

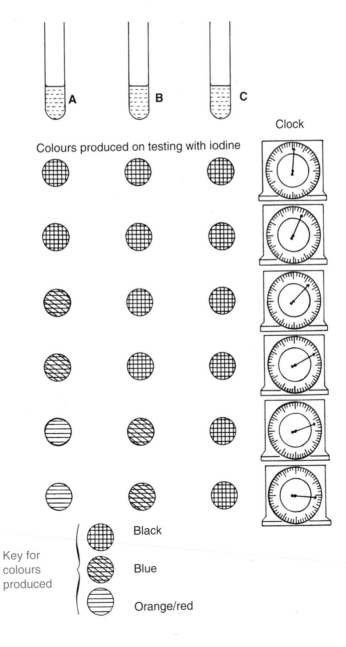

(a) By means of a table clearly show the results which were obtained with the iodine solution test. (7)

(b) What colour was obtained as a result of testing the contents of test tube **C** with Benedict's reagent? (1)

(c) What conclusions can you make from these results about the effect of pH on the activity of amylase? (3)

(d) Suggest **one** way in which this experiment could be improved to make it a more accurate investigation of the effect of pH on the activity of amylase. (1)

SEG 1993

6 The circulatory system

1 The diagrams **A** and **B** show vertical sections through the heart in two stages of the heart beat.

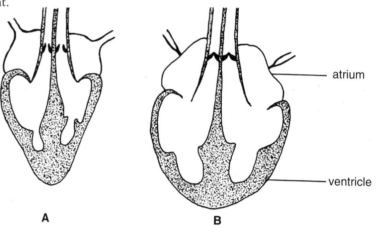

Complete the table by using the letters **A** or **B**. (5)

Actions happening during the heartbeat.	Shown by diagram **A** or diagram **B**.
Contraction of the ventricles.	
Blood entering the heart.	
Blood entering the ventricles.	
Blood leaving the heart.	
Contraction of the atria.	

SEG 1993

2 (a) The diagram shows the transport of oxygen in the blood.

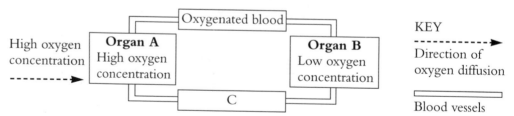

(i) Use the letters in the diagram to help you complete the following table.

	Letter
Respiring muscles	
Lungs	
Deoxygenated blood	

(3)

(ii) Add **arrows** to the diagram to show the direction of blood flow. **(1)**

(b) The table shows the composition of blood from three different patients, **P**, **Q** and **R**.

Patient	Red blood cells (mm³)	White blood cells (mm³)	Platelets (mm³)
P	6 500 000	5600	250 000
Q	5 100 000	8100	260 000
R	2 200 000	5000	500

Use the information in the table and your knowledge to answer the following questions. Give reasons for your answers.

(i)   Suggest which patient had a diet which was low in iron. **(2)**
(ii) Suggest which patient has blood which takes a long time to clot. **(2)**
(iii) Suggest which patient has an infection. **(2)**

(c) When giving blood transfusions, doctors must cross match the donor blood to make sure it is compatible with the recipient blood.

Recipient blood group	Donor blood group			
	O	A	B	AB
O	✓	✗	✗	✗
A	✓	✓	✗	✗
B	✓	✗	✓	✗
AB	✓	✓	✓	✓

Key: ✓ compatible with recipient
     ✗ incompatible with recipient

Use the information in the table and your knowledge to answer the following questions.

(i) Which group is known as the Universal recipient and which is known as the Universal donor? Give reasons for your answers. **(4)**
(ii) Explain why it is important to screen all donated blood. **(1)**

(d) Human blood carries a rhesus factor. People with rhesus negative (Rh−) blood do not have antibodies to the rhesus factor but would produce antibodies if they were in contact with rhesus positive (Rh+) blood.

Explain why this can be dangerous for a rhesus positive baby (Rh+) carried by a rhesus negative mother (Rh-). **(2)**

NICCEA 1995

3 (a) A person who has lost a lot of blood in an accident may be given a blood transfusion. It is important to know the blood group of the donor (person giving the blood) and of the recipient (person receiving the blood) as some transfusions are not safe. If the antibodies in the recipient's blood match the antigens on the red cells of the donor then the transfusion will not be safe.

(i) Complete the table to show transfusions which are safe with a tick (✓) and to show which transfusions are unsafe with a cross (✗). **(3)**
     (*One line of the table has been completed for you as an example.*)

(continued overleaf)

Blood group of donor	Antigens of donor	A	B	AB	O	Blood group of recipient
		anti-B	anti-A	none	anti-A + anti-B	Antibodies of recipient
A	A	✓	✗	✓	✗	
B	B					
AB	A + B					
0	none					

(ii) In an unsafe transfusion, the antibodies of the recipient stick together the red blood cells from the donor to form clumps of red cells. A typical blood capillary has an internal diameter of 10 μm (0.01 mm) and a red blood cell has a diameter of 8 μm (0.008 mm). If a patient received blood of the wrong group, explain what would happen in the blood capillaries and to the body cells served by these capillaries. **(6)**

(b) In a law court, Miss X accused Mr. Y of being the father of her child. Miss X had blood group A, Mr. Y had blood group AB and the child had blood group O. Was it possible for Mr. Y to be the child's father? Give a biological explanation of your answer. **(6)**

Use the following symbols in your explanation:

I^A = allele for blood group A.
I^B = allele for blood group B
I^O = allele for blood group O

SEG 1995

7 Regulation/Homeostasis

1 (a) The diagram shows a vertical section through a human kidney.

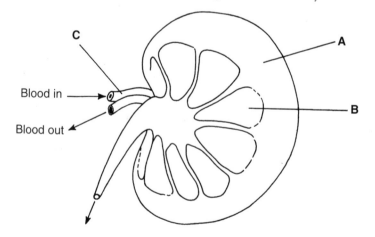

(i) Name regions **A** and **B**. **(2)**
(ii) Is blood vessel **C** the renal artery all the real vein? Give **two** reasons for your answer. **(2)**
(b) The table shows the composition of blood plasma, the filtrate in the Bowman's capsule and the urine.

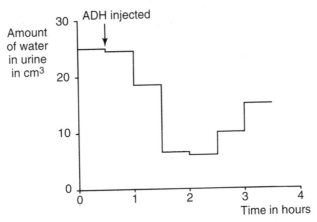

	Concentration in g per 100 cm³		
	Blood plasma	**Filtrate in the Bowman's capsule**	**Urine**
Urea	0.03	0.03	2.0
Glucose	0.10	0.10	0.0
Amino acids	0.05	0.05	0.0
Salts	0.72	0.72	1.5
Proteins	8.00	0.00	0.0
Water	92.00	97.00	95.0

(i)   Name **one** substance in the table which is **not** filtered out of the blood.   (**1**)

(ii) Name **two** substances in the table which are filtered out of the blood and then are completely reabsorbed back into the blood by the kidney.   (**1**)

(iii) **A** What is the name of the organ of urea production in the human body?   (**1**)

   B The concentration of urea in urine is much higher than in blood plasma. Suggest what may have caused this.   (**1**)

(c) Antidiuretic hormone (ADH) is released by the pituitary gland and helps to regulate the amount of water reabsorbed by the kidney. When ADH was injected into a person, the volume of water produced was altered. The graph below shows this.

Amount of water in urine in cm³

ADH injected

Time in hours

(i)   **From the information given in the graph**, does ADH increase or decrease the amount of water reabsorbed by the kidney?   (**1**)

(ii) Which **three** of the following circumstances would normally cause an increase in the amount of ADH released by the pituitary gland into the blood?   (**1**)

(*Tick **three** of the boxes*)

   A   eating salty food

   B   drinking a large volume of fresh water

   C   loss of water by sweating on a hot day

   D   drinking a large volume of salty water

(iii) Explain what would happen to the body cells if the kidneys failed to remove enough water from the blood.   (**5**)

SEG 1995

2   The diagram below shows part of the human urinary system and its blood supply.

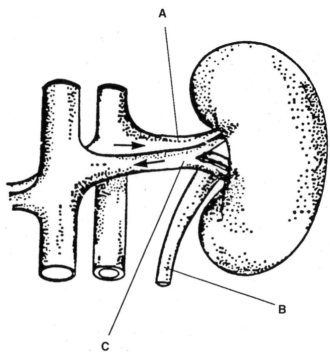

(a) Name the parts labelled **A**, **B** and **C**.

(b) Copy the table below and show two differences in composition between the blood in vessel **A** and vessel **B**.

Composition of blood in vessel **A**	Composition of blood in vessel **C**

(c) Sometimes a patient's kidneys fail. One method of treating such a patient is to transplant a healthy kidney.
Explain why transplanted kidneys sometimes fail.   (2)

(d) Another way of treating patients suffering from kidney failure is to use a dialysis machine.
The diagram below shows a section through part of a dialysis machine.

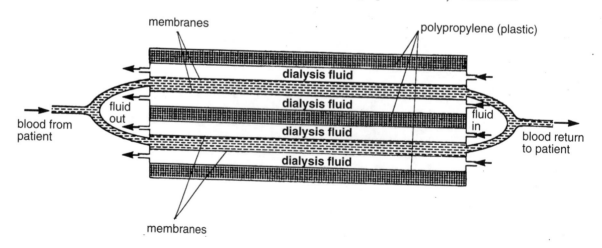

Describe how the composition of the patient's blood changes as it flows through the dialysis machine.   (3)

NEAB 1993

3 The figure shows a kidney tubule.

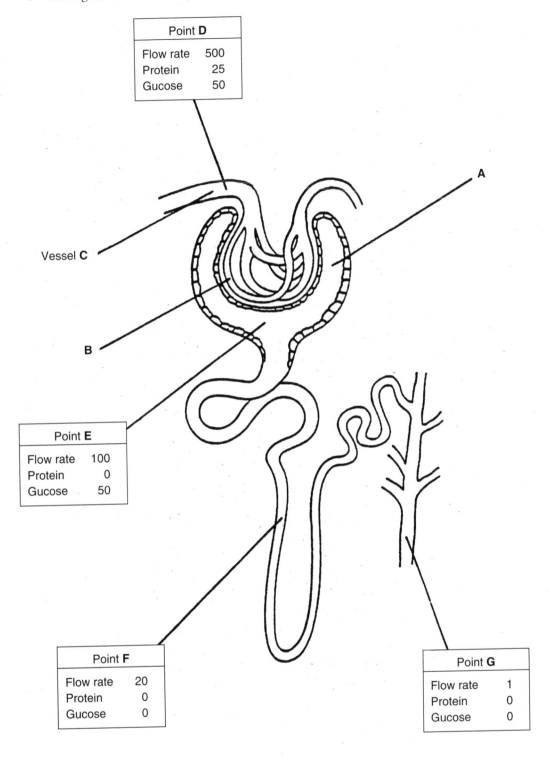

Point **D**	
Flow rate	500
Protein	25
Gucose	50

Vessel **C**

B

A

Point **E**	
Flow rate	100
Protein	0
Gucose	50

Point **F**	
Flow rate	20
Protein	0
Gucose	0

Point **G**	
Flow rate	1
Protein	0
Gucose	0

(a) Name the parts labelled **A** and **B**.   (2)

(b) On the diagram, draw an arrow to show the direction of blood flow in the vessel
   labelled **C**.   (1)

Points **D**, **E**, **F** and **G** show the concentrations of protein and glucose in samples of
the fluid at those points. Use this information to answer the following questions.

(c) Name the fluids sampled at: Point **D**; Point **E**; Point **G**.   (3)

(d) (i) What process brings about the decrease in flow rate from **E** to **G**?   (1)

   (ii) Why is this process necessary?   (1)

(e) Explain the absence of protein at **E**. (2)

(f) (i) Look at the levels of glucose at **E** and **F**. What has happened to the glucose between these two points? (2)

(ii) Doctors test for glucose in the urine. Which organ is not working correctly if glucose is present? (1)

(g) The table shows the volume of urine collected from one person over a period of 10 days during the winter and a further 10 days during the summer.

Winter		Summer	
Day	Volume of urine collected/cm³	Day	Volume of urine collected/cm³
1 January	1395	1 July	900
2 January	1415	2 July	895
3 January	1405	3 July	985
4 January	1400	4 July	988
5 January	1400	5 July	1000
6 January	1386	6 July	895
7 January	1431	7 July	897
8 January	1426	8 July	887
9 January	1413	9 July	935
10 January	1406	10 July	978

(i) What difference do you observe between urine output in Winter and Summer? (1)

(ii) Suggest an explanation for this difference. (2)

(h) A group of students decided to repeat the investigation described in (g)

(i) Suggest **three** ways to make the investigation more reliable. (3)

(ii) How could the results of the new investigation be presented to make them easier to understand? (1)

MEG 1993

8 Coordination

1 (a) The diagram shows a section through a human eye which is focusing light rays **from a near object**.

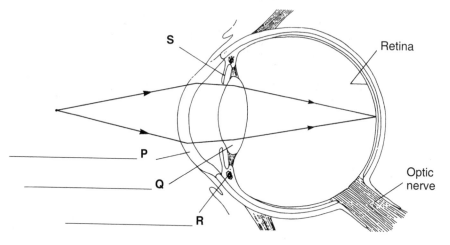

(i) **On the diagram**, label structures **P**, **Q** and **R**. (3)

(ii) If the object were moved further away from the eye,

    A what would happen to shape of structure **Q**? (1)

    B What must structure **R** do to cause this change in the shape of **Q**? (1)

(iii) How do changes in structure **S** help us to see clearly? (2)

(b) The diagram shows the eye of a person who suffers from an eye defect. The light rays are shown coming from a **very distant** object.

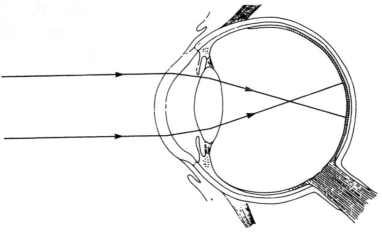

(i) Is this person long-sighted or short-sighted? (1)

(ii) Explain why this person would not see the object clearly. (2)

(iii) On the diagram draw, in front of the eye, the type of lens needed to correct this eye defect. (1)

(c) What do the retina, the optic nerve and the brain each do to help a person to see?

- Retina (2)
- Optic nerve (1)
- Brain (1)

SEG 1996

2 (a) The diagram shows the side view of part of the human nervous system.

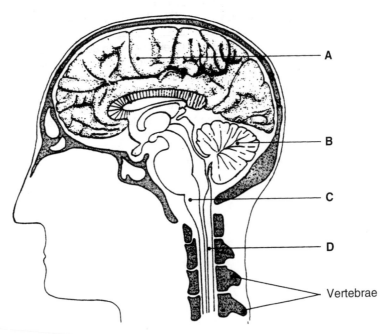

(i) Name the parts labelled **A**, **B**, **C** and **D**. (4)

(ii) What is the function of the vertebrae? (1)

(iii) What structures make up the central nervous system? (1)

(b) The diagram shows a reflex action which occurs when a person's hand is burnt.

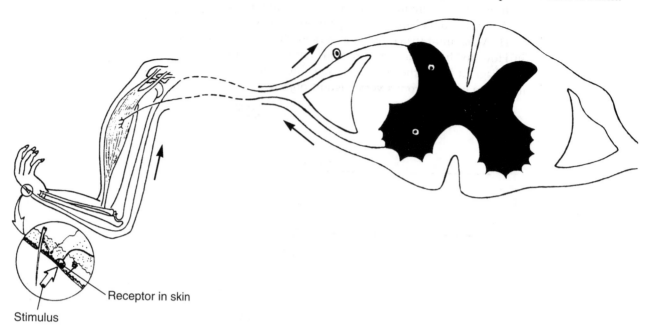

Receptor in skin

Stimulus

(i) Use the diagram to describe how this reflex action occurs, starting with the receptors in the skin being stimulated. **(5)**

(ii) Suggest why the reflex action would be the same whether a person is conscious or unconscious. **(1)**

(iii) Why are reflex actions important to our body? **(1)**

(iv) Suggest **two** reflex actions other than the reaction to pain. **(2)**

(v) Design an experiment to measure the reaction time of a **named** reflex action. **(3)**

NICCEA 1995

3 (a) The level of glucose in the blood is controlled by a negative feedback system. What is meant by negative feedback? **(1)**

(b) The following passage describes the control of blood glucose.

> Normal blood glucose level is between 80–100 mg glucose per 100 cm³ blood. In the pancreas special types of cell in the Islets of Langerhans respond to blood glucose level; alpha cells detect low glucose and beta cells detect high glucose. The alpha cells respond by secreting a hormone which causes the liver to increase the rate of production of glucose. The beta cells respond by secreting a hormone which causes the liver to increase the rate of storage of glucose.

Use the information in the passage to complete the flow diagram of the control of blood glucose on the opposite page. **(6)**

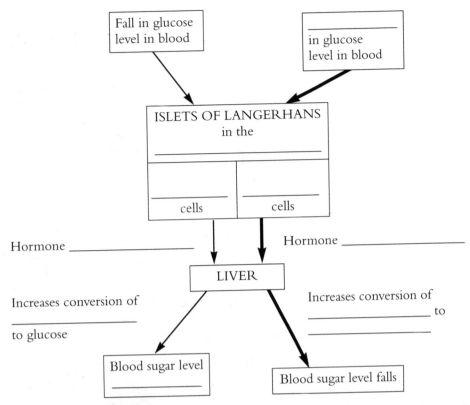

Flow diagram of the control of blood glucose level

(c) State which part of the control system for glucose is
   (i) the receptor
   (ii) the effector? **(2)**

(d) Explain how the water content of the body is regulated by a negative feedback system. (Up to two marks will be given for the way in which your answer is expressed.) **(9)**

NEAB 1996

9 Human reproduction and development

1 (a) The diagram shows a sectional view of the male reproductive system.

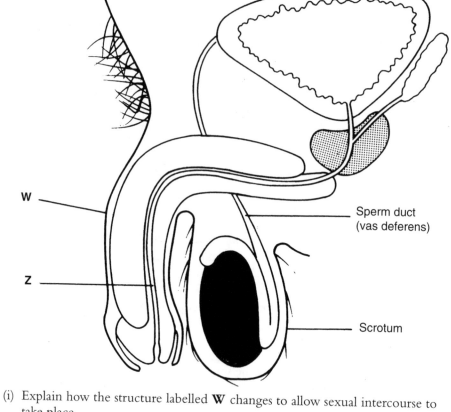

(i) Explain how the structure labelled **W** changes to allow sexual intercourse to take place. **(3)**

(ii) List the following structures in increasing order of size, as shown on the diagram:

  BLADDER
  PROSTATE GLAND
  TESTIS **(2)**

(iii) What evidence does the diagram give about the age of the person whose reproductive system is drawn? Explain your answer. **(2)**

(iv) Name part **Z**. **(1)**

(b) The diagram shows a sperm cell and an egg cell (ovum).

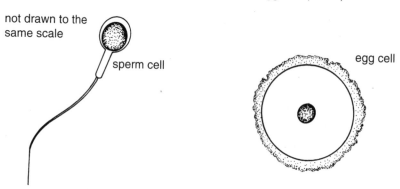

(i) State **two** differences, visible in the diagram, between the two cells. **(2)**

(ii) State **one** similarity, **not** visible in the diagram, between the two cells. **(2)**

(c) Explain the term 'fertilisation'. **(3)**

SEG 1993

2   The diagram shows the sexual cycle of a human female, with changes in the thickness of the uterus wall and the levels of the hormones, oestrogen and progesterone.

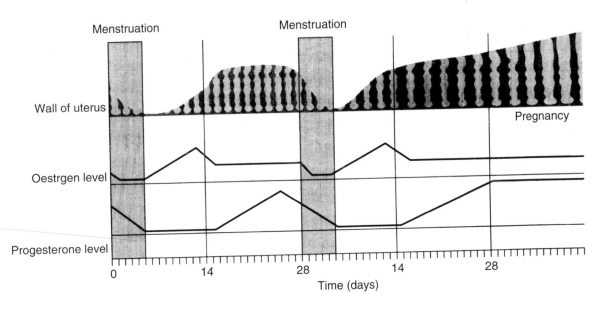

Use the diagram to help answer the following questions.
(a) How long is the menstrual cycle?   **(1)**
(b) Which hormone reaches its maximum 1 to 2 days before menstruation?   **(1)**
(c) Explain what is meant by menstruation.   **(2)**
(d) Explain what is meant by ovulation.   **(2)**
(e) When does ovulation occur?   **(1)**
(f) Which hormone reaches its maximum 1 to 2 days before ovulation?   **(1)**
(g) Describe the changes, shown in the diagram, when the human female
      becomes pregnant.   **(4)**
(h) Oestrogen and progesterone are hormones. What is a hormone?   **(3)**
(i) Name the system to which oestrogen and progesterone belong.   **(1)**

NICCEA 1995

3   (a) The diagram below shows a developing fetus.

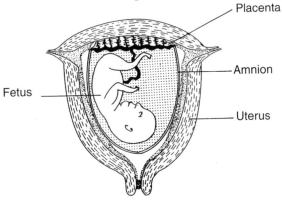

(i) Name **one** substance which the fetus obtains from its mother.   **(1)**
(ii) Explain how the fetus obtains this substance which passes from the mother. **(4)**

(b) The placenta develops after fertilisation. The graph shows changes in the level of a hormone produced by the developing placenta.

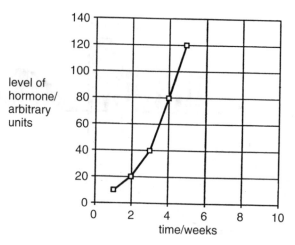

(i)   What is the name of this hormone? **(1)**
(ii) What is the effect of this hormone on the ovaries? **(1)**
(iii) Explain why this effect on the ovaries is important for a successful pregnancy.

(c) Some couples have difficulty in conceiving a child.
(i)   Explain how hormones can be used to treat infertility. **(3)**
(ii) Describe **one** other method by which an infertile couple could be helped to have a child. **(3)**

NEAB 1996

10 Genetics

1 (a) The flow diagram shows the main steps in the process of cell division leading to the formation of reproductive cells.

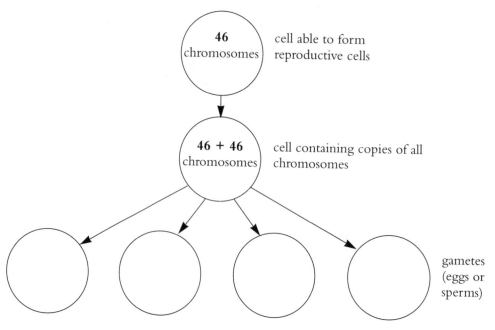

(i)   In each of the circles, write in the number of chromosomes present in each reproductive cell. **(1)**
(ii) How many sets of chromosomes are present in each reproductive cell? **(1)**
(b) Describe how pairs of male sex chromosomes differ from pairs of female sex chromosomes. **(1)**

(c) Polydactyly is an inherited condition which causes extra fingers and toes to develop on the hands and feet. The allele of the gene (**P**) which causes this condition is dominant to the other allele of the gene (**p**).
Using the symbols given, state the two alleles which would be present in a person without polydactyly. **(1)**

(d) The family tree shows the inheritance of polydactyly.

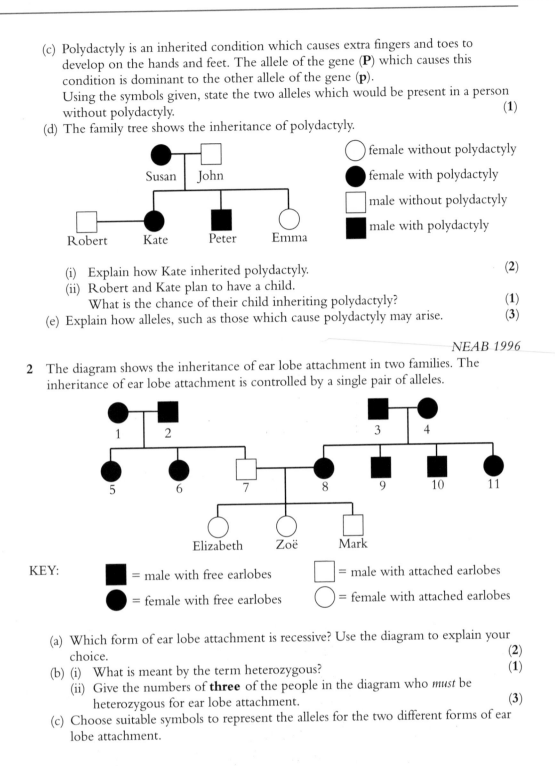

○ female without polydactyly

● female with polydactyly

□ male without polydactyly

■ male with polydactyly

  (i) Explain how Kate inherited polydactyly. **(2)**

  (ii) Robert and Kate plan to have a child.
    What is the chance of their child inheriting polydactyly? **(1)**

(e) Explain how alleles, such as those which cause polydactyly may arise. **(3)**

NEAB 1996

2 The diagram shows the inheritance of ear lobe attachment in two families. The inheritance of ear lobe attachment is controlled by a single pair of alleles.

KEY:

■ = male with free earlobes   □ = male with attached earlobes

● = female with free earlobes   ○ = female with attached earlobes

(a) Which form of ear lobe attachment is recessive? Use the diagram to explain your choice. **(2)**

(b) (i) What is meant by the term heterozygous? **(1)**
    (ii) Give the numbers of **three** of the people in the diagram who *must* be heterozygous for ear lobe attachment. **(3)**

(c) Choose suitable symbols to represent the alleles for the two different forms of ear lobe attachment.

Use your symbols to complete the following genetic diagram to explain how persons **7** and **8** could produce children with either type of ear lobes. **(5)**

Parents	7	8
Phenotypes	attached	free
Genotypes	_____	_____

Gametes

Offspring genotypes

Offspring

phenotypes   A _____   B _____   C _____   D _____

Genotypes of: Elizabeth _____
                Zoë _____
                Mark _____

(d) Elizabeth, Zoë and Mark are triplets, but each was adopted by a different family and so they grew up separately. The table gives some information about them at the age of 19 years.

	Sex	Height in cm	Weight in kg	Blood group	Ear lobe attachment	Intelligence (IQ)
Elizabeth	female	173	62	O	attached	126
Zoë	female	170	51	O	attached	140
Mark	male	173	80	A	attached	128

(i) Two of the triplets are identical twins. Identify which two are identical twins and give **two** reasons for your choice. **(3)**

(ii) Three of the features in the table show continuous variation and three show discontinuous variation. Identify the **three** features which show **continuous variation**. **(1)**

SEG 1996

3 Brachydactyly is a condition caused by a dominant allele. In the homozygous state there are such severe defects in the bones that death occurs shortly before or shortly after birth.

In the heterozygous state there is also some bone defect shown by a short middle finger on each hand.

Using **B** to represent the allele for brachydactyly and **b** to represent the allele for normal bone development, answer the following questions.

(a) What are the **three** possible genotypes for this bone development which can exist in a population? **(1)**

(b) What is the genotype of a person who has normal bone development? **(1)**

(c) (i) Explain why brachydactyly can be passed on only by parents who are heterozygous. **(2)**

(ii) What is the possibility of two parents, both with brachydactyly, having a child who is normal? With the help of a clear genetic diagram fully explain the reason for your answer. **(7)**

SEG 1995

11 Interdependence

1 (a) The diagram shows the nitrogen cycle.

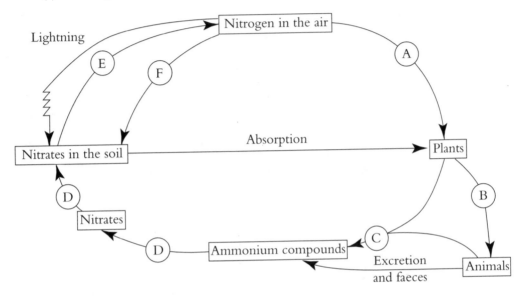

Use the diagram and your knowledge to answer the following questions.
  (i)   Name the processes, **B** and **E**. **(2)**
  (ii) Some of the processes in the nitrogen cycle involve bacteria.
        Which process represents:
        ● bacteria producing nitrates in the root nodules? **(1)**
        ● bacteria increasing the nitrates available for plants? **(2)**
  (iii) Name the process and the organisms involved in **C**. **(2)**

(b) Farmers use fertilisers to supplement the nitrogen content of their land. The table shows some information about fertilisers.

	Natural fertiliser	**Artificial fertiliser**
Cost	Low	High
Speed of action	Slow	Fast
Availability	Limited availability	Always available

  (i)   Give an example of a natural fertiliser. **(1)**
  (ii) Using your own knowledge and the information in the table, suggest why the majority of farmers do not use natural fertilisers despite their advantages. **(3)**
  (iii) Suggest why it is necessary to add fertilisers to farmland but not to forests. **(1)**

NICCEA 1995

2 Two groups of pupils carried out surveys in seven different parts of their local river, (shown as **A–G** on the map). The surveys were carried out in early summer.

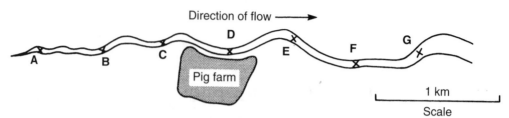

(a) One group was comparing the concentration of oxygen in the water with the number of mayfly nymphs. Their results are shown on the graph.

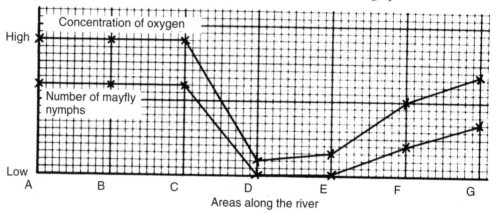

(i) Describe what happens to the concentration of oxygen in the water as it flows from **C** to **G**.   **(1)**
(ii) What could have caused this sudden change in the concentration of oxygen? **(1)**
(iii) Explain how this change will affect the fish.   **(2)**
(iv) An area of water in another river contains lots of mayfly nymphs. What should the pupils be able to say about the concentration of oxygen in the water? **(1)**

(b) The other group investigated the feeding relationships at areas **A**, **B** and **C**. The food web shows some of their results.

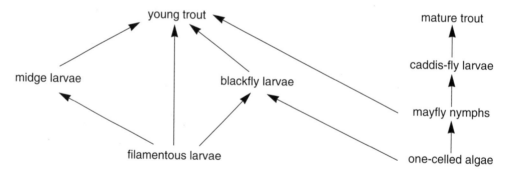

(i) Write down the longest food chain shown in this web.   **(2)**
(ii) The algae are called *producers*. Explain why.   **(2)**
(iii) From the food web, name the prey of the caddis–fly larvae.   **(1)**
(iv) From the food web, name the predator of the blackfly larvae.   **(1)**
(iv) The pupils knew that the blackfly larvae change into flies and fly away.   **(1)**
    [A] This change could cause the population of **mayfly nymphs to go down**. Explain why.   **(2)**
    [B] This change could cause the population of **mayfly nymphs to go up**. Explain why.   **(2)**

SEG 1995

12 Disease

1 Some people in a town developed a bacterial disease which caused coughing, chest pains and a rash on the face.

The graph shows some of the effects of the disease on one person.

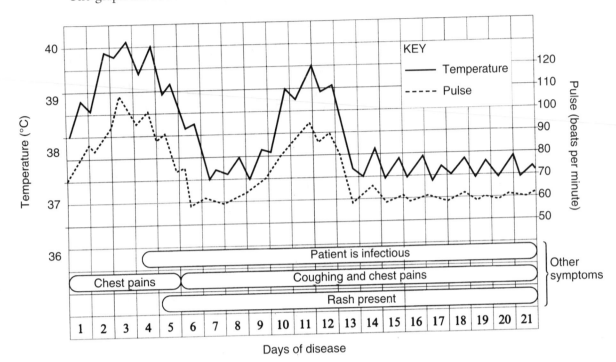

Use the graph to help you answer the following questions.

(a) When did the body temperature reach its maximum? **(1)**

(b) What was the maximum temperature? **(1)**

(c) The disease could only be diagnosed when all the symptoms were present. On which day was this possible? **(1)**

(d) Describe what was happening to the bacteria between days 9–11 and 12–13. **(2)**

(e) Describe the relationship between the body temperature and pulse rate. **(1)**

(f) Suggest **two** other symptoms of the infection, apart from those described, which you would expect the patient to show. **(2)**

(g) Give **two** methods of transmitting bacterial disease and name an example of each. **(2)**

(h) The people who suffered from the disease developed active immunity to the bacteria causing it. Describe the differences between active and passive immunity. **(4)**

NICCEA 1995

2 (a) What is a malignant tumour (cancer)? **(2)**

(b) The bar chart shows the results of a survey of the incidence of some types of cancer.

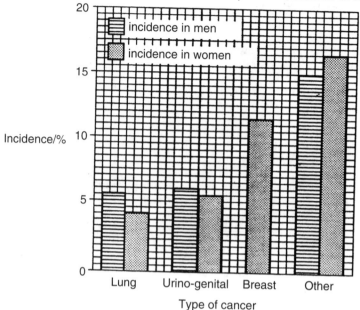

(i) What is the incidence of urino-genital (kidney, bladder and reproductive organs) cancer in men? **(1)**

(ii) Recent surveys suggest that the incidence, in men, of cancers of the urino-genital system (kidney, bladder and reproductive organs) may be much higher than this. Suggest **one** reason why the data may be inaccurate. **(1)**

(iii) Suggest **one** reason why the incidence of lung cancer is lower in women than in men. **(1)**

(iv) The bar chart shows a category for 'other' types of cancer. These include leukaemia and melanoma (skin tumours).
State one possible cause for each of these types of cancer.
- leukaemia **(1)**
- melanoma **(1)**

(c) The following bar chart is adapted from a publicity leaflet produced by an insurance company. It shows the causes of death of 100 men and 100 women in 1954 and in 1984.

(i) The pattern of causes of death in 1984 is different from the pattern in 1954. Describe **three** of these differences. **(3)**

(ii) Suggest **two** reasons for the changes in causes of death between 1954 and 1984 in
   - Infectious diseases
   - Cancer
   - Circulatory diseases. (6)

NEAB 1996

13 Personal health and hygiene

1   A company has produced a new disinfectant.
Company scientists carried out the following experiment to find out the most effective strength of disinfectant to use.
Bacteria from a stock culture were first grown in nutrient broth and then transferred to six sterile agar plates.

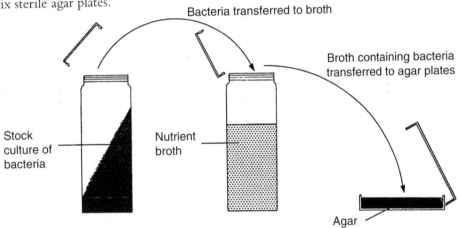

(a) Name a suitable piece of apparatus that could be used to transfer the bacteria from the broth to the agar plate. (1)
(b) Give **one** way of preventing contamination when transferring the bacteria from the stock culture to the nutrient broth. (1)
(c) Each agar plate was incubated for 24 hours.
Discs of filter paper soaked in different strengths of disinfectant were placed on each agar plate.
The diagrams below show the results after a further 24 hours

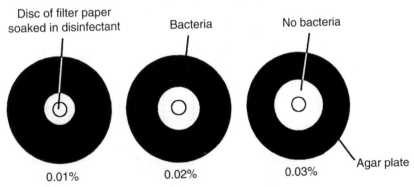

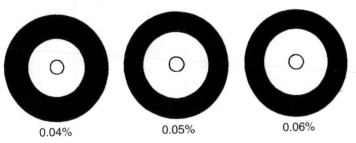

(i) Which strength of disinfectant would you recommend for sale? (1)

(ii) Give **two** reasons why you chose this strength. (2)

NEAB 1993

2 The female housefly usually lays its eggs in decomposing organic matter, including kitchen waste. Two groups of flies were kept at different temperatures and the numbers of eggs they produced per week were counted. The two line graphs show these results.

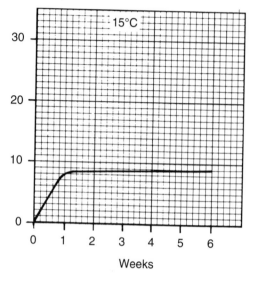
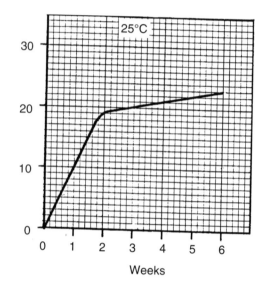

(a) Another group of female flies was kept at 35°C and the number of eggs they laid were counted over a period of six weeks. The results are shown in Table A below. Use the results in the table to plot a line graph on the grid.

Table A

Week	Number of eggs per female
0	0
1	7
2	7
3	8
4	8
5	8
6	9

(4)

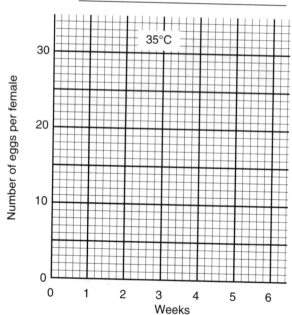

(b) At what temperature is egg laying
    (i) at its highest? **(1)**
    (ii) at its lowest? **(1)**
(c) Use the graphs to help you complete the following table B.

Table B

Temperature °C	Number of eggs per female at week 4
15	——
25	——
35	8

(2)

(d) Suggest **two** precautions you might take to reduce the number of houseflies round the home. For each precaution, suggest a **reason** why it would be effective. **(4)**

MEG 1993

4 The diagram shows the teeth in the lower jaw of a human adult. If the person chewed a disclosing tablet, this would stain any plaque on the teeth.

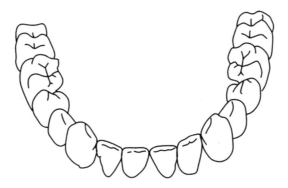

(a) **On the diagram**, use a pencil to shade in the different areas most likely to be stained by the disclosing tablet. **(2)**
(b) Plaque on the teeth might lead to tooth decay.
    (i)   What type of micro-organism is found in plaque and causes tooth decay? **(1)**
    (ii) What type of substance is released by these micro-organisms which damages tooth enamel? **(1)**
    (iii) Brushing the teeth after meals helps to stop tooth decay. Tooth paste is slightly alkaline. State **two** different ways in which brushing the teeth with tooth paste will help to stop tooth decay.

SEG 1995

14 Public health

1 (a) Householders in the United Kingdom produce approximately 20 million tonnes of domestic waste each year. Local authorities would like the amount of domestic waste reduced.
    (i) Give **one** method of domestic waste disposal on land. **(1)**
    (ii) Suggest **one** reason why local authorities want to reduce the amount of domestic waste. **(1)**
(b) The diagram shows the average composition of domestic waste.

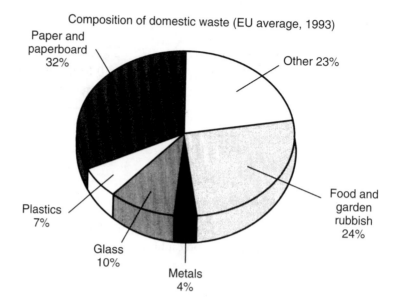

Composition of domestic waste (EU average, 1993)

Paper and paperboard 32%

Other 23%

Food and garden rubbish 24%

Metals 4%

Glass 10%

Plastics 7%

Use the diagram and your knowledge to answer the following questions.
  (i)   Give **one** example of domestic waste that is biodegradable. **(1)**
  (ii) Explain the term biodegradable. **(2)**
  (iii) Name a material, other than glass, that can be recycled. **(1)**
  (iv) Name a domestic waste material which is hard to recycle and non-biodegradable. Suggest how the quantity of this material could be reduced. **(2)**
  (v)   Give **two** reasons why it is important to recycle as much domestic waste as possible. **(2)**
(c) A river flows through farmland. In summer the river looked green and a number of dead fish were found floating on the surface.
  (i)   Explain why the river looked green. **(2)**
  (ii) Explain why the fish died. **(3)**

NICCEA 1995

2   Sulphur dioxide gas produced in Britain can cause acid rain both in Britain and in other countries. The map shows how quickly sulphur dioxide can spread from Britain.

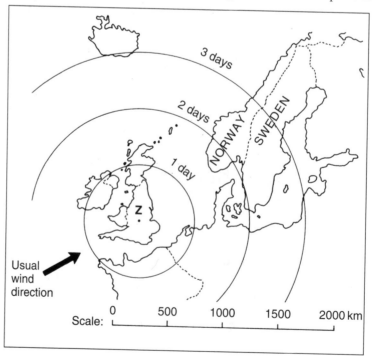

(a) (i) Give **one** human activity which releases large amounts of sulphur dioxide into the air. **(1)**

(ii) How far can the sulphur dioxide produced in Britain at point **Z** travel each day? **(1)**

(iii) Much of the sulphur dioxide produced in Britain falls as acid rain in Norway and Sweden. Use the map to explain why these two countries are affected most. **(1)**

(b) Write down **three** harmful effects of sulphur dioxide on living organisms. **(3)**

SEG 1995

3 The diagram shows the main stage of the "activated sludge" method to sewage treatment. Activated sludge is rich in micro-organisms and is added to the sewage in large open tanks. Air is bubbled through the sewage/sludge mixture continuously to supply the micro-organisms with oxygen.

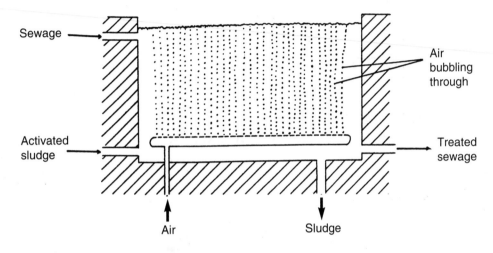

(a) For what biological process do the micro-organisms need oxygen? **(2)**

(b) Describe how micro-organisms in the activated sludge make the sewage harmless. **(4)**

SEG 1993

Answers

Please note that the answers that follow are the author's only and that the various examining groups accept no responsibility for the methods or accuracy of working in the answers given.

1 Man's position in the living world

Quick test

(a) **D** (b) **A** (c) **C** (d) **A** (e) **D** (f) **B** (g) **C** (h) **A**

1 (a) Artwork of cell, labelled as below. One mark is given for each correct label (**3**).

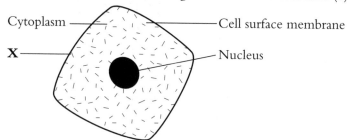

(b) One mark is given for **X** pointing to the cell membrane (**1**).

2 (a) (i) Irregularly shaped (**1**) with a nucleus (**1**) and cytoplasm (**1**).
(ii) 1000 × (**1**).
(b) (i) Cell wall (**1**). Vacuole (**1**). Chloroplasts (**1**).
(ii) *Marks:* (**1**) *for correct size (length 10 cm),* (**1**) *for correct width,* (**1**) *for accuracy of contents.*

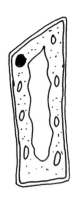

3 (a)

Structure found in	
Plant cells only	**Animal and plant cells**
Chloroplasts	Cell membrane
Cell wall	Cytoplasm
Starch grains	Genes
Vacuole	Mitochondria
	Nucleus

(**9**)

(b) They have no nucleus so that all the volume is taken up by haemoglobin (**1**). They have an elastic cell membrane to enable them to squeeze through capillaries (**1**).

4 (a) The air provides oxygen (**1**). The enzyme speeds up oxidation (**1**).
(b) Add a known volume of Vitamin C (ascorbic acid) to piece of apple exposed to air (**1**). Leave for a known time (**1**) and observe whether browning has taken place (**1**). Add the same volume of citric acid (**1**) to the same size piece of apple exposed to air (**1**). Leave for the same length of time (**1**) and observe whether browning has taken place (**1**).

2 The skeleton and movement

Quick test
(a) **C** (b) **B** (c) **A** (d) **D** (e) **C** (f) **D**

1 (a) Support, movement, protection, storage of calcium, manufacture of blood cells. Any three of these answers (**3**).

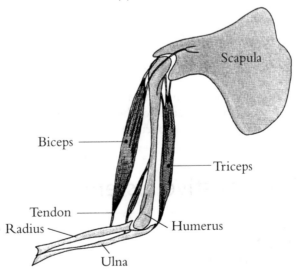

(b) (i) See diagram for labels (**3**).
(ii) To allow movement (**1**). To allow flexibility (**1**).
(iii) X, triceps (**1**). Y, biceps (**1**).
(iv) Because it must pull on the bone across a joint without stretching to produce movement (**1**).
(v) The lower arm is straightened (**1**). Muscle Y relaxes (**1**).
(c) **A, B, E** (**3**).

2   (a) (i) **A** Femur (**1**). **B** Pelvis (**1**).
     (ii) Support (**1**)
     (iii) Cartilage (**1**). Synovial fluid (**1**).
     (iv) Cartilage may wear out and arthritis occurs (**1**).
     (b) (i) Hard wearing/strong (**1**) Smooth (**1**) Not biodegradable (**1**).
         (ii) Movement at the elbow is in one plane. (**1**) Movement at the hip is universal (**1**).
     (c) (i) Ball does not move smoothly in the socket. Movement is restricted (**1**) and it is painful (**1**).
         (ii) The skeleton is still growing (**1**) at its fastest rate (at puberty) (**1**).

3 The respiratory system

Quick test
(a) **C** (b) **D** (c) **C** (d) **B** (e) **C** (f) **D**

1   (a) (i) **A** Sound production (**1**). **B** Support of trachea and bronchi (**1**). **C** Breathing movements (**1**).
         (ii) Large surface area (**1**). Thin walled (**1**). Richly supplied with blood (**1**).
     (b) (i) **A** 9.5 dm³ (**1**). **B** 16 dm³ (**1**).
         (ii) They need to pay back the oxygen debt (**1**) so they take in large volumes of air (**1**).
         (iii) Realease of energy from glucose without oxygen (**1**).

2   (a) **A** trachea. **B** Pleural membrane. **C** Intercostal muscle. **D** Diaphragm (4 × (**1**))
     (b) (i) An increase in carbon dioxide causes an increase in breathing rate (**1**).
         (ii) There is an increase in carbon dioxide in exhaled air (**1**) which when breathed in by a person causes an increased rate of breathing (**1**).
     (c) Oxygen diffuses (**1**) in solution (**1**) into the red blood cells where it combines with haemoglobin (**1**).
     (d) Causes lung cancer (**1**). Destroys air sacs (**1**).

4 Food and nutrition

Quick test
(a) **B** (b) **D** (c) **A** (d) **B** (e) **C** (f) **C**

1   (a) The person has too much fat in the diet (**1**).
     (b) Substitute boiled potatoes for the chips (**1**). Do not have cream with the apple pie (**1**). Do not eat crisps for supper (**1**).

5 The digestive system

Quick test
(a) **A** (b) **C** (c) **D** (d) **A** (e) **B** (f) **C**

1

(a) Time in minutes	1	4	7	10	12	16
Colour in tube **A**	Black	Black	Blue	Blue	Orange/red	Orange/red
Colour in tube **B**	Black	Black	Black	Black	Blue	Blue
Colour in tube **C**	Black	Black	Black	Black	Black	Black

(*Marks:* (**1**) *for time columns.* (**1**) *for units of time.* (**1**) *for accurate clock readings.* (**1**) *For* **A**, **B**, *and* **C** *recorded.* (**1**) × 3 *for correct colours for* **A**, **B**, *and* **C**.)

(b) Blue (**1**).

(c) Amylase digests starch quickest in neutral conditions (**1**). It does not digest starch in alkaline conditions (**1**). It begins to digest starch in acid conditions after 10 minutes (**1**).

(d) Temperature should remain constant (**1**).

6 The circulatory system

Quick test

(a) **C** (b) **B** (c) **C** (d) **A** (e) **C** (f) **C**

1   Contraction of ventricles **A** (**1**). Blood entering the heart **A** (**1**). Blood entering the ventricles **B** (**1**). Blood leaving the heart **A** (**1**). Contraction of the atria **B** (**1**).

2   (a) (i)

	Letter	
Respiring muscles	B	(**1**).
Lungs	A	(**1**).
Deoxygenated blood	C	(**1**).

   (ii) The arrows should go from **A** to **B** to **C** to **A** (**1**).

(b) (i)   **R** because the patient has the lowest red blood cell count (**1**).

   (ii)   **R** because the patient has the lowest platelet count (**1**).

   (iii) **Q** because the patient has the highest white blood cell count (**1**).

(c) (i)   Universal recipient is group **AB** because it can receive blood from any group within the **ABO** system (**1**).
         Universal donor is group **O** because it can be given to any blood group within the **ABO** system (**1**).

   (ii)   To make sure that it is not contaminated with disease-causing organisms (**1**).

(d) Blood could seep through the placenta and enter the baby's circulation (**1**).
    This could cause agglutination of the baby's blood (**1**).

3   (a) (i)

Blood group of donor	Antigens of donor	A anti-B	B anti-A	AB none	O anti-A + anti-B	Blood group of recipient Antibodies of recipient
A	A	✓	✗	✓	✗	(**1**) for row
B	B	✗	✓	✓	✗	(**1**) for row
AB	A + B	✗	✗	✓	✗	(**1**) for row
0	none	✓	✓	✓	✓	(**1**) for row

   (ii) The blood cells would clump together (agglutination) (**1**).
        The clump would fill the diameter of the capillaries (**1**) and would prevent blood flow (**1**) and therefore oxygen and glucose supply (**1**) to the cells (**1**).
        The cells would die because they could not respire (**1**).

(b) **Blood group of Miss X**   **Blood group of Mr Y**
        IᴬIᴬ   IᴬIᴮ   (1)
     or IᴬIᴼ   (1)

Possible children are:
Parents genotypes   IᴬIᴬ   IᴬIᴮ   (1)
    Children   IᴬIᴬ or IᴬIᴮ
              or   IᴬIᴼ   IᴬIᴮ
           IᴬIᴬ or IᴬIᴮ or IᴬIᴼ or IᴮIᴼ   (1)
Mr Y could not be the father (1) because the possible blood groups of the children could only be **A** or **B** or **AB**.

7 Regulation and homeostasis

Quick test

(a) **A** (b) **A** (c) **C** (d) **D** (e) **A** (f) **C**

1   (a) (i)   **A** Cortex (**1**). **B** Medulla (**1**).
        (ii) Renal artery. *Reason 1*: it takes blood to the kidney (**1**).
              Reason 2: it has a thick wall (**1**).
    (b) (i)   Protein (**1**).
        (ii) Glucose and amino acids (**1**).
        (iii) **A** Liver (**1**). **B** Reabsorption of water (**1**).
    (c) (i)   It increases it (**1**).
        (ii) A, C, D (**1**).
        (iii) Water would pass into cells (**1**) by osmosis (**1**) because there would be a greater amount of water molecules outside the cells (**1**). Water molecules would therefore diffuse (**1**) through the selectively permeable cell membrane (**1**).

2   (a) **A** Renal artery (**1**). **B** Ureter (**1**). **C** Renal vein (**1**).

(b) Composition of blood in vessel **A**	Composition of blood in vessel **C**
Rich in oxygen	Not much oxygen
Rich in urea	Not much urea

    (c) If the recipient's antibodies react with antigens produced by the donor's kidney the kidney will fail (**1**). It is more likely to be successful if tissue types are correctly matched (**1**).
    (d) Urea is filtered out of the blood (**1**) under pressure from the patient's heart (**1**). Mineral salts and glucose will also pass out and will have to be replaced if the composition of the dialysis fluid is not similar to blood plasma (**1**).

3   (a) **A** Bowman's capsule (**1**). **B** Glomerulus (**1**).
    (b) Arrow should point towards glomerulus (**1**).
    (c) **D** Blood plasma (**1**); **E** Glomerular filtrate (**1**); **G** Urine (**1**).
    (d) (i) Reduction in pressure (**1**).
        (ii) So that re-absorption can take place. (**1**)
    (e) The molecules are too big (**1**) to pass through the glomerulus (**1**).
    (f) (i) It has been reabsorbed (**1**) into the blood supply (**1**).
        (ii) The pancreas (**1**).
    (g) (i) There was less in the summer than in the winter (**1**).
        (ii) In the summer more water is lost through the skin (**1**) during sweating (**1**).
    (h) (i) Increase the number of people tested to obtain an average (**1**); Control their water intake (**1**); Control their protein intake (**1**).
        (ii) As a histogram or graph (**1**).

8 Coordination

Quick test
(a) **B** (b) **B** (c) **B** (d) **C** (e) **D** (f) **D**

1 (a) (i)   **P** cornea (**1**); **Q** lens (**1**); **R** ciliary muscle (**1**).
     (ii) **A** It would become thinner (**1**).
          B Relax (**1**).
     (iii) It controls the amount of light entering the eye (**1**) so that the light sensitive cells are not stimulated (**1**).
   (b) (i)   Short-sighted (**1**).
     (ii) The light rays are focused in front of the retina (**1**) so that the light sensitive cells are not stimulated (**1**).

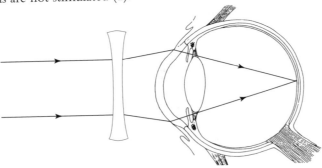

     (iii) Diagram as shown (**1**). (Eye with bi-convex lens in front of it.)
   (c) Retina converts light energy into electrical energy (**1**) and starts a nerve impulse (**1**). Optic nerve sends impulse to the brain (**1**). The brain interprets the impulse as an image (**1**).

2 (a) (i)   **A** Cerebral hemisphere (**1**); **B** Cerebellum (**1**); **C** Medulla oblongata (**1**); **D** Spinal cord (**1**).
     (ii) Protection of the spinal cord (**1**).
     (iii) Brain and spinal cord (**1**).
   (b) (i)   A nerve impulse begins at the receptor and travels along the sensory nerve (**1**) to the grey matter where it forms a synapse (**1**) with the relay nerve (**1**). It then passes across another synapse to the motor nerve (**1**) which carries it to the effector (muscle) (**1**).
     (ii) The conscious brain is not necessary for a reflex action (**1**).
     (iii) They protect it from harmful changes in the surroundings (**1**).
     (iv) Pupil constriction / blinking / coughing / sneezing / knee jerk. Any two of these (**2**).
     (v)   One person holds a 30 cm rule vertically, while the other places a thumb and forefinger at the bottom end without touching it (**1**). The first person lets the rule drop without warning and the second catches it as quickly as possible by closing the thumb and forefinger together (**1**). Record how many cm the ruler fell. The more rapid the reflex, the shorter will be the distance through which the ruler is allowed to fall (**1**).

3 (a) The rate of a reaction is controlled by the accumulation of the product of the reaction (**1**). Or a change from a steady rate results in changes that bring about a return to a steady state.

(b)

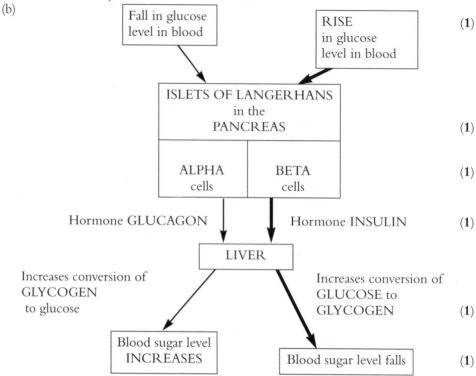

Fall in glucose level in blood

RISE in glucose level in blood (**1**)

ISLETS OF LANGERHANS in the PANCREAS (**1**)

ALPHA cells | BETA cells (**1**)

Hormone GLUCAGON | Hormone INSULIN (**1**)

LIVER

Increases conversion of GLYCOGEN to glucose

Increases conversion of GLUCOSE to GLYCOGEN (**1**)

Blood sugar level INCREASES

Blood sugar level falls (**1**)

(c) (i) Pancreas / Islets of Langerhans / Alpa cells / Beta cells (**1**).
(ii) Liver (**1**).
(d) **Seven** marks for the following explanations:
Water content monitored by pituitary / hypothalamus;
Fall below normal causes release of ADH;
Kidney reabsorbs more water;
Urine becomes more concentrated;
Water level rises to normal;
The mechanism illustrates negative feedback;
If water intake is too high, ADH production is reduced;
This leads to little reabsorbtion by the kidney.
There are **two** marks for the account being clear and concise.

9 Human reproduction and development

Quick test

(a) **D** (b) **B** (c) **C** (d) **D** (e) **A** (f) **C**

1 (a) (i) It becomes erect (**1**) because the rate of inflow of blood (**1**) is greater than its rate of exit (**1**).
(ii) Prostate. Testis. Bladder. (**2**).
(iii) The person has reached adolescence (puberty) because of pubic hair (**1**) and the position of the testis in the scrotum (**1**).
(iv) Urethra (**1**).
(b) (i) The sperm has a tail (**1**). The egg has more cytoplasm in proportion to its size (**1**).
(ii) Both have the same (**1**) haploid number of chromosomes (**1**).
(c) Fusion (**1**) of the nuclei (**1**) of a male and female gamete (**1**).

2 (a) 28 days (**1**).
 (b) Progesterone (**1**).
 (c) It is the shedding of the lining of the uterus (**1**) which has built up in preparation
 for pregnancy (**1**).
 (d) The release of an egg (**1**) from the ovary (**1**).
 (e) At approximately day 14 after menstruation (**1**).
 (f) Oestrogen (**1**).
 (g) The wall of the uterus continues to thicken (**1**) and becomes well supplied with
 blood (**1**). Progesterone production remains at a high level (**1**) and oestrogen
 remains steady (**1**).
 (h) A chemical secretion (**1**) of a ductless gland (**1**) producing a physiological effect (**1**).
 (i) Endocrine (**1**).

3 (a) (i) Glucose/sugar/amino acids/vitamins/named example of vitamin/
 mineral salt/named example of mineral/oxygen/water. Any of these (**1**).
 (ii) The named substance passes across the placenta (**1**) by diffusion (**1**) to the
 blood of the fetus (**1**). The umbilical artery carries fetal blood to the placenta
 and the umbilical vein carries blood from the placenta (**1**).
 (b) (i) Gonadotrophin (**1**).
 (ii) Maintains secretion of hormones/oestrogen/progesterone (**1**).
 (iii) Prevents any further cycles/inhibits follicle stimulating hormone (**1**); prevents
 menstruation (**1**).
 (c) (i) Follicle stimulating hormone/hormones in the female causes extra ovulation
 (**1**); oestrogen/progesterone maintain lining of uterus (**1**); hormones in male
 increase sperm production (**1**).
 (ii) *Either:* artificial insemination (**1**); sperm of donor/father collected
 artificially(**1**) and artificially introduced into the vagina/uterus/womb (**1**).
 Or: Eggs removed from mother (**1**) and fertilised outside the body (**1**).
 Fertilised eggs/developing embryo placed back into womb (**1**).

10 Genetics

Quick test
(a) **C** (b) **D** (c) **B** (d) **C** (e) **A**

1 (a) (i) 23 in each circle (**1**).
 (ii) One (**1**).
 (b) Males have XY, females have XX (**1**).
 (c) **pp** (**1**).
 (d) (i) Inherits **P** which is the dominant allele/gene (**1**) from mother/Susan (**1**).
 (ii) 50% / 1:1 / 1 in 2 (**1**).
 (e) Mutation (**1**) of alleles/genes (**1**) by radiation/sub-atomic particles (**1**).

2 (a) Recessive: attached ear lobes (**1**).
 Explanation: the character does not show in the parents **1** and **2** but shows in child
 7 although **5** and **6** do not show it (**1**).
 (b) (i) An individual receiving unlike genes from both parents (**1**).
 (ii) **1, 2,** and **8** (**3**).
 (c) Free ear lobe **F**. Allele for attached ear lobes **f**.

Genotypes	**ff**	**Ff**	(**1**)
Gametes	f + f	F + f	(**1**)
Offspring genotypes	A fF; B ff; C ff, D ff		(**1**)
Offspring phenotypes	A Free lobes. B Attached lobes		
	C Free lobes. D Attached lobes		(**1**)

 Genotypes of Elizabeth, Zoë and Mark must all be **ff**. (**1**).
 (d) (i) Elizabeth and Zoë (**1**). They are of the same sex (**1**) and have the same blood
 groups (**1**).
 (ii) Height, weight and IQ (**1**).

3 (a) **BB, Bb, bB** (1).
   (b) **bb** (1).
   (c) (i)   Genotype **BB** never reach maturity (1). Brachydactyly is dominant (1).
       (ii) **B** = brachydactyly (dominant). **b** = normal (recessive)   (1)
             Parental genotypes   **Bb x Bb**   (1)
             Gametes   **B + b**   **B + B**
             Children   **BB   Bb   bB   bb**   (3)
             Parents must be heterozygous for brachydactyly, otherwise they would not
             have survived (1). The possibility of the child being normal is 1 in 4 (1).

11 Interdependence

Quick test

(a) **A** (b) **A** (c) (i) **A** (ii) **C** (d) **B** (e) **C** (f) **B** (g) **D** (h) **D**

1 (a) (i)   **B** feeding (1). **E** Dentrification (1).
       (ii) **A** (1). **C, D** (2).
       (iii) Decay (1) is caused by putrefying bacteria / fungi (1).
   (b) (i)   Manure / compost / animal waste (1).
       (ii) There is limited availability and so the supply is not dependable (1). The speed
             of action is slow (1) so this limits productivity when quick profit is needed (1).
       (iii) In forests there is natural cycling of materials because there is no crop
             harvesting (1).

2 (a) (i)   It drops sharply and then rises slowly (1).
       (ii) Pollution from the pig farm. Waste material will have bacteria which will use
             the oxygen (1).
       (iii) The fish population will decrease (1) because of lack of oxygen which has
             been used by the bacteria (1).
       (iv) The concentration of oxygen is high (1).
   (b) (i)   One-celled algae → mayfly nymphs → caddis-fly larvae → mature trout
             One mark for four organisms; one mark for correct direction of arrows (2)
       (ii) Algae are plants (1). Plants are the only organisms to produce food (1).
       (iii) Mayfly nymphs (1).
       (iv) Young trout (1).
       (v)   **A** Trout would not have black-fly larvae to feed on (1) so they would eat
             more mayfly nymphs (1).
             B Black-fly larvae would not feed on one-celled algae (1) so there would be
             more food for mayfly nymphs so their population would increase (1).

12 Disease

Quick test

(a) **D** (b) **D** (c) **C** (d) **D** (e) **C** (f) **D**

1 (a) On day 3 (1).
   (b) 40°C (1).
   (c) On day 6 (1).
   (d) On days 9–11 the bacteria are increasing (1). On days 12–13 bacteria are
       decreasing.
   (e) As the temperature increases and decreases, so does the pulse rate (1).
   (f) Sweating (1) and a flushed appearance (1) at times of high temperature.
   (g) Through contaminated food: food poisoning – *Salmonella* (1).
       Through contaminated water: Typhoid (1).

(h) Active immunity is long lasting (**1**). Active immunity is caused by the body producing its own antibodies over a long period (**1**).
Active immunity is artificially induced by vaccination of antigens (**1**). In passive immunity, antibodies are introduced to the body (**1**).

2 (a) Abnormal cells carrying out abnormal cell division (**1**).
(b) (i) 6 (**1**).
(ii) Ignoring symptoms/no screening (**1**).
(iii) Fewer women smoke (**1**).
(iv) Ionising/nuclear radiation/radioactive substances (**1**).
Ultra violet exposure (**1**).
(c) (i) Increase in circulatory disorders; increase in cancer; decrease in infectious diseases (**3**).
(ii) *Infectious disease*: mass vaccination; improved medicines/antibiotics; mass screenings; less overcrowding. Any two of the above (**2**).
Cancer: increase in environmental pollution; more exposure to ultra violet; more use of nuclear reactors; increase in smoking. Any two of the above (**2**).
Circulatory disorders: increased stress; diet changes to higher fat intake; less exercise; increase in smoking. Any two of the above (**2**).

13 Personal health and hygiene

Quick test

(a) **B** (b) **D**

1 (a) A sterile loop (**1**).
(b) Flame the loop and quickly transfer the bacteria with the lid off for the minimum time (**1**).
(c) (i) 0.05% (**1**).
(ii) The maximum number of bacteria are killed (**1**) with the minimum concentration (**1**).

2(a)   ((**4**) *marks for all plots correct,* (**3**) *for one error,* (**2**) *for two errors,* (**1**) *for 3 errors.*)

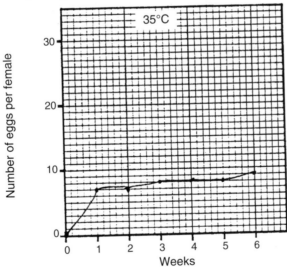

P(4)

(b) (i) 25°C (**1**).
(ii) 35°C (**1**)
(c) 9 at 15°C (**1**); 21 at 25°C (**1**).
(d) Use an insecticide (**1**) to kill insects (**1**). Cover refuse (**1**) to prevent flies laying eggs (**1**).

3 (a) Shading should be at the base of the teeth (**1**) and between them (**1**).
   (b) (i) Bacteria (**1**).
       (ii) Acid (**1**).
       (iii) The alkali will neutralise the acid produced by the bacteria (**1**). The abrasive effect will remove food debris between the teeth (**1**).

14 Public health

Quick test
(a) **C** (b) **D** (c) **C** (d) **D** (e) **B** (f) **A**

1 (a) (i) Land fill disposal (**1**).
       (ii) It causes pollution (**1**).
   (b) (i) Food and garden rubbish (**1**).
       (ii) Material can be broken down (**1**) by microbes (**1**).
       (iii) Metals (**1**).
       (iv) Plastic (**1**). Use a substitute which can be recycled (**1**).
       (v) There is a limited amount of non-replaceable resources, e.g. minerals (**1**). There will be a reduction in pollution (**1**).
   (c) (i) Waste from farm animals acted as fertiliser in the river (**1**). This caused growth of green plants in the river (**1**).
       (ii) The plants multiplied so much that one layer grew on top of the other, killing those below because of lack of light for photosynthesis (**1**). Bacteria caused decay of the dead plants (**1**) and used the oxygen, therefore causing the fish to die (**1**).

2 (a) For aerobic (**1**) respiration (**1**)
   (b) Microorganisms are aerobic (**1**) and ingest (**1**) anaerobic (**1**) pathogens (**1**).

3 (a) (i) Combustion of fossil fuels (**1**).
       (ii) 500 km (**1**).
       (iii) The usual wind direction is towards Norway and Sweden (**1**).
   (b) Acid rain kills trees by releasing toxic aluminium from salts in the soil (**1**). Acid rain kills fish by lowering the pH of water and affecting their gills and eggs (**1**). It kills most lichens (**1**).

Experimental skills and coursework

GCSE syllabuses in Human Biology and Human Physiology and Health include 'coursework' as part of the assessment. There are certain skills which are best tested via continuous assessment of coursework over a long period of time. Indeed, skills such as handling apparatus and setting up experiments in the laboratory cannot be judged by any other means. Some possible benefits of coursework are:

1 Coursework can be fairer to you if you are hard-working and never receive proper credit in formal examinations because of nervousness.
2 You may also suffer because of difficulty in understanding and expressing yourself in written English. Discussion with your teacher may give a clearer picture of your understanding than a written answer.
3 Coursework can stimulate a sense of investigation and discovery through experiments in the laboratory.
4 Coursework will help your understanding of the role that Human Biology plays in the everyday world, its links with other subjects and its relevance to your life. Examination questions which test knowledge of the applications of Human Biology may be unfair because they depend on knowledge 'outside the syllabus'. If you are encouraged to find facts from various sources, this kind of understanding can be tested. You will be able to learn by using up-to-date information on social and technological issues during coursework.

Guidelines for Coursework

General points to remember:
1 Your coursework assessment will account for at least 20% of your final mark in the examination.
2 You must always carry out practical work with due regard to safety.
3 Practical work will be assessed during coursework over two years but there will not be formal practical tests.
4 Your practical assessment will cover the following skills:
    (a) observation and recording
    (b) measurement
    (c) procedure
    (d) handling apparatus
    (e) formulation of hypotheses and experimental design
5 Each of the skills (a)–(d) will be assessed on widely separated occasions, using different experiments.
6 In many exercises, there may be an overlap in the skills to be assessed, e.g. observing and measuring a biological structure may be assessed by means of a scale drawing. In this case, skill (b) (measurement) and skill (a) (observation and recording) overlap.
7 Assessments will be based on the principle of positive achievement. You will be given opportunities to show what you understand and *can* do.
8 Evidence of the actual practical work that you have undertaken and on which you have been assessed, must be kept. This could include practical work sheets, drawings, etc., because the examination group under which you have entered the examination, will want to see samples of the work to maintain national standards.

The assessment of coursework via scientific investigation

During this assessment you will be given the opportunity to:

1. formulate questions, predictions or hypotheses based on your knowledge and understanding;

2. put together a sequence of investigative processes (such as identifying key variables, observing and measuring) into an overall strategy to test hypotheses or predictions;

3. collect results and use them to draw conclusions;

4. Evaluate your findings in the light of your original hypotheses and predictions;

5. develop the way you tackle problems in the light of your increasing knowledge and understanding.

Investigative work

You should:

1. make your own observations;

2. make 'I think … because …' statements, which you can test;

3. plan how to proceed with the investigation;

4. make decisions about what to change, what to measure or judge and what to keep the same;

5. select the most appropriate instruments and apparatus for your investigation;

6. decide which is the most appropriate way to record and display your results;

7. recognise a possible variety of routes to a solution and possibly refine concepts during the investigation.

The importance of recognising variables in an investigation

What are variables? Variables are factors that will change and can be measured.
Independent variable. The variable which the investigator changes systematically.
Dependent variable. The variable which is measured or judged by the investigator. The value of the dependent variable depends on the value chosen for the independent variable.

In investigations variables can be of the following types:

Categoric e.g. colours;

Discrete – can only have certain values e.g. number of people;

Continuous – a continuous variable can have any value. e.g. weight, volume, length, temperature, time;

Control variables – these are variables which must be controlled and held constant by the investigator and which make the results of the investigation valid, i.e. a fair test.

Advice on completing an investigation

Your investigation

On your own:

- Think of a question to test.
- Write an outline plan for your investigation. Use the check list below.
- State what you think you will find out and why.

In your group:

- Decide which plan to follow.
- Check with your teacher whether you can start your investigation.
- Collect all the equipment you will need and carry out your investigation.
- You may change your plan as you go along, but note any changes you make.

On your own:
Write up your investigation. Use the second check list below.

Your plan – a check list
In planning your investigation, think about these things:

1. what you are trying to find out;
2. what you think will happen;
3. why you think this will happen using scientific ideas;
4. what you will measure/ observe;
5. what you will alter between measurements/ observations;
6. what you will keep the same to make it a fair test;
7. how many measurements/ observations you will take;
8. how you will space out your measurements/ observations;
9. what instruments you will use to make your measurements/ observations;
10. safety problems that could arise.

Writing up your investigation – a check list.
In your report, think about including:

1. what you were trying to find out;
2. what you altered;
3. what you measured or observed;
4. how you made your investigation a fair test;
5. what instruments you used to make your measurements;
6. your results, e.g. in a table;
7. a graph if suitable;
8. a description of any pattern;
9. a conclusion which matched your results;
10. a comment on how you could have improved your investigation;
11. an explanation of your results using scientific ideas.

Examples of investigations

A Enzymes in living things

Background
All living things contain an enzyme called *catalase* which cause hydrogen peroxide to be broken down to oxygen and water. This process is necessary to change harmful waste products into harmless chemicals.

Use your knowledge and understanding of enzymes to predict what the effect of changing conditions would have on how quickly the catalase works. Then use the apparatus provided by your teacher to test your predictions.

You will need to consider:
- Independent variables (those you can change). e.g. temperature, pH, type of tissues, surface area of tissues, substrate concentration.
- Dependent variables (those you could measure). e.g. rate of bubble production or total volume of oxygen produced per unit time.

Technical notes
Material such as liver or potato can be used as a source of enzyme.

Eye protection must be worn.

You should not use high concentrations of hydrogen peroxide. *See C.O.S.H.H. (Control Of Substances Hazardous to Health) regulations in your school/ college laboratory.*

B Digesting egg white

Background

Food reaches the stomach in large pieces. It must be digested into small pieces before it can be used by the body. Chemicals called *digestive enzymes* help to break the food down. Egg white, which is a protein, is broken down quickly by an enzyme called *protease*. The protein can only be used by the body if it is broken down quickly.

What conditions will affect the break down of egg white by protease?

Carry out an investigation to test your ideas.

You should consider:

● Independent variables (those you can change). e.g. temperature, pH, amount of enzyme, amount of substrate.

● Dependent variables (those you could measure). e.g. rate of disappearance of egg white.

Technical notes

The egg white can be drawn into glass tubing, sealed and boiled in water. The resulting tubes may be cut into equal lengths to provide a controlled amount of substrate.

Index